DECADES
Of
DOMINANCE

Auburn Football
in the Modern Era

Also by Van Allen Plexico and John Ringer:

Season of Our Dreams: The 2010 Auburn Tigers

DECADES

Of

DOMINANCE

Auburn Football
in the Modern Era

Van Allen Plexico
& John Ringer

"Wishbone" Columnists
from *TheWarEagleReader.com*

WHITE ROCKET BOOKS

Van and John would like to gratefully acknowledge and express their appreciation to Jeremy Henderson and the War Eagle Reader for publishing our original columns and our Wishbone Podcast. Visit the site at www.thewareaglereader.com

Chapter 8, "The AUdacity of Hope," originally appeared in the Maple Street Auburn Football Preview *magazine for the 2011 season.*

CONTENTS

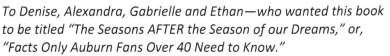

To Denise, Alexandra, Gabrielle and Ethan—who wanted this book to be titled "The Seasons AFTER the Season of our Dreams," or, "Facts Only Auburn Fans Over 40 Need to Know."

—John

To my family—one small segment of the larger Auburn Family. We believe in Auburn, and love it.

—Van

– INTRODUCTION –

We named this book *Decades of Dominance*, with the subtitle *Auburn Football in the Modern Era*. We want to be very clear what we mean by each of those phrases—and very clear that we most definitely *mean* them.

First, however, a quick word about who exactly "we" are, and what comprises our War Eagle *bona fides*.

"We" are the columnist/podcasting duo of Van Allen Plexico and John Ringer. We attended Auburn in the late 1980s (Van returned for graduate school in the early-mid 1990s) and during that time we witnessed some of the most amazing events in Auburn history firsthand, from Sugar Bowls to earthquake games to interception fiestas. Graduation hardly dimmed our love for the Tigers, and eventually we decided to pour that affection for the program into a column series, "The Wishbone," for the *War Eagle Reader* web site beginning in September of 2010—just in time for Cam and Nick and the rest of the gang to carry us along on a totally unexpected *Season of Our Dreams*. (A certain remarkably popular book later emerged from those early columns.) Then, early in the 2012 season, we added a semi-weekly podcast—named, creatively enough, "the Wishbone Podcast"—to the mix. And now, here we are again, with a collection of thoughts and lists and essays and statistics of a more historical (and fun!) nature, united in their theme of stressing the "dominance" of the Tigers, stretching across all of what we refer to as "the Modern Era" of Auburn football. But—what exactly does that entail?

When we say "the Modern Era," we mean "beginning in 1981," as in, the first year of Pat Dye's tenure as head coach on the Plains. All throughout this book, we maintain that definition of the term "modern," and we will focus almost exclusively upon those years—the years since the Doug Barfield administration ended and Pat Dye was hired. That moment marked a very dramatic change in Auburn's ambitions and in its fortunes, and the thirty-plus seasons (as of this writing) that followed it deserve to be examined as a thing apart from the earlier periods of Auburn history. That is not meant in any way as a slight against the accomplishments of Shug Jordan or Mike Donahue or even John Heisman or Doug Barfield. It's simply a way of focusing on a singular, specific period in Auburn history—and a period that both authors of this book witnessed in its entirety, with their own eyes, and mostly in person.

When we say "Dominance," we mean that during the aforementioned period, Auburn's football program has been one of the most dominant in the SEC and in the nation. That fact has not always been adequately recognized, in our opinion—certainly not by the supporters of another program on the other side of the state of Alabama. As we will demonstrate and document here, Auburn football reached remarkable heights of accomplishment and glory under its four official head coaches between 1981 and 2012, with Heisman winners, All-Americans, conference and national titles, a majority of Iron Bowl wins, and winning records against almost the entirety of the rest of the Southeastern Conference. In the final chapter, we lay out our vision for where we see the program going in the years to come.

A few quick statistics bear out our contentions:

* Auburn is one of only 4 programs in NCAA Division 1 college football history to finish a season 14-0.

* Auburn is the only program in the country to have recorded *three* undefeated seasons in the past twenty years.

* Auburn is (as of this writing) the last program in the SEC to finish a season undefeated.

*   Auburn is one of only three SEC programs to record an undefeated season since the conference expanded and split in 1992. Auburn is the only one to have done so *three* times.

*   For most of the Modern Era, Auburn has enjoyed a winning record against nearly every team in the SEC—including Alabama. Only Florida holds a notable edge over the Tigers, as a direct result of Steve Spurrier's early seasons when he was dominating *everyone* in the league.   But even that record is sliding toward obscurity; Auburn leads Florida 4-1 in head-to-head contests since the current century began.

*   In the current century, Auburn holds a 5-0 edge over the other traditional Eastern power, Tennessee, and still has never lost a game to South Carolina while the Gamecocks have been members of the SEC.

*   In the Modern Era, Auburn players have won two Heisman Trophies.   Only Florida can match this; only three other SEC programs during all that time won *one*.   (Texas A&M's Johnny Manziel marked the third in 2012.)

Factoids and statistics like this go on and on. The conclusions are clear: Auburn has enjoyed decades of dominance in the SEC and in the nation since Pat Dye took the reins in 1981. In the pages to come, we look at many specific instances that support that assertion.

If you read our previous Auburn football-related book, *Season of Our Dreams*, you know that we wear our emotions on our sleeves when it comes to the Tigers. There is little objectivity with us, and little claim to it. In the famous words of the Creed, we believe in Auburn and we love it. We make every effort in the pages ahead to be fair and balanced when such an approach is warranted, but be warned: We are generally as "objective" as Jim Fyffe calling an Iron Bowl, and we make no apologies for it. If you root for some other team, you're welcome to soak up the glory of the Tigers from these pages; perhaps you'll become converted to supporting the *good* guys—the guys in burnt orange and navy blue. But if you have issues with Auburn and want to nitpick our arguments here, we'd just as soon you go and read something else.

Still here? AUsome! Now—kick back, pour yourself a tall, cool glass of Toomer's lemonade, put on a recording of a winning Auburn game in the background (we know you have one!) or of the Auburn

University Marching Band, turn the volume down a bit, and enjoy with us a walk down memory lane. A walk through the Decades of Dominance.

The stands are full. The ball's being teed up. Let's go!

War Eagle!

--Van Allen Plexico & John Ringer—
"The Wishbone"
April 2013

1

Dye Hard:
Ten Memorable Things
about the Pat Dye Era

"You can talk about the Alabama mystique and the Georgia mystique, but they've done it with people. Hell—we've got people, too." –Coach Pat Dye

We discuss many of the specific football games of the Pat Dye Era at Auburn—and pretty much all of the big ones, whether wins or losses—in subsequent chapters of this book. Here we simply wanted to take ten *other*, non-game-specific moments, players, and situations from the Dye Era—moments that truly sum up Coach Dye's impact—and evaluate what they meant to Auburn's fans and its program in the short term and the long run.

1. RESPECT.

Patrick Fain Dye believed in "tough, hard-nosed" football, and that approach was reflected in most everything he did as our coach. His first practices at Auburn in the spring of 1981 became legendary in a "Junction Boys" sort of way. He ran off some players and worked others nearly to death. The end result, of course, was that those who remained were committed and determined to succeed—to *win* for Auburn. One former player later said he and the other players talked about getting T-shirts made that read, "I SURVIVED SPRING PRACTICE 1981." Another said that Dye made them more afraid of him than they were of any of their opponents.

Dye himself talked about "wolf sign" on the ground after those early practices; that's hunting talk for ground that's all chewed up, with blood and bits of fur scattered around. In short, no prisoners were taken that first spring. Dye wasn't worried about how many players he'd lose to attrition; he knew that those still with him come the fall would be players he could count on through thick and thin. The foundations for all the subsequent successes of the decade were being laid. That first team only won five games, but the seniors could look back with pride, knowing that they were the start of it—the start of something unparalleled in Auburn history.

The Modern Era was beginning, and lord help the rest of the SEC.

In his interview before being hired, he was asked how long it would take him to beat Alabama. The Tigers hadn't managed that feat in eight years and counting. Dye responded with one of the greatest answers in the history of job interviews: "Sixty minutes." There it was: No equivocations, no excuses. He would build a team that could go toe-to-toe with the Tide for sixty minutes and come out on top. And that's exactly what he did. It didn't happen immediately, but in his second season, he took down the mighty Bear and ended Alabama's streak.

He did it with the physical and mental toughness that he had been determined from day one to instill in the Tigers. This was easiest to see in the way the defense played—with vast improvement and a much more physical nature—and in the emphasis on the run game. He rarely brought in the top recruiting class in the country, but he molded the players he could get into tough, "hard-nosed" competitors who could get the job done.

Other coaches, players and fans came to respect Dye during his tenure at Auburn. They didn't much like him—but who wants their head coach liked by other teams and fans? That's usually the clearest sign your coach is doing something very wrong, or else not winning many games. Dye won, and he won consistently, and he wasn't shy about it, and thus he wasn't liked. But he was most definitely *respected*.

2. Bo Jackson.

If any one player is most identified with the Pat Dye era, it has to be Bo Jackson.

A true freshman on Dye's second team in 1982, Bo went on to a career so legendary you scarcely need us to explain it to you now. He played three of his four seasons in the wishbone formation, sharing carries with another halfback, a fullback, and the quarterback, who carries the ball occasionally in that scheme. Despite that situation, Jackson ended his career on the Plains with 4,303 rushing yards (a 6.6 yards-per-carry average—breaking the SEC record) and 4,575 all-purpose yards, along with 45 touchdowns.

Dye said it best when explaining to Bo why Auburn needed him so badly: "With you, we have a chance to beat any team in the country." For four glorious years on the Plains, that's exactly what he did.

It's hard to imagine now that Bo nearly left the team the week before the 1982 Iron Bowl—the game where he would go "over the top" and score the points that broke Alabama's nine-year streak. The story goes that Dye met him at the bus station and convinced him to return to the team. That Saturday, he capped off the huge 23-22 win over the Crimson Tide.

Bo went on to be named MVP of the Sugar Bowl following the 1983 season (a year in which 11-1 Auburn should have been awarded the national championship) and to win the 1985 Heisman Trophy following his stellar senior season, in which he ran for over 1,700 yards.

One can only imagine what Bo might have accomplished in a more modern offense, perhaps running the "Wildcat" as the quarterback. In any case, he turned in four spectacular seasons and helped put Auburn on the national map in a big, big way.

3. National Championships—Almost.

Four times in the Dye Era, Auburn teams found themselves in contention for the national championship. Three additional seasons saw the Tigers ranked #1 or predicted to win it all. That makes seven of Dye's twelve seasons occasions in which at least someone in a position to evaluate such things felt Auburn deserved to be considered.

The three occasions where it mattered the least were 1984, '85 and '90. In each of those seasons, someone (AP; *Sports Illustrated; etc.*) ranked Auburn as preseason or early-season #1. In each of those cases, the Tigers lost at least four games and never came close to challenging for a title.

The most flagrant and painful of those occasions upon which Auburn seriously flirted with a title in the Dye Era came in 1983. In his third year on the Plains, the Tigers played what was clearly the most difficult schedule in the country—*and the fifth most difficult of all time!*—and won all but one of those games. The Tigers defeated high-scoring Florida State, tough (and fifth-ranked) Florida, seventh-ranked Maryland (with Boomer Esiason), Tennessee, Georgia Tech, and fourth-ranked and defending conference champ Georgia all on the road, as well as top twenty-ranked Alabama (at Legion Field) and #8 Michigan in the Sugar Bowl. Their only loss was an early defeat at the hands of second-ranked Texas—a team that later lost to Georgia, a team Auburn defeated.

Of course, we all know the sad ending to this glorious story. The AP voters inexplicably voted #5 Miami (losers of an early game to Florida—another team Auburn had beaten!) national champions over Auburn, which at #3 was the highest-ranked team to win its bowl game.

Had there been a BCS, and had the computer rankings back then mattered, Auburn's lead over Miami in the rankings would have been too great for the Hurricanes to overcome after the bowls. The *New York Times* rankings, which relied upon computers, named Auburn the national champs for that season.

The 1987, '88, and '89 Auburn teams were all national-title-caliber squads. The first of these ended the regular season with a loss and a tie; play East Carolina that year instead of Florida State and you're undefeated. The 1988 team was without question one of the best squads in Auburn history, and only a tough, one-point loss in Baton Rouge (about which more later) kept them from facing Notre Dame in the Sugar Bowl for the national title. The 1989 team suffered two gut-wrenching losses on the road (at Tennessee and at Florida State) but won everything else, including a certain game over undefeated and second-ranked Alabama, and finished the year with a share of the conference title and looking like one of the best teams around.

Pat Dye never won a generally-recognized national title at Auburn, but he came oh-so-close multiple times, and he made the very idea of Auburn as a legitimate title contender on an annual basis something that the rest of the country took seriously for the first time since the heart of the Jordan years.

4. Adapting to the Times.

Coach Dye was flexible and adaptable to the times, and to the players at hand. In his first four seasons, he utilized the wishbone formation in order to take advantage of good running backs, good blocking tight ends and linemen, and quarterbacks who were perhaps smarter decision-makers than they were great pocket passers.

When Bo Jackson emerged as a force in college football and a contender for the Heisman Trophy in his senior season, Dye shifted the offense to the I-Formation to feature Bo as the single back, and to try to generate more of a passing attack.

The following year, 1986, with Bo gone to the Royals, Dye tossed out the almost run-exclusive offense he'd used up till then and incorporated a mixed attack that featured the forward pass in a much more prominent role. Jeff Burger stepped up as the trigger man and a corps of very solid receivers and tight ends emerged, including stars Lawyer Tillman, Freddy Weygand, Walter Reeves, Alexander Wright, Shane Wasden and Duke Donaldson. The running game dropped off somewhat after Brent Fullwood and Tommie Agee completed their careers at running back and fullback with the conclusion of the 1986 season, but serviceable backs like Stacey Danley and James Joseph kept the chains moving for the next three years.

By the early 1990s, with Tommy Bowden on board as Offensive Coordinator, the Tigers began to incorporate more shotgun formations and a more sophisticated mix of run and pass— something that Tommy's brother Terry would build upon in his first year as head coach.

5. Expansion of Jordan-Hare.

When Pat Dye took over as Auburn head coach in 1981, the West Upper Deck had just been added. It featured regular seating and a new press box area underneath it, and it took the capacity of the facility from 61,261 to 72,169. Dye immediately recognized the value of potentially having the largest football stadium in the State of Alabama on the Auburn campus, and pushed through another expansion, completed for the start of the 1987 season, that increased capacity to over 85,000 and added two rows of glass-fronted luxury suites beneath the new East Upper Deck.

Having made Jordan-Hare the largest stadium in Alabama, Dye had the leverage to force Alabama to play Auburn's home games in the Iron Bowl series on the Plains—and two years later, that happened.

Dye later referred to the East Upper Deck—and the subsequent moving of the home games with Alabama, culminating in the huge 1989 win—as "the last brick in our house."

6. The Missing Piece?

The 1987-'89 Auburn teams were among the best in the conference and in the nation in their respective years. Each of them won at least a share of the conference championship. Together the three teams suffered only four regular-season losses. But—what might have been, had one player made a slightly different choice?

The story has it that running back Emmitt Smith of Pensacola, Florida, was highly coveted by Dye, and his final choice came down to Auburn and Florida. Allegedly, Smith's mother at the last minute told him he couldn't go to school north of the Florida state line, and so he ended up in Gainesville—where he promptly exploded onto the scene, dominating the SEC at running back for three seasons.

Following his junior year at Florida, he turned pro and went on to greatness with the Dallas Cowboys.

But—what if he'd played for Auburn instead? It can be argued that the one missing piece on those three Tigers squads was a true home run threat at running back. Added into the mix with Jeff Burger and Reggie Slack and all those great receivers and those dominating defenses, it's entirely plausible that Auburn might have won at least two national championships during that time. Might he have made a difference in Baton Rouge in 1988? Very possibly. Might he have altered the outcome in the rain against Tennessee in 1989? Maybe.

Alas, Emmitt chose the Gators—and finished his college career winless against Auburn. And we will never know what might have been.

7. Always a Contender.

Nearly every season under Pat Dye, there was a sense that "This could be the year!" His defenses were always rugged and overpowering and dependable; his offenses were hard-nosed and would not be pushed around. His teams demonstrated continual excellence over a long period of time—something quite different from one-and-done, and much, much harder to accomplish. Any team can hitch its wagon to a star for a season; Dye built a solid foundation and then added to it, year by year.

While it never quite worked out for a generally-recognized national championship, the Tigers came so close, so many times, that fans always felt the big prize was just around the corner. The big games in Dye's era wouldn't have been nearly so big, had Auburn not always been in or near contention for even bigger prizes and honors during that time.

8. No Overtime.

The current system of overtime tie-breakers in major college football dates back only to the 1996 season. Prior to that, games that ended regulation in a draw went into the record books as draws. Pat Dye retired four years before this change, and he never got the opportunity to coach an overtime game. But he never let that stop him from ending a game in a draw. In fact, during his twelve-year tenure, he coached Auburn to four draws: two in 1987 (Tennessee and Syracuse), one in 1990 (Tennessee again), and one in 1992 (Arkansas).

Dye's philosophy was to take the points for the tie if he felt that his defense could then get the ball back one last time and allow him the opportunity for a final score and the win. The justification seemed to be, we might score again—but, if we don't, at least we don't *lose*. The best example of this was the 1990 Florida State game, in which Dye had Auburn kick the extra point (rather than go for two) after scoring to pull even late in the game. On that occasion, his defense did manage to (miraculously!) regain possession in the closing moments, and Jim Von Wyl nailed the game-winning field goal.

But with the two Tennessee ties, one might be forgiven for getting the impression that he and his Volunteer counterpart, Johnny Majors, didn't really mind ending up in a draw—particularly when there was a larger prize still to be had. Dye said more than once that, because the Auburn Tennessee game came so early in the year, the loser was at a profound disadvantage the rest of the way through the conference season. Those two draws with Tennessee, on the other hand, allowed Auburn to go on and win a share of the SEC title on both occasions.

Then there was Syracuse and the 1987-'88 Sugar Bowl. There was no longer-term justification for that one. Dye said at the time that his players didn't deserve to lose, and he didn't believe the referees were going to allow the Tigers a fair shot at scoring at the end. So he took the field goal and the deliberate draw. And the brains of every Orangemen fan exploded. Syracuse sent Dye crates of ugly neckties; he autographed them and sold them for charity. Auburn fans sent Syracuse crates of sour grapes. And so it goes.

9. Eric Ramsey.

We don't want to have to go there—indeed, the Ramseys crop up again in our Hall of Fame Bowl chapter later on—but the Eric Ramsey controversy was an integral part of the Dye Era, and of his decline and ultimate fall.

We have no desire to rehash all the gory details. The story is out there, from a variety of perspectives. In (very) brief: Dye and/or some assistants and/or boosters allegedly gave defensive back Ramsey and his wife and young child assistance when they desperately needed it. Dye also tried to get Ramsey on with an NFL team after his eligibility expired, despite general lack of interest in him on that level. Ramsey wrote a paper for one of his classes comparing Auburn's football program to an antebellum plantation complete with slavery, and also attempted to record meetings with the coaches, allegedly attempting to create a blackmail situation.

The media, ever hungry for a controversial story about Auburn, jumped all over the affair. The next thing you knew, Auburn was being called a racist institution (despite the strong denials of virtually every other player of any race on the team) and the program was being investigated by the NCAA. Ultimately, Dye would announce his retirement prior to the 1992 Iron Bowl, and later the NCAA would hit Auburn with a two-year bowl ban and one-year television ban. It was a sad situation turned into an ugly incident by the actions of selfish and greedy individuals, and it mostly brought the Dye Era to a disappointing finish.

10. The Legacy.

Even before the controversy came to light, however, the program appeared to be in sharp decline. The 1990 season had begun with at least one magazine predicting Auburn would win the national championship that year, but in reality the team was a hollow shell of its former self. The vast array of top-drawer talent that had carried Auburn to the heights of 1986-'89 was mostly gone by then. The 1990 squad limped to an 8-3-1 finish. The real signal that times were changing came in the horrific 48-7 loss to Florida in Gainesville. Steve Spurrier's first Gator team lit the Tigers up and made them look slow on the field by comparison. The two seasons that followed represented a slow-motion plunge to the bottom.

If not for the Ramsey mess, might Pat Dye have reinvented himself (and Auburn football) one more time? It's entirely possible. He'd done it before, most notably after the ugly Cotton Bowl loss in 1985. But it seems somehow unlikely. The old fire appeared to be dimming. The game was rapidly changing. The old era was at an end and a new one was beginning.

That being said, there is simply no denying the magnitude of the positive impact the man had on Auburn University, its football program, and its people during his time as head coach (and athletics director for several of those years). He came to Auburn at a time when, five years after the retirement and death of Shug Jordan, the program was floundering and directionless, playing all its games with Alabama in Legion Field, lacking any sort of defense, and scaring nobody. Twelve years later he left behind a program that easily filled its 85,000-seat stadium, commanded fear and respect across the football world, and had been able to look Alabama in the eye and say, "We are playing our home games in our home stadium. Period."

They named the field after him for a reason. And much of what has been accomplished in the years since he stepped down has been done at least in part by standing on his shoulders. His accomplishments on the Plains will resonate long after petty and overblown scandals have been forgotten, and his legacy will live forever in orange and blue.

2

The Top Ten Auburn Games
Played in Jordan-Hare Stadium,
1981-2000

Auburn played roughly 150 football games within the friendly confines of Jordan-Hare Stadium during the twenty years beginning with the arrival of Pat Dye and ending with the close of the 2000 season. (For the record, the first was a 24-16 win over TCU on September 5, 1981; the last was a 29-26 overtime win over Georgia on November 11, 2000.)

Here we present our views on the ten greatest games Auburn played *in Jordan-Hare* during that period. We have ranked them in what we feel is the proper order of importance, but such measurements are extremely subjective and surely everyone who reads this will prefer a different order to the list.

Honorable mentions:

Before we get to the Top Ten, here are a few great games that didn't quite make the cut:

*1983 Florida State, in which linebacker Greg Carr intercepted a late pass to preserve the 27-24 win.

*1988 Tennessee, in which the Big Blue defense put a hurtin' on the Big Orange offense, to the tune of 38-6!

*1990 Tennessee, which was a tie rather than a win (after all, it featured Johnny Majors against Pat Dye!), but in which Stan White stepped up to lead a furious comeback by the Tigers.

*1995 Alabama, in which the Tigers weathered a furious Tide comeback attempt and held on for a 31-27 victory at home.

*2000 LSU, in which Tim Carter's 100-yard kickoff return for a touchdown capped off a big 34-17 win over Nick Saban's first LSU squad.

*2000 Georgia, the last home game of this period, in which Rudi Johnson carried the load and Ben Leard snuck it over the goal line in OT to beat the Dawgs for the first time in Jordan-Hare in a decade.

And now—the Top Ten:

10. Texas, 1987 season.

Other games—perhaps any of the Honorable Mentions above—could fill this spot as easily as the 1987 Texas game. After all, nothing much was on the line here; no conference titles, no championships, and heck—it wasn't even a bowl game. It was in fact the opening game of the year. That being said, this game did mean a lot to Auburn players and fans alike. Texas had ruined Auburn's shot at the national championship in 1983, dealing the Tigers their only loss of the season. A year later, in Austin, the Longhorns had won again and dislocated Bo Jackson's shoulder in the process. Payback was more than due, and the '87 Tigers

26

delivered it by the truckload, crushing Texas 31-3 to start off a memorable season.

The Longhorns, who had dismissed Fred Akers as coach following the previous season and replaced him with David McWilliams, appeared to expect that Auburn would run the ball every play. To the contrary, Auburn had every intention of throwing the ball, and the passing game (which had been in use since the beginning of the previous season) clicked on all cylinders. Senior Jeff Burger connected with a powerful squadron of receivers that included Freddy Weygand, Lawyer Tillman, Alexander Wright, and Duke Donaldson, among others. For the defense, in his first game as a Tiger, Greg Staples at safety made an eye-popping interception when he crashed into a Texas receiver in midair and literally tore the ball away, and Kurt Crain at linebacker helped stuff the Texas run game and at one point even hugged the referee.

No, this wasn't an earth-shatteringly consequential game in the big picture, but it was a big, emotionally satisfying win over the Texas Longhorns, after two very damaging losses to them. And that's plenty.

9. Florida, 1989 season.

The Auburn-Florida series in the 1980s generally gave us great defensive performances by both teams, and the '89 edition was no different. Twelfth-ranked Auburn's spirits were high coming into this game, which marked the fiftieth anniversary of Jordan-Hare Stadium, and even featured a reenactment at halftime of Auburn's touchdown pass scored during the very first game against Florida in the stadium. The #19 Gators, on the other hand, were in turmoil. Defensive Coordinator Gary Darnell had taken over as head coach of Florida five games into the season, amid suggestions of NCAA violations by Coach Galen Hall. Things quickly went south for the Gators, who would finish the season 7-5 after starting out 6-1.

Even so, the Gators—led by running back Emmitt Smith—gave Auburn a hard-nosed game that came down to the final play. Florida's lone score came after Auburn fumbled deep within their own territory; otherwise, the Gators were unable to move the ball. Neither were the Tigers, however; they had mustered only a field goal before their final drive of the game.

With time running out, Reggie Slack put together a scoring drive that culminated with a rollout pass to Shane Wasden stumbling backwards and falling down in the end zone. Jim Fyffe summed it up in his inimitable style: *"I have seen the impossible happen!"* Auburn held on to win, 10-7.

Emmitt Smith turned pro after this season and thus finished his college career 0-3 against Auburn.

After the game, Darnell engaged in a shouting match with numerous fans in the Auburn student section on his way out of the stadium, and a number of Auburn students were actually restrained (by plastic wrist-ties) and detained by AU police. Darnell would not return at the helm in Gainesville in 1990; instead, the Gators brought in a former Duke coach you may have heard of: Steve Spurrier. Things would never be the same.

8. Florida, 1983 season.

This game was a huge win for Auburn in Pat Dye's best season as Tigers coach. The '83 Gators were a strong unit—ranked fifth in the country—and were in fact the only team to defeat the future national champion Miami Hurricanes that year. Lots of future NFL players dotted the lineups of both squads. It was an epic clash in a season of epic clashes for then-#4 Auburn.

The Tigers got off to a big start following a 55-yard touchdown run by Bo Jackson and then a short Randy Campbell scoring run. Florida hung in there when QB Wayne Peace connected with Ricky Nattiel for a touchdown. The Tigers tried to pull away again by way of a 17-yard Lionel "Little Train" James score. But the Gators weren't done. They marched down to the Auburn goal line in the third quarter and threatened to punch it in—only for RB Neal Anderson to fumble the ball out the back of the end zone. Auburn took over on the twenty and on the very next play, in quintessential Bo Jackson style, the Great One rumbled eighty yards for a touchdown. (He would end the day having amassed nearly two hundred yards rushing.)

Florida managed two scores of their own in the fourth quarter and even recovered an onsides kick, but it wasn't enough—the Tigers held on for the huge 28-21 win and remained on track for the SEC title and a shot at the national championship. And of course any win over Florida is a big win—which brings us to:

7. Florida, 1987 season.

Auburn fans were beyond hungry for a victory over Florida in 1987, having lost three straight to the Gators following the '83 win. The 1984 game had been a 24-3 embarrassment, with Bo Jackson returning to the lineup after missing six games with a separated shoulder, only to play somewhat tentatively. The game the following year was a hard-fought affair—a "Game of Steel," as the *Birmingham News* called it—that nevertheless went Florida's way. The 1986 game in Gainesville was hardest of all to swallow; Auburn had the win in their pockets only to lose at the last moment when limping quarterback Kerwin Bell somehow hobbled across the goal line to score a two-point conversion and steal the 18-17 win. It hadn't helped that Florida had pulled to within 17-10 earlier in the game due to a long field goal by Robert McGinty—a former Auburn kicker Pat Dye had essentially shoved out the door after he missed a potential game-winner against Alabama in 1984. Thus in 1987 Tigers fans were desperate to beat Florida, and beat them soundly.

At the beginning of the national telecast of the 1987 game, the CBS announcer summed up the zeitgeist of the day perfectly: "It's the irresistible force—Florida's Emmitt Smith—against the immovable object—Auburn's Aundray Bruce." Now, looking back, we know that the actual "immovable object" of that defense was probably Tracy Rocker, not Bruce. But Bruce had recently put together one of the most remarkable individual performances in some time against Georgia Tech in Atlanta and so he's who the media and fans were focusing on at the time.

The game was played on Halloween night and T-shirts beforehand proclaimed a "Nightmare at Jordan-Hare." Indeed, the tenth-ranked Gators were spooked from the first moment, with every phase of the game coming together for sixth-ranked Auburn. The Gators were held to only six points and Emmitt Smith was mostly held in check, failing to reach a hundred total rushing yards. Auburn, meanwhile, scored 29 points and cruised to victory in what was one of the most satisfying wins against a big rival in Auburn history.

6. Florida State, 1990 season.

This game brought the Auburn-Florida State series to a close; as of this writing, the teams have not faced one another since. It's been so long, many young Auburn fans today have no real understanding of how intense this rivalry became during the 1980s. Both programs were on the rise under iconic head coaches (Pat Dye/Bobby Bowden). Both had developed stout defenses to go along with exciting offenses. (It was as if, one day in the middle of 1986, Florida State came around to the idea of playing defense at the exact same moment that Auburn came around to the idea of attempting the forward pass.)

This game was the rubber match of what had turned out to be a seven-game series. Auburn had won in exciting shootouts in 1983, 1984, and 1985, while FSU struck back with a blowout win in

Jordan-Hare in 1987 (the very week after the above Florida game!) and a controversial Sugar Bowl win at the end of the 1988 season (featuring a no-call on a Dedrick Dodge pass interference of Freddy Weygand as Auburn was driving for what would have been the winning score). The Seminoles brought the series level in 1989 by holding on in the face of a furious Auburn comeback to win in Tallahassee. So 1990 would decide the series winner and would also provide the Tigers a chance to break the three-game losing streak. Auburn fans were ravenous for victory over the Seminoles and this would be the last chance to get it.

Auburn's defense ultimately would make the difference. They shut out FSU in the second half, and two of their plays in particular stand out from this game—along with one interesting coaching decision by Pat Dye.

First came the "fumblerooksi." A staple of the Bowden playbook in those days, FSU would save this (now-banned) trick play for critical situations. Unfortunately for the Seminoles, AU's defensive line had been well-versed in how to spot it. When the FSU center placed the ball on the ground to start the play, a Tiger lineman (we think it might have been "Pig" Goff) immediately leapt upon it. Boom: "fumblerooski" becomes just plain "fumble."

With Florida State ahead very late, 17-14, an Auburn drive stalled out and Pat Dye called for a field goal. This brought back memories of the Sugar Bowl tie with Syracuse after the 1987 season, as well as the tie with Tennessee earlier in the season. This time, however, Dye was proven right in his decision. Auburn leveled the game at 17-17 with very little time remaining, but FSU would have one more chance to score. Quickly the Seminoles drove into Auburn territory, and things appeared bleak.

Then Auburn's defense stepped up, getting a huge sack on the Seminole QB after pursuing him across what seemed like half the length of the field. The play lost what must have been twenty yards at the very least, taking the Seminoles out of field goal range.

Getting the ball back, Auburn moved into field goal range themselves and, as time expired, Jim Von Wyl nailed the kick that gave the Tigers an absolutely shocking and improbable 20-17 victory.

As Tigers fans celebrated in the stadium after the win, many of them spontaneously broke out into the Seminole tomahawk chop and war chant—directed at the visitors' section of the stands. The FSU crowd, perhaps not as well-versed at that time as most SEC fan bases on the maxim, "When you lose on the road, get out of the stadium immediately," simply stood there, agape, watching. They couldn't quite seem to believe what had happened, or that they were getting their annoying gesture chopped back at them. Ahh, sweet victory.

The seven-game FSU series belonged to Auburn, 4-3.

5. LSU, 1994 season.

Hollywood couldn't have written a script this bizarre and unbelievable.

Auburn had won thirteen games in a row coming into the 1994 contest at home against LSU. In his second season as Tigers coach, Terry Bowden had yet to lose. Before this game was over, most observers could be forgiven for concluding that they were about to see the fabled "Streak" come to an end—but it didn't. Remarkably, astonishingly, *unbelievably*—it didn't.

For the entire game, Auburn's offense proved wholly ineffectual against a stout LSU defense, converting only one of thirteen (!!) third-downs. Dameyune Craig came on at quarterback in place of a mostly-floundering Patrick Nix but was unable to jumpstart the attack. LSU, meanwhile, ran and passed with relative ease and held the blue-clad Tigers offense to only a 40 yard field goal early in the second quarter.

The Tigers did have more than three points on the board, however. Prior to halftime, Auburn's Chris Shelling leapt on an LSU fumble in the end zone. The defense had done something the offense could not on this day—score a touchdown. Little did anyone guess that they were only getting started.

Early in the fourth quarter, LSU kicked a field goal to increase their lead to 23-9. Auburn displayed virtually no signs of life at this point. Then came one of the more shocking turns of events in college football history.

Attempting to convert a fourth down, LSU's quarterback, Jamie Howard, threw downfield—into the arms of Auburn defensive back Ken Alvis, who returned the interception forty-two yards for a touchdown. A few plays later, it was Fred Smith's turn to pick Howard off and take it to the house. As hard as it was to believe, the game was suddenly tied.

A field goal pushed LSU back out to a 26-23 lead, but then Coach Curly Hallman inexplicably called for another Howard pass on third down. This one was snagged by Brian Robinson, who took it in for the decisive score. The game ended with Chris Shelling grabbing his second of the game, this time in the Auburn end zone, to fend off a late LSU comeback attempt.

Auburn had pulled out the miraculous 30-26 win. LSU, having outgained Auburn 407-163 in yardage, was defeated and demoralized. They had turned the ball over a staggering eight times, with four of those resulting directly in touchdowns for Auburn. The Streak lived on and would endure for another seven games.

LSU's Curly Hallman was shown the exit at Baton Rouge at the end of the season.

This game is still the standard for coaching stupidity. Les Miles only dreams of coaching LSU to an ending this bizarre. When coaches go boring on offense when they have a lead, this game is why. Just Say No to throwing the ball into coverage when protecting a lead late.

(John points out—even on the first LSU touchdown pass, Howard does not throw a good, catchable pass. Van counters that the Auburn secondary clearly found his passes quite catchable...)

4. Florida, 1993 season.

The 1993 Auburn-Florida game certainly gave those of us lucky enough to witness it firsthand our money's worth—and a lot more. It provided enough entertainment, enough action, enough scoring, enough back-and-forth lead changes, and enough drama for any three games. And it ended with an Auburn victory. The three games that rank ahead of it on this list had a little more going for them in terms of what was at stake—and of course they were all Iron Bowls, which really says it all—but none of them quite matched this one for sheer fireworks and "head on a swivel," "don't blink or you'll miss something" action.

Auburn, of course, was serving the first of two years probation for violations during the previous regime, and the game was not allowed to be televised. The Tigers were riding a six-game winning streak—the early stages of the famous twenty-game "Streak" of Terry Bowden—but #4 Florida was expected to bring that run to a quick end.

Florida got out to a quick lead at 10-0 and was threatening to go up by seventeen. Such a lead might well have proven demoralizing and insurmountable. Thankfully, we will never know. As Danny Wuerffel zipped a pass toward the Auburn end zone, Calvin Jackson stepped in front of it and picked it off, returning it ninety-five yards for a touchdown.

From there the game went back and forth with long passes and reverses and all forms of entertaining football until finally, very late, Florida scored a touchdown and two-point conversion to tie the game at 35. As the last seconds drained away, Auburn's Scott Etheridge nailed a long field goal to secure the 38-35 win.

The game marked Auburn's first win over a Steve Spurrier-coached Florida team—a team that would go on to win the SEC Championship Game. Afterward, an obviously drained but still hyper Terry Bowden commented, "I never thought we could get into a scoring contest with Florida and win." Yet somehow the Tigers had done just that.

It was apparently very exciting even to non-Auburn fans in attendance: When a newly-hired professor handed Van back a research paper on the Monday after the game, "War Eagle!" was marked in red on the cover page! "My parents from North Carolina were in town and they had a blast," the Poly Sci prof reported. Well, of course they did.

The game is also notable for yielding the cover photo for *Sports Illustrated*'s special issue celebrating Auburn's undefeated season; the player sacking Wuerffel on the cover is none other than backup defensive lineman and now superstar crime novelist Ace Atkins.

3. Alabama, 1997 season.

For this game, John was safely ensconced before his television in Jackson, Mississippi, along with his wife and his then-infant daughter, where he could scream at the screen to his heart's content. Van was actually in the stadium—but it was a very close-run thing, and he nearly didn't get in!

In retrospect, of all the seasons during the second half of the 1990s that Van could have chosen to attempt the "don't buy season tickets; try scalping them before each game" approach, 1997 was the worst option. Yet that's just what he did. As a consequence, he nearly missed out seeing on the Florida game altogether, and had to haunt the alumni parking lot for an hour prior to kickoff, begging and pleading and digging deep into his wallet, in order to scrape up a pair of tickets for the Iron Bowl. By the time he sat down in his precious and hard-won seat, his nerves were frazzled. As it turned out, the game would do little to improve that mental state. It was a doozy.

The Auburn Tigers had a lot on the line, heading into the 1997 Iron Bowl in Jordan-Hare, including a Western Division title and their first-ever trip to Atlanta for the SEC Championship Game. Alabama, meanwhile, was suffering through one of their worst years in memory, having won only one game since September (!!) and even having fallen to Louisiana Tech.

This being the Iron Bowl, however, you just knew the Tide would rise up and give Auburn their best effort—and they certainly did.

After two early Jarret Holmes field goals, Auburn led 6-0. But then Alabama stormed back to take a 17-6 lead deep into the second half. Fred Beasley's one-yard scoring dive brought Auburn to within five at 17-12, but the Tigers failed on a two-point conversion. Another Holmes field goal closed the gap even more, to 17-15, but then Alabama got the ball back with less than three minutes to go. Once the Tide converted a first down, the situation appeared dire indeed.

And then the almost unthinkable happened, as Alabama faced a third down on its own 36 with less than a minute to go. Freddie Kitchens threw a screen pass to fullback Ed Scissum, who was immediately hit by Auburn's Martavious Houston, knocking the ball loose. Quinton Reese recovered at the 33, and Jaret Holmes knocked through his fourth field goal of the game to win the Iron Bowl for the Tigers.

Perhaps the only thing better than soundly thrashing the Tide is outright stealing a big win from them, and this game more than qualifies. Alabama ended the season at 4-7 while Auburn went on to play in Atlanta twice in December—in the conference title game and then again in the Chik-Fil-A (Peach) Bowl.

And Jim Fyffe's deliriously screamed, *"It's gooooood! It's gooooood! It's gooooood!"* still vibrates happily in the ears of Tigers faithful worldwide.

2. Alabama, 1993 season.

It is an odd truism of the last few decades of Auburn and Alabama football that a strange symmetry seems to assert itself on occasion. In 2009 Alabama won every game, the BCS title, and the Heisman Trophy; the next year, Auburn duplicated all of those feats. In 1997, Alabama managed only four wins; the next season—only a year removed from losing the SEC Championship Game by a single point—Auburn utterly collapsed and finished with only three wins. And in 1993, Auburn followed up an undefeated Crimson Tide season by racking up a very unexpected one of their own. With the Tigers prohibited from postseason play, the game that clinched that perfect 1993 season was the Iron Bowl.

So many things stand out as noteworthy (if not downright unusual) about this game. It was only the second Iron Bowl ever played at Jordan-Hare, though it had been four years since the previous (and first) occasion. Auburn's "Streak" was on the line. The game wasn't televised, so Alabama aired a closed-circuit broadcast in Bryant-Denny Stadium—and sold out every available seat, making it the first college football game to sell out two stadiums at once. The game's radio play-by-play was broadcast over telephone lines for those who wished to call in, and the phone interchange received so many calls that it actually melted. (John called in from Virginia, got bumped off the connection—and then came the interchange meltdown, so he eventually had to call a friend in Alabama and have them set the phone down next to the radio!) It was Stan White's final game as an Auburn Tiger, yet he didn't get to finish it or throw the winning score. And Auburn trailed for most of the game, yet ended up winning by eight.

As with the 1997 Iron Bowl, Auburn allowed the Tide to get out to an early lead before scratching and clawing their way back. A field goal and a safety accounted for all of the Tigers' points at halftime and they trailed, 14-5, to Gene Stallings' defending national champions. In the second half, the Tigers drove to Alabama's 35 yard line where they faced a fourth-and-15. Unfortunately, four-year starting quarterback Stan White was injured on the previous play and had to leave the game. Even with White out, Terry Bowden decided the distance was too long for a field goal and too short for a punt, so he sent backup Patrick Nix onto the field. What Nix did next will live forever in Iron Bowl lore: He lofted a pass to receiver Frank Sanders (not the last time we would cheer for that combination), who caught the ball on about the three yard line, spun around, and dived into the end zone for the touchdown. Alabama's best defensive back, Antonio Langham, had been shadowing Sanders previously but, for reasons never explained, he crossed over to the far side of the field on the play, leaving Sanders in single coverage. Nix spotted the mismatch and put the ball where it needed to be.

During this play, because he was jumping up and down and screaming, Van's trusty radio flew out of his jacket pocket and impacted the concrete steps of the stadium at his feet, exploding into pieces. Thus he didn't get to hear Jim Fyffe's elated, perfect description of the play until much later: *"Ohh—he caught it! And he's in! Touchdown Auburn!!"*

Despite this spectacular play, Auburn still trailed by two, but Alabama was done with scoring and had been for some time. Auburn would record a field goal to take the lead in the fourth quarter, 15-14, and then later faced a short-yardage third down situation deep in their own territory while trying to run the clock out. As the Tide defense bunched up tight against the line of scrimmage, Tigers RB James Bostic burst through the line and rambled for the score that iced the game, 22-14. The fact that Bostic wasn't exactly a speed demon only added to the spectacle of the play, as he rambled along, shedding Tide defenders along the way.

Rarely has Toomer's Corner been rolled as thoroughly or comprehensively as it was that night. Van, a graduate student at Auburn at the time, supplied navy blue t-shirts to his friends that he had ordered printed up beforehand—so confident was he in victory—that read "11-0" in big orange numbers on the front, and "Oh Hell Yes!" on the back. He and his roommate stood atop the metal fencing near the Oaks and exulted with the vast celebratory throngs in orange and blue long into the night.

The National Championship Foundation awarded the Tigers their title as the only major college program to finish the year undefeated; ironically, the AP winner, Florida State, was coached by Terry Bowden's father. Terry himself was named Coach of the Year by the National Sportswriters and Sportscasters Association; in yet more irony, he and every Auburn head coach since has won this trophy, which was named the "Bear Bryant Award."

39

Much of the disappointment of Auburn being denied a berth in the SEC Championship Game was assuaged by the exultation of such a satisfying victory over the arch-rival, and the successful completion of a perfect season on the Plains.

1. Alabama, 1989 season.

For so many reasons, reasons most Auburn fans will immediately and implicitly understand, this game towers above all the others played in Jordan-Hare. It is without question the single greatest—and most important—game *ever* played in Auburn's home stadium. Here are some of those reasons:

It was an Iron Bowl—though of course not just *any* Iron Bowl.

Auburn had won the previous three clashes with Alabama. An entire graduating class of Crimson Tide players faced the very real and nearly unthinkable prospect of having spent their entire college careers at Tuscaloosa never having beaten Auburn.

The SEC Championship was on the line; Alabama was undefeated while Auburn had suffered one conference loss, at Tennessee. A win by Auburn would force a three-way tie for the title, and give the Tigers their third straight SEC crown.

It was a game against the second-ranked team in the country, and so there were national championship implications, as well.

Most importantly of all, though, it was the game that has come to be known simply as "First Time Ever." It marked the first time in history that the University of Alabama played a football game against Auburn University in the confines of Jordan-Hare Stadium. As Pat Dye said beforehand, the fact that the game was being played at all in Auburn was a bigger story than whatever the outcome might turn out to be.

The game had been played in a variety of locations prior to 1989, settling finally and seemingly permanently in Birmingham's Legion Field. The teams alternated "home" years in that same stadium, and the crowd was always (allegedly) divided 50/50 between the two schools. Even so, Alabama clearly enjoyed a tremendous advantage by playing the game there every year, for a variety of reasons including the playing surface of the field, the overwhelmingly pro-Alabama nature of Birmingham, the fact that the Tide played several other home games each season in that stadium, and the statue of their coach right outside the gates. Bear Bryant knew full well that his teams enjoyed an advantage playing there every year and he took steps to prevent any changes from happening. He worked out a contract with Auburn, prior to Pat Dye's arrival, that would see the game played in Birmingham at least through the end of the decade—and well beyond, if things remained the way they always had been.

Things would not remain the way they always had been. Patrick Fain Dye intended to see to that.

When discussion between the two universities turned to a heretofore-perfunctory renewal of the Legion Field contract, Dye informed the powers at the Capstone that Auburn intended to move the game in Auburn's home years to Jordan-Hare Stadium. By Auburn's reading of the contract, that meant 1989 would be the year it moved to the Plains.

Alabama begged to differ. According to their reading of the contract, the game was set to be played at Legion Field at least through the 1991 season.

When informed that Auburn intended to bring the game home to Jordan-Hare, then-Alabama head coach Ray Perkins infamously replied, "It won't happen." (That Perkins quote graced a huge sheet on the roof of the Auburn gymnastics building across from the stadium on the morning of the game, followed by the line, "It happened.")

Perhaps the conflict was already worked out; perhaps it would have been under any circumstances. But it didn't hurt that the intransigent Perkins left Tuscaloosa for the Tampa Bay Buccaneers following the 1986 season, replaced by new head coach Bill Curry and new Athletic Director Steve Sloan. Sloan in particular had a different view on the situation, stating publicly that home-and-home arrangements didn't harm other big traditional rivalries such as Ohio State-Michigan or Southern Cal-Notre Dame. In any case, soon after Curry and Sloan arrived at Alabama, the Tide's position changed in principle and they agreed that the games in odd-numbered years would be played in Auburn.

One sticking point remained, however. Auburn had to play the 1989 game in Birmingham instead of Auburn, Sloan and company stated, as per their interpretation of the contract. In response to this, Pat Dye simply dug in his heels and said *no*, the 1989 game would be played in Auburn. Finally, to break the impasse, Dye agreed to play the 1991 Iron Bowl in Legion Field—a "bone thrown to Alabama," as he later described it, to reach a peaceful agreement.

(As it turned out, the 1991 team was one of Pat Dye's weakest squads, finishing with a 5-6 record and losing that bizarre Auburn "home game" in Legion Field, with its "AU" logo painted on the cheap Astroturf. Had the game been played in Auburn, it is entirely possible the Tigers' lock on beating the Tide in Jordan-Hare would have lasted only one game rather than an entire decade. Maybe things worked out for the best, after all.)

So the 1989 Iron Bowl was coming to Jordan-Hare Stadium. Tigers fans rejoiced. Quickly, however, thoughts turned to the game itself: What if, after all the acrimony and threats and bombast, we actually *lost* the game? Surely that wasn't likely though—right? After all, Auburn was on a three-game winning streak over Alabama coming into 1989, and the previous year's Tigers team had been one of the best in school history. Just how good could the Tide be, to actually threaten to defeat Auburn in the "First Time Ever" game?

The answer, almost horrifyingly for Auburn fans, turned out to be "very, very good." As the 1989 season rolled around and the weeks and games flew by, Alabama looked more and more like a powerhouse. The '89 Auburn team, on the other hand, seemed to be struggling to find itself. Yes, we would get Alabama in our stadium at last—and it looked increasingly as if they would beat us there. A sort of dull, sinking feeling set in among many of the Tiger faithful. We didn't give up hope—none of us did. But we worried. Each in our own quiet, introspective way, we worried.

Part of the reason for concern was that the Tigers still hadn't quite come together as a solid team most of the way through the '89 season. In previous years, Dye's teams had a way of suddenly clicking on offense and defense in one game—usually one *early-season* game—and then rolling along into the tough season-ending stretch of "Amen Corner" contests at top gear. But the '89 squad sputtered and stumbled, never quite seeming in synch, dropping road games (to quality opponents) at Knoxville and Tallahassee. Alabama, meanwhile, rolled up the yards and points against Tennessee; their offense, under the command of Homer Smith, appeared unstoppable. Yes, we'd finally gotten what we wanted—Alabama in Jordan-Hare—and it looked very much as if we were going to live to regret it.

So it was with a strange blending of anticipation, excitement, concern, and stomach-churning nervousness that we awoke on the morning of December 2, 1989, to head out for the stadium. En route, we were treated to the then-almost unthinkable sight of actual, crimson-clad Alabama fans in the hundreds roaming around our campus. This was something, remember, that we had never ever witnessed before, in all the years of Auburn football history. In a way it was gratifying—"You're here! We made you come, whether you liked it or not!"—but in another way it was almost...dare we say, *disgusting*? "Take your beating," we collectively, almost psychically yelled at them, "and then *get out of here!*"

We could only hope that a beating would indeed be administered later that afternoon, and that the guys in blue and white would be doing the beating.

For one of your intrepid Wishbone columnists, the previous twenty-four hours had been quite literally gut-churning. Early on December 1, then-AU junior Van drank a half-gallon of fruit juice that, unbeknownst to him, one of his roommates had left out of the refrigerator all day. The resulting hours of utter misery almost convinced him he could not under any circumstances attend the game—he would be too busy attending his own funeral. Fortunately, by the time every drop of juice (and everything else) had evacuated his stomach several hours later, he realized with gratitude that he just might be able to attend after all—even if it meant crawling to the stadium with a barf bag in tow. (It would be seventeen years before he could again taste Dole's Pine-Orange-Banana juice without gagging.)

Before the game, rumors swirled that Tide fans planned to roll Toomer's Corner with red toilet paper if the unthinkable happened and Alabama won. In a strange foreshadowing of much darker and more recent events, Tigers fans quickly drew up contingency plans to rendezvous post-game at the Corner and protect the Oaks at all costs.

Auburn students began gathering outside the gates to the stadium before dawn, though kickoff on CBS was not until 1 pm. Your Wishbone columnists' group made its way past RVs that had been parked in vast numbers all over campus as early as Monday of game week; in all the time John and Van attended Auburn prior to that game, neither had seen more than a few campers arriving on campus earlier than Thursdays of game weeks.

The atmosphere outside the stadium was electric. Some people had brought cards or games and attempted to play while waiting for the gates to open, but no one could really focus on anything other than what was to come later in the day. Nearly everyone seemed to float on air. "Body Getta" and "Two Bits" and other Auburn cheers were shouted and echoed back over and over, with scarcely a break in between, for hours. "War Eagle" tumbled easily and often from every pair of lips.

"From the cradle to the grave," intoned CBS's Jim Nantz from atop Haley Center in the broadcast lead-in, "football borders on religion in the state of Alabama." Truer words were never spoken, as the national viewing audience was about to find out.

Finally, after what seemed like an eternity of waiting, the gates opened and students dashed for their "first come-first served" seats. The game itself could have been almost anticlimactic, except that Alabama had come to play and had every intention of ruining the day for the better part of the 85,314 attendees.*

In brief, the contest played out thusly:

Auburn went up 7-0 on a James Joseph one-yard plunge. Alabama struck back with a field goal and touchdown of their own— and would have added more, but a fake field goal attempt was snuffed out by the Tigers defense. Even so, at the half, terrifyingly, Alabama led, 10-7.

The second half would be nearly all Auburn. Two long passes from Reggie Slack—one to Shane Wasden, the other to Alexander Wright—set up another touchdown and a Win Lyle field goal.

Suddenly Auburn was back in front, 17-10. A Darrell "Lectron" Williams touchdown run put the Tigers ahead by fourteen, and another Lyle kick appeared to have pushed the game out of reach at 27-10. Auburn players celebrated on the sidelines with as much glee as most of the fans in the stands at that point. Alas, the scoring was not done yet. Alabama came back to ring up ten more points in the final eight minutes, pulling within only seven of Auburn, but an onsides kick failed. Lyle knocked home one last field goal for the Tigers to make the final score 30-20.

The crowd was delirious. For the first time ever, Alabama had come to Auburn to play the Iron Bowl—an undefeated, second-ranked Alabama, no less—and Auburn had won. A literal "purple haze" floated over the stands, a result of the 60,000-plus orange and blue paper shakers that had been distributed before kickoff. (The Auburn Student Government Association had been setting aside shakers all year so that almost everyone in the stadium could have one for this game.) Fans were coughing and sneezing "shaker dust" for hours afterward; many joked that we would probably come down with some strange orange-and-blue variety of lung cancer later in life—but it had been for a worthy cause!

For years afterward, Alabama fans, notorious in their tendency to seek any available excuse for a loss, countered any mention of this game with, "There was no way Alabama could have been expected to win *in that environment*." Auburn fans didn't care what excuse the Tide fans wanted to console themselves with, though. The good guys had won. That was all that mattered.

The playing of the game in Jordan-Hare instead of Legion Field was compared by some, at the time, to the fall of the Berlin Wall, which had happened only a few weeks earlier. Then-Sports Information Director David Housel evoked images of "the children of Israel" coming out of bondage and into the Promised Land. Some in the national media, not fully understanding the depth of passion and cultural history involved, made light of these remarks. Only Auburn people truly understood just how apt such comparisons were, however, at least in the social and emotional realms. After years of Alabama dominating the rivalry to the point of even controlling the parameters of where the game would be staged, the playing (and winning) of the game *in Auburn* was a milestone of epic proportions for the entire *state* and its history, not just for a university or for the world of sports. Pat Dye called it "the last brick in our house," meaning that with the successful relocation of the game to our own stadium, we had become a complete program, fully in control of our own destiny, no longer at the mercy of anyone else. Our house was at last complete.**

The 1989 Iron Bowl was the *last* football game Auburn University played during the 1980s*** and it was a perfect conclusion to what had been the greatest decade in Auburn football history. So much was accomplished on that December day in Jordan-Hare, so many old demons laid to rest. Walls came down; bricks were forged; Israelites found the Promised Land. Mainly, though, a group of young men in orange and blue stepped up and did what they had to do—what thousands and thousands of Auburn men and women and children who looked on with nervousness and trepidation but also with hope and brimming confidence wanted them to do, depended on them to do, and virtually *willed* them to do:

They faced the mighty Tide in their own house for the *First Time Ever*.

And they *won*.

* The stated maximum capacity of Jordan-Hare during the 1989 season, and for several years afterward, was 85,214. For this game, however, an additional one hundred attendees were somehow allowed inside, thus causing this game to hold the record for the largest attendance at a football game in the history of the state of Alabama for quite some time. Some accounts claim attendance was only 85,214 for this game as well, but that is simply not accurate.

**It says a great deal about both programs that there was a "brick" associated with each program during the Dye/Curry era. The Auburn brick is the one Pat Dye had engraved with the score of this game, to keep on his desk, after referring to the game as "the last brick in our house." The brick associated with Alabama, of course, is the one a disgruntled Crimson Tide fan threw through Coach Bill Curry's window after the Tide lost a game to Ole Miss.

***Depending on how one calculates decades, of course; it was the last game played while the calendar read "198_." Auburn's bowl game that season was the Hall of Fame Bowl, played on Jan. 1, 1990.

Running Back U:
Auburn's Top Rushers in the Modern Era

Auburn is so widely known within the college football world as "Running Back U" that an in-depth, specific analysis of statistics would seem at first unnecessary.

The great backs of the Eighties and early Nineties stand out, of course, from Lionel James and Bo Jackson through James Bostic and Stephen Davis. In the past decade, however, the Tigers have been blessed with the services of another tremendous batch of runners with power and/or speed, beginning with Rudi Johnson and continuing through Cadillac Williams, Ronnie Brown, Kenny Irons, and most recently Ben Tate, Mike Dyer and Onterio McCalebb. A recent study by the *Bleacher Report* revealed that even in just the past twelve years, Auburn is still Running Back U, beating out USC and Miami for that distinction.

Here we present a look at the numbers behind the backs. In the first four charts, the top runners of the Modern Era are listed *by season*, with stats broken down into the categories of Yards (for that Season), Attempts, Touchdowns, Average Yards Per Carry

(APC), and Yards Per Game. Each table ranks the players in the order of each of those categories, beginning with *Yards Per Season*. We had intended to include only the top twenty players in each chart, but we allowed a couple of them to run longer because of the interesting information revealed by including the players further down the lists. In this first case, we present the *Top 28*:

Auburn Running Backs in the Modern Era, by Yards per Season

#	Year	Player	Gm	Yards	Att	TD	APC	YPG
1	1985	Bo Jackson	12	1915	309	18	6.20	159.6
2	2000	Rudi Johnson	13	1652	349	14	4.73	127.1
3	1986	Brent Fullwood	12	1543	194	11	7.95	128.6
4	2009	Ben Tate	13	1362	263	10	5.18	104.8
5	1983	Bo Jackson	12	1343	180	12	7.46	111.9
6	2003	Carnell Williams	13	1307	241	17	5.42	100.5
7	2005	Kenny Irons	12	1293	256	13	5.05	107.8
8	1994	Stephen Davis	11	1263	221	13	5.71	114.8
9	2011	Michael Dyer	12	1242	242	10	5.13	103.5
10	1993	James Bostic	11	1205	199	12	6.06	109.5
11	1995	Stephen Davis	12	1188	192	14	6.19	99.0
12	2004	Carnell Williams	13	1165	239	12	4.87	89.6
13	2010	Michael Dyer	14	1093	182	5	6.01	78.1
14	2002	Ronnie Brown	11	1008	175	13	5.76	91.6
15	1988	Stacy Danley	11	945	198	7	4.77	85.9
16	2004	Ronnie Brown	12	913	153	8	5.97	76.1
17	2007	Ben Tate	13	903	202	7	4.47	69.5
18	1982	Bo Jackson	12	893	141	11	6.33	74.4
19	2006	Kenny Irons	11	893	198	4	4.51	81.2
20	1992	James Bostic	10	819	186	5	4.40	81.9
21	1989	James Joseph	11	817	172	4	4.75	74.3
22	2010	Ont. McCalebb	14	804	95	9	8.46	57.4
23	1982	Lionel James	12	779	113	7	6.89	64.9
24	2002	Carnell Williams	7	745	141	10	5.28	106.4
25	1989	Stacy Danley	10	737	170	4	4.34	73.7
26	1983	Lionel James	11	728	124	4	5.87	66.2
27	1988	James Joseph	11	721	118	5	6.11	65.5
28	1985	Brent Fullwood	11	709	97	6	7.31	64.5

Just 85 yards short, Bo! So close to a 2000-yard season; but at least he did win the Heisman for that spectacular 1985 campaign. And on 309 carries, second only to Rudi Johnson's workhorse-like 2000 season. The real victim of Bo's Heisman march in 1985 was likely Brent Fullwood, who would've been a star anywhere else in the country that year (and possibly challenged Bo for the Heisman!) Fullwood's '86 campaign ranks third in yards for a season, but he did it with 115 fewer carries than Bo in '85, and (good heavens) 155 fewer carries than Rudi Johnson in 2000!

Where does Cam Newton fit into the Yards Per Season list? In his one year with the Tigers, playing quarterback, he rushed for 1473 yards on 264 carries, placing him fourth ahead of Ben Tate (2009) in the Modern Era. In Gus Malzahn's three years with Auburn as offensive coordinator, his running backs achieved the fourth, ninth, and thirteenth spots in yards per season, along with Cam at QB finishing higher than any of those. And another of his backs, Onterio McCalebb, rules the roost overall in the yards per carry category.

Now we shift from Yards Per Season to Yards Per *Game* for a given year of a player's Auburn career. This time we stretch the list out to the *Top 22* in order to include James Joseph and Stacy Danley, for reasons we will get into just after the table:

Auburn Running Backs in the Modern Era, by Yards per <u>Game</u>

# Year	Player	Gm	Yards	Att	TD	APC	YPG
1 1985	Bo Jackson	12	1915	309	18	6.20	159.6
2 1986	Brent Fullwood	12	1543	194	11	7.95	128.6
3 2000	Rudi Johnson	13	1652	349	14	4.73	127.1
4 1994	Stephen Davis	11	1263	221	13	5.71	114.8
5 1983	Bo Jackson	12	1343	180	12	7.46	111.9
6 1993	James Bostic	11	1205	199	12	6.06	109.5
7 2005	Kenny Irons	12	1293	256	13	5.05	107.8
8 2002	Carnell Williams	7	745	141	10	5.28	106.4
9 2009	Ben Tate	13	1362	263	10	5.18	104.8
10 2011	Michael Dyer	12	1242	242	10	5.13	103.5
11 2003	Carnell Williams	13	1307	241	17	5.42	100.5
12 1995	Stephen Davis	12	1188	192	14	6.19	99.0
13 2002	Ronnie Brown	11	1008	175	13	5.76	91.6
14 2004	Carnell Williams	13	1165	239	12	4.87	89.6
15 1988	Stacy Danley	11	945	198	7	4.77	85.9
16 1992	James Bostic	10	819	186	5	4.40	81.9
17 2006	Kenny Irons	11	893	198	4	4.51	81.2
18 2010	Michael Dyer	14	1093	182	5	6.01	78.1
19 2004	Ronnie Brown	12	913	153	8	5.97	76.1
20 1982	Bo Jackson	12	893	141	11	6.33	74.4
21 1989	James Joseph	11	817	172	4	4.75	74.3
22 1989	Stacy Danley	10	737	170	4	4.34	73.7

Bo Jackson (1985) dominates this category—yards per game—but by virtue of 115 more carries than second-ranked Brent Fullwood (1986). Rudi Johnson holds down the third spot by virtue of his relentless, seemingly tireless efforts and raw endurance more than because of spectacular long runs of the style typified by the top two backs; Rudi always seemed to get stronger as the game went on and as he got more carries. Bo's 1983 season ranking fifth is a testimony to his abilities, because he was sharing carries on a purely run-oriented team with Lionel James at the other halfback spot, Tommie Agee at fullback, and Randy Campbell at quarterback in the wishbone set often keeping the ball as well. Bo rang up right at 112 yards per game as one of four players carrying the ball—the highest total of any wishbone-formation player on this chart. (In fact, the only other entry here in the top 20 for a wishbone back is Bo again, in his freshman season of 1982, down at 18.)

It's interesting to see James Joseph and Stacey Danley (both from 1989) making the last two spots on this list. They essentially split time at running back that season, posting remarkably similar numbers. Combine them and you basically have Rudi Johnson's solo numbers from 2000—though without nearly as many touchdowns.

Also of note: Carnell Williams places eighth—not *despite* playing in only seven games, but likely *because* he played in only seven games. That run of contests did not include, for example, having to face the defenses of LSU, Georgia, or Alabama. (In fact, because of injuries and the rescheduling of the 2001 LSU game, Williams did not get to play against the Bayou Bengals until his junior season.)

Where does Cam Newton fit into the Yards Per Game chart? He gained 105.2 yards per game in his one season with the Tigers, ranking him ninth—just ahead of 2009 Ben Tate and just below 2002 Carnell Williams.

Now let's break it down by *Yards Per Carry*:

Top 20 Auburn Running Backs in the Modern Era, by <u>Yards per Carry</u> (APC)

# Year	Player	Gm	Yards	Att	TD	APC	YPG
1 2010	Onterio McCalebb	14	804	95	9	8.46	57.4
2 1986	Brent Fullwood	12	1543	194	11	7.95	128.6
3 1983	Bo Jackson	12	1343	180	12	7.46	111.9
4 1985	Brent Fullwood	11	709	97	6	7.31	64.5
5 1982	Lionel James	12	779	113	7	6.89	64.9
6 1982	Bo Jackson	12	893	141	11	6.33	74.4
7 1985	Bo Jackson	12	1915	309	18	6.20	159.6
8 1995	Stephen Davis	12	1188	192	14	6.19	99.0
9 1988	James Joseph	11	721	118	5	6.11	65.5
10 1993	James Bostic	11	1205	199	12	6.06	109.5
11 2010	Michael Dyer	14	1093	182	5	6.01	78.1
12 2004	Ronnie Brown	12	913	153	8	5.97	76.1
13 1983	Lionel James	11	728	124	4	5.87	66.2
14 2002	Ronnie Brown	11	1008	175	13	5.76	91.6
15 1994	Stephen Davis	11	1263	221	13	5.71	114.8
16 2003	Carnell Williams	13	1307	241	17	5.42	100.5
17 2002	Carnell Williams	7	745	141	10	5.28	106.4
18 2009	Ben Tate	13	1362	263	10	5.18	104.8
19 2011	Michael Dyer	12	1242	242	10	5.13	103.5
20 2005	Kenny Irons	12	1293	256	13	5.05	107.8

What really stands out on this chart to us is Brent Fullwood's average yards per carry (APC). While Onterio McCalebb rang up even gaudier numbers in that category, he was utilized in a very specific role that season (gaining only 57.4 yards per game on just 95 attempts) and in all likelihood would not have gained that kind of yardage if he had been an every-down back lining up in the backfield. (See, for example, 2012.) Fullwood, on the other hand, was the starting tailback for a run-first, I-formation team, and everyone knew he was getting the ball; there was no risk of QB Jeff Burger taking off on a fifty-yard jaunt to the end zone. Yet Fullwood still gained an eye-popping 7.95 yards per carry in 1986, his senior campaign. Had the coaching staff made the decision to push Fullwood for the Heisman and feed him the ball even close to the number of times they gave it to Jackson the season before, he might well have eclipsed Bo's record yardage number. Fullwood did, after all, gain only about 350 fewer yards for the season, and on more than a hundred fewer carries than Bo had!

The other thing remarkable here is the average yards per carry of Lionel James in his junior season of 1982: 6.89, placing him fifth overall. His senior season ranks 13th.

Where does Cam Newton fit into this chart? His 5.58 average yards per carry would place him at 16, bumping Cadillac's 2003 and 2002 campaigns down a spot each. The threat of his carrying the ball also likely contributed to Mike Dyer's APC being nearly a full yard higher in 2010 than in 2011.

For the last of the four "by Year" tables, let's look purely at the number of *Touchdowns* these backs scored in a single season:

Top 20 Auburn Running Backs in the Modern Era,
by __Touchdowns__ per Season

# Year	Player	Gm	Yards	Att	TD	APC	YPG
1 1985	Bo Jackson	12	1915	309	18	6.20	159.6
2 2003	Carnell Williams	13	1307	241	17	5.42	100.5
3 1995	Stephen Davis	12	1188	192	14	6.19	99.0
3 2000	Rudi Johnson	13	1652	349	14	4.73	127.1
5 1994	Stephen Davis	11	1263	221	13	5.71	114.8
5 2002	Ronnie Brown	11	1008	175	13	5.76	91.6
5 2005	Kenny Irons	12	1293	256	13	5.05	107.8
8 1983	Bo Jackson	12	1343	180	12	7.46	111.9
8 1993	James Bostic	11	1205	199	12	6.06	109.5
8 2004	Carnell Williams	13	1165	239	12	4.87	89.6
11 1982	Bo Jackson	12	893	141	11	6.33	74.4
11 1986	Brent Fullwood	12	1543	194	11	7.95	128.6
13 2002	Carnell Williams	7	745	141	10	5.28	106.4
13 2009	Ben Tate	13	1362	263	10	5.18	104.8
13 2011	Michael Dyer	12	1242	242	10	5.13	103.5
16 2010	Onterio McCalebb	14	804	95	9	8.46	57.4
17 2004	Ronnie Brown	12	913	153	8	5.97	76.1
18 1988	Stacy Danley	11	945	198	7	4.77	85.9
18 2007	Ben Tate	13	903	202	7	4.47	69.5
18 1982	Lionel James	12	779	113	7	6.89	64.9

When it comes to rushing touchdowns, Bo Jackson and Carnell Williams were in a class by themselves (not counting that superhero playing QB in 2010). As the final chart will reveal, Williams actually owns the all-time touchdowns record at Auburn by two TDs over Bo.

How potent was the 2004 rushing attack? Cadillac Williams finished with 1165 yards and 12 touchdowns, while Ronnie Brown ran for 913 yards and 8 touchdowns. Together they accounted for 2078 yards and 20 touchdowns.

Interestingly, Stephen Davis didn't gain as many yards in 1995 as he did in 1994, but had more carries, a higher per-carry average, and more touchdowns in '95. Meanwhile, Kenny Irons and James

Bostic lurk around the lower half of the top ten in this and seemingly every other statistical list of running backs.

Ronnie Brown's numbers for 2002 are particularly noteworthy in that he really didn't get substantial playing time until after Carnell's season-ending injury at Florida on Oct. 19—this is why his yards per game number is relatively low—yet he still gained over a thousand yards and scored 13 (!!) touchdowns on just 175 carries.

Where does Cam fit in here? In terms of total number, he's the greatest ever, with 20 rushing touchdowns in 14 games (the same number as Caddy and Ronnie together in 2004). Bo Jackson wins in Average TDs per Game, with 1.5 in his Heisman season of 1985; Cam's 2010 average was 1.43 TDs per game. Interestingly, that 1.43 is the same average Cadillac Williams rang up in his injury-shortened 2002 campaign, playing in only 7 games. Cadillac's average in his first full (non-injury-shortened) season, 2003, was 1.31 TDs per game. No other back has an average substantially above 1.0 per game.

Finally, we come to *Career Yardage Leaders*. This chart lists the twenty running backs in the Modern Era with the most yards across all of their games played at Auburn:

Top 20 Auburn Running Backs in the Modern Era, by Total Yards (Career)

# Player	Years	Games	Att	Career	TDs	APC	YPG
1 Bo Jackson	1982-85	47	650	4313	43	6.6	91.8
2 Carnell Williams	2001-04	44	741	3831	45	5.2	87.1
3 Ben Tate	2006-09	47	678	3321	24	4.9	70.7
4 Stephen Davis	1993-95	31	488	2811	30	5.8	90.7
5 Brent Fullwood	1983-86	47	390	2797	24	7.2	59.5
6 Ronnie Brown	2000-04	48	513	2707	28	5.3	56.4
7 Ont McCalebb	2009-12	50	406	2546	24	6.3	50.9
8 Stacy Danley	1987-90	48	526	2427	14	4.6	50.6
9 Michael Dyer	2010-11	26	424	2322	15	5.5	89.3
10 Kenny Irons	2005-06	34	454	2186	17	4.8	64.3
11 Lionel James	1980-83	45	350	2106	12	6.0	46.8
12 James Bostic	1991-93	32	396	2084	18	5.3	65.1
13 James Joseph	1986-89	48	358	1851	13	5.2	38.6
14 Tommie Agee	1983-86	47	356	1733	10	4.9	36.9
15 Brad Lester	2004-08	41	371	1689	19	4.6	23.8
16 Rudi Johnson	2000-00	13	349	1652	14	4.7	127.1
17 Fred Beasley	1994-97	44	282	1241	18	4.4	28.2
18 Tre Mason	2011-12	21	199	1163	9	5.8	55.0
19 Mario Fannin	2007-10	51	179	1348	10	6.2	26.4
20 Tre Smith	2002-06	54	196	1023	13	5.2	18.9

Rudi Johnson's Yards Per Game number really jumps out here, but this is because he came to Auburn from junior college as a third-year player, and only played one year, serving as the featured back (and virtually the only legitimate rushing threat) for that squad. For the other players, most of whom played at least three or four years, their early years (as in the case of, for example, Ben Tate) or injury years where they only played in a few games (Cadillac and Bo) served to lower that "Per Game" stat for them.

It might at first be surprising to see Ben Tate all the way up at *third* in career yardage, but several factors are at work there. Tate arrived in 2006 and was immediately able to serve as Kenny Irons' backup, and for the three years that followed, he was the primary back, getting the bulk of the work. He finished his Auburn career with 678 carries—more than any other back on the list, and likely *more than any back in Auburn history, period*. The great backs just below him on that chart played in far fewer games, had nearly equal competition in the backfield for carries, or both. That's not to diminish in any way his great accomplishments for the Tigers; it's simply to point out that important factors contributed to his being in position to receive so many carries and compile so many yards in his career, relative to the others.

A couple of Tigers who played primarily at fullback managed to crack this list, including Tommie Agee and Fred Beasley. That's particularly noteworthy for Agee, who served mainly as a blocker and had to compete for carries during his career with the likes of Bo Jackson, Lionel James, and Brent Fullwood!

Brad Lester finally makes an appearance at a high spot on one of these tables. While he never had a huge individual season, he did contribute continuously over his career, comprising the latter stages of the Tuberville Era, and eventually he compiled a nice career resume, including nineteen touchdowns—enough to place him eighth on the career TD list for running backs.

Mike Dyer's two seasons land him at ninth in career rushing, but because he was a (somewhat) featured back from the moment he set foot on the grass of Jordan-Hare Stadium, his 89.3 Yards Per Game for his career rank him fourth, behind only Rudi, Bo, and Stephen Davis. It truly makes you wonder where he would have ended up on this chart if things had turned out better for him and he had been able to play all four years at Auburn. His total yards through those two seasons (2322) had him well on pace to surpass Bo Jackson's career rushing record of 4313 yards.

Although this book focuses specifically on 1981 and beyond, we thought it might be interesting to see how the two great Auburn backs from just before Pat Dye's arrival fit into the chart above:

3 James Brooks	1977-80	44	621	3523	24	5.7	80.1
4 Joe Cribbs	1976-79	44	657	3368	34	5.1	76.5

. As you can see here, James Brooks and Joe Cribbs rank third and fourth all-time in Auburn career yards, trailing only Bo and Cadillac, and bumping everyone else down two spots.

And what about Cam? His 1473 yards in 2010 would place him seventeenth on the Career Rushing Yards list. Cam rushed for more yards in one season than Mario Fannin gained (on the ground) in his entire Auburn career. (Fannin, of course, also rang up quite a few *receiving* yards.)

So there you have it: the greatest running backs in Auburn history and in the Modern Era, with the stats revealing both the expected (domination by Bo Jackson) and perhaps the somewhat unexpected (Brent Fullwood and Ben Tate's remarkable stats, among others).

One thing that is as clear as a crystal football is that Auburn has been fortunate to attract great players at the running back position over the years, and they have, for the most part, flourished during their time on the Plains.

Fame Game:
The 1989-90 Hall of Fame Bowl

For the Auburn Tigers, the 1980s did not end on December 31, 1989. They didn't even end a few weeks earlier, on December 2, when Auburn faced Alabama in Jordan-Hare Stadium for the "First Time Ever" and defeated them.

No, for Auburn football, the decade of the Eighties actually ended on a slick field in Tampa, Florida on January 1, 1990. For on that day, the same squad of Tigers that had beaten the second-ranked Crimson Tide at home—and many of the same players that had given Auburn faithful three straight SEC Championships—faced the Buckeyes of Ohio State in the Hall of Fame Bowl.

Wait. The *what?* The *Hall of Fame Bowl?*

It does seem like an odd choice of bowl games in which to find the SEC Co-Champions. However, at that time, the Hall of Fame Bowl was a New Year's Day game (when that still meant something) and was in the process of trying to boost its reputation. Players called it the "Fame Game," and there was just a hint of a growing cachet to it—though of course as we know now, that wouldn't last long.

The game itself is not really remembered among Auburn's greatest contests of the modern era, but a couple of things do sort of stand out about it, making it well worth the time to re-examine.

First in the minds of many, when thinking back to this game, is the incredible shot suffered by running back Stacey Danley early in the second quarter—possibly the most famous (or infamous) blow dealt an Auburn player in modern history (and made all the more remarkable for the fact that he walked off the field and then played throughout the second half!).

Equally important, we would argue, is that this was the game *after* the "First Time Ever" game. The same squad that beat Bama got to take the field against a powerful Big Ten team in Ohio State. It was the first game Auburn played in the 1990s—and it was the last game for the great 1980s teams.

So let's sit down and watch the game—for the first time in two decades, for some of us—and talk about it. (For whatever reason, NetFlix actually has it available on DVD. Hardly any other Auburn games, but they do have this one. Van also still has his old VHS tape.) Okay, so—ready? Here we go:

"Championship Monday?"

NBC Sports. "Championship Monday." There's Pat Dye in classic Pat Dye form: sport coat and tie and baseball cap. Pat Sullivan stands next to him in his orange sweatshirt, waving frantically between plays. Reggie Slack is under center, one last time. Stacey Danley and James Joseph swap into and out of the backfield, along with occasional appearances by Darrell "Lectron" Williams. Alexander Wright and Greg Taylor and Shane Wasden and Victor Hall catch the passes. Win Lyle kicks the field goals. Ogletree and

Riggins and Billingslea and Crawford chase down Buckeye ballcarriers. And look there, back in the secondary—it's Eric Ramsey. Oh, my.

The viewer of today can't help but notice the gigantic white Hall of Fame Bowl patches on the shoulders of the Auburn jerseys, in place of the usual numbers. These had to have been among the largest and most obnoxious bowl patches in football history. To make things worse, the Ohio State players aren't wearing them, so they look even more ridiculous on our guys. Oh well. Moving along:

Auburn comes out slinging the ball around, with Reggie Slack throwing deep for Alexander Wright at every opportunity. (He even runs back kickoffs—and does pretty darned well.) After one early completion, though, the Buckeye defense seems to figure out how to take Wright out of the game. With the other Tigers receivers slipping down on the wet grass (apparently a recurring problem in Auburn bowl games) and otherwise bobbling and dropping catchable balls, nobody seems able to hang on to it.

The Buckeyes score first and look pretty strong in the process. Trailing 7-0, Auburn finally gets down to the Ohio State two yard line, but the Buckeyes defense looks pretty danged tough up the middle against the run at this stage, and so Pat Dye elects on fourth down to settle for a short Win Lyle field goal. A little while later the Buckeyes score another touchdown, and the Tigers are down 14-3 early in the second.

And then comes the big hit on Danley.

The Hit

If you weren't old enough at the time and no one's shown it to you or told you about it before, here is—briefly, because it happened just insanely quickly—what happened.

63

Slack took the snap and dropped back. Danley curled around out of the backfield into the right flat. Nothing but green (muddy, slick) grass in front of him at that point. Slack lofts a gentle pass over to him. He looks back at Slack, watching the approaching ball. Meanwhile, a Buckeye defender comes straight at him, full-bore.

THE INSTANT THE BALL LANDS IN HIS HANDS, THE BUCKEYE PLAYER COLD-COCKS HIM.

It was rough. Visceral. Violent. It was *insanely* violent. And, above all, it was *fast*.

The Ohio State players nearly walked over the prone Danley in their rush to celebrate. Sideline personnel swarmed out, bending over him. The story goes that Pat Dye told him, "If you can run off, run off." The TV broadcast doesn't show it—they went to commercial, and when they came back, he was on the bench, not looking terribly well—but supposedly he did just that: he jogged off, or at least walked off under his own power.

Considering that for a long moment it appeared as if they'd be searching for his *head*, this was very impressive.

As I said earlier, he would re-enter the game in the second half and perform quite well. Meanwhile, the rest of the Auburn squad seemed to decide that now would be a good time to wake up, get off the team bus, and actually *play up to their potential*. And that they did.

This, at least, is the popular conception. But it is a *mis*conception.

The Surreal Life

The Auburn passing game actually got *worse* after the Danley hit. A short time later, Slack was intercepted on a deflected pass by—we kid you not—Bo Pelini! The screen graphic identifies him as "Mark

Pelini," but announcer Don Criqui makes it clear that he's known as "Bo." (He also points out that Pelini has played with a broken jaw, broken collar bone, etc.) Does this make Reggie Slack the only Auburn quarterback to have a pass intercepted by the head coach of the Nebraska Cornhuskers?

If you're watching the game (as we are) in the present day, things only get more surreal from there. First the Danley hit, then the Pelini interception, and then Criqui (and his color analyst, Ahmad Rashad) throw it down to their sideline reporter, who is in the stands visiting with none other than Twilitta Ramsey. She has her little boy sitting on her lap and is telling the reporter his name is "Eric Ahmad Rashad Ramsey." That may well be his name. But it says a lot about Twilitta that those of us watching today instantly found ourselves wondering if that really was the young man's name, or if she only made it up to get on television.

Back to the action: Shane Wasden returns a Buckeye punt for a then-Hall of Fame Bowl record 30 yards, but Slack throws another interception—his second of the quarter—on the next play. Ohio State looks to be trying to run out the clock and get to the half, but the Tigers defense holds and forces another punt. Retreating to field the kick, Wasden then breaks his own barely-four-minute-old record with a 34-yard return down the right sideline. Then Slack hits Alexander Wright inside the 20, and on the next play he hooks up with Greg Taylor for the touchdown with only eleven seconds left until halftime.

The quick score before the half was great, but the stats at halftime were not. Auburn had rushed for just 61 yards and thrown for only 74, along with Slack's two interceptions. This from the team that, in its previous outing, had rolled up 30 points on the undefeated Crimson Tide. Clearly, something had to change.

And it did.

Breathing Fire in the Second Half

The great Auburn football author and friend, Will Collier, was in attendance that day, and he tells us: "I talked to several players at a rest stop on the way home from that game. I asked them what the hell Pat Dye said at the half [that fired the team up]. All they did [in reply] was wince and say, "Oooooo!" We can just imagine.

(Will also amusingly points out that the Ohio State fan sitting next to him at the game observed, "Youse guys' colors clash." Meanwhile, the guy was wearing maroon and gray pajamas.)

The second half begins with Ohio State receiving the kickoff. Auburn's defense is fired up and the Buckeyes can't move the ball. Their punt is terrible and Auburn takes over on the Buckeyes' end of the field, just inside the fifty. After run plays from seemingly every member of the backfield (Joseph, Danley, and "Lectron" Williams), Slack rolls out and hits Taylor again for the go-ahead score. Two TD passes from Reggie, two TD catches by Taylor.

After some third quarter back-and-forth, Slack is sacked and leaves the game, and we get a rare Frank McIntosh sighting. It's interesting to note that Big Frank's passer rating at that point in the season was in the mid-twenties, with three completions in ten attempts. Eeek. At this moment, however, he comes through like a champion—albeit without winging the ball. He simply gives on the quick draw handoff to Danley, who fights his way for sixteen yards on a third-and-fourteen. Mission accomplished, Frank. Have a seat, son.

Slack re-enters the game after that single play. He quickly makes his presence known, running for another critical first down conversion and then, toward the eight-and-a-half minute mark in a very long drive, running into the end zone for the score. Auburn is starting to pull away now, 24-14.

Ohio State clearly realizes at this point that things are going against them in a big way. The Tigers defense is breathing fire and smothering everything the Buckeyes are trying to do. That last drive by the Tigers not only pushed the lead to ten but also took the game deep into the fourth quarter before it ended. Facing another fourth down, John Cooper calls for the "Bummerooski," a fake punt play in which the ball is actually snapped to the blocking back, who then hands it to another player to run with, even as the punter pretends to grab for it as it seemingly sails over his head. Auburn sniffs the trick play out instantly and the Tigers crush the ball carrier for little or no gain. A bad situation for the Buckeyes has become much worse: Auburn now has the ball deep in Ohio State territory.

The Tigers waste little time in striking again. Danley rips off a run down to the three, and then Slack rolls out and hits Herbert "the Weapon" Casey (oh, yes—Herbert "the Weapon" Casey) for the score. Now it's 31-14 and the hay is pretty much in the barn.

(Interestingly, and to give some real "wow" perspective on how long ago this was: Following the last Auburn touchdown, NBC cuts to Bob Costas, who reports that following the Orange Bowl late that night, Lou Holtz's top assistant at Notre Dame, Barry Alvarez, will be leaving to become the head coach at Wisconsin. Wow. And another odd twist—sixteen years later, Alvarez would coach his final game at Wisconsin in another Florida bowl, the Capital One, against none other than the Auburn Tigers.)

Ohio State threatens one more time, but Quentin Riggins steps in front of a short pass over the middle for the drive-killing interception and, hey—as NBC actually rolls the credits over the game action—it's Frank McIntosh, one more time! He hands off a few times, the clock is quickly eaten up and the game ends.

It was nice of Ohio State to show up, at least for the first half. Another in their long line of bowl losses to SEC teams goes into the record books, ladies and gentlemen.

Reggie Slack gets the nod for MVP, and is carried onto the field on the shoulders James Joseph and Stacey Danley.

The Coda

And there you have it. A game that ended more than two decades ago—a game in some ways nearly forgotten today, a game always overshadowed that season by the monolithic, megalithic contest that immediately preceded it—yet a game that contained very visible and memorable shards of both the past and the future of Auburn football at that singular moment in time.

Certainly there were big moments still to come in the Pat Dye Era. The 1990 season would see titanic battles with Tennessee and Florida State, among others. Ultimately, however, that campaign proved to be disappointing, and somewhat foreshadowed the downward spiral of the following two years that would culminate with scandal and investigation and Pat Dye's resignation in the hours before the 1992 Iron Bowl.

If "First Time Ever" on December 2, 1989 was therefore Pat Dye's Wagnerian operatic climax to his brilliant Auburn career, this Hall of Fame Bowl in south Florida served as a sort of early coda presaging the end of the Dye Era. It gave us one last real look at Dye in his prime, and one last visit with so many of the players that had carried Auburn football to new heights during the decade just ended—before the 1980s themselves evaporated into history like the steam coming off of Tampa Bay.

Auburn's Ten Greatest Bowl Games

As of this writing, Auburn has played in twenty-three bowl games in the Modern Era, beginning with the win over Boston College in 1982's Tangerine Bowl and most recently marked by the Tigers defeating Virginia in the Chick-Fil-A Bowl. The record breaks down this way:

- Nine bowls under Pat Dye, with a record of 6-2-1.

- Three bowls under Terry Bowden, with a record of 2-1. (Bowden also would have coached the Tigers to bowls in 1993 and '94, as well as the 1993 SEC Championship Game, if not for probation.)

- Eight bowls under Tommy Tuberville, with a record of 5-3.

- Three bowls under Gene Chizik, with a record of 3-0.

Thus every coach in the Modern Era has taken the Tigers bowling, and every one of them has attained a winning record in bowls in the process. But of course some of those bowl games stand out as particularly special. Here, then, are our choices for the Ten Greatest Auburn Bowl Games.

Honorable Mentions:

Arkansas, Liberty Bowl, 1984 season.

The 1984 season was a bit of a disappointment overall. It followed the spectacular 1983 campaign that should have resulted in a national championship (we still remember that, Miami). Hopes were high that '84 would represent a real breakthrough for the Tigers, seeing them ascend to the top of the polls on a mostly permanent basis—and, indeed, they were ranked #1 by the AP coming into the season. But early losses to Miami at the Meadowlands in New Jersey and at Texas (during which Bo separated his shoulder) and later on to Florida and Alabama brought the regular season to a somewhat disappointing 8-4 end.

Facing Arkansas (still of the old Southwestern Conference at that point) for the first time ever, in the Liberty Bowl in cold, rainy Memphis, didn't seem terribly exciting to most of the Auburn faithful. The Tigers pretty much shut down the Hogs' vaunted "Flexbone" attack and prevailed, 21-15. If nothing else, it gave the Tigers at least nine wins for a third straight season, and an early victory over a program that would soon become an annual divisional foe.

Boston College, Tangerine Bowl, 1982 season.

The battle of future Heisman Trophy winners: Bo Jackson vs. Doug Flutie. The Eagles played hard, but the War Eagles played harder. Auburn won. A nice capper to the season in which Pat Dye turned Auburn's fortunes around and made us all believe the future would be very bright.

10. Clemson, Peach Bowl, 1997 season.

Auburn returned to the Georgia Dome just a month after having lost to Tennessee in the final seconds of their first-ever appearance in the SEC Championship Game. Clemson had a good defense and solid special teams but not much of anything on offense. Auburn had a nice passing attack but (with apologies to Rusty Williams) no running game whatsoever. Clemson actually took the lead on a blocked Auburn punt, but the great Dameyune Craig (in his final appearance in an Auburn uniform) brought the Tigers roaring back for the 27-17 win. Auburn finished the year with a 10-3 record, losing in the regular season only to Mississippi State and Florida.

The outcome meant the Tigers' almost inexplicable domination of Clemson would continue, and not be broken until the 2011 season.

9. Wisconsin, Music City Bowl, 2003 season.

The 2003 season was unusual in several ways. It began with hopes as high as they had probably ever been on the Plains. Just as in 1984, the Tigers were coming off a big New Year's Day bowl win from the previous season and all the signs seemed to point to even bigger things on the horizon. Preseason magazines rated the Tigers very highly.

We should have known, however, that the situation was not really as bright as it seemed. Offensive guru Bobby Patrino had departed to become head coach at Louisville, and Tommy Tuberville made the mistake of handing the OC/playcalling duties over to O-line coach Hugh Nall and tight ends coach Steve Ensminger. The offense never got on track all year long, despite having a stable of four talented running backs in Cadillac Williams, Ronnie Brown, Tre Smith, and Brandon Jacobs, along with one of the finest squadrons of wide receivers ever to take flight on the Plains—and a future NFL first-round draft pick available at quarterback in Jason Campbell.

How this group failed to produce points—even failing to score a touchdown until the third game, at Vanderbilt!—is still a mystery.

By the time the Tigers arrived in Memphis for their bowl matchup with Wisconsin, they had tumbled to 7-5, including losses to LSU and Georgia by a combined score of 57-14. The big cheese-heads from the upper Midwest were just what the doctor ordered, and a good running attack coupled with some opportunistic plays on defense led to a 28-14 win. Having not beaten a Big 10 foe in a bowl game since 1990 (Indiana), it was nice to beat up on one for a change.

8. Clemson, Chik-fil-a Bowl, 2007 season.

What a strange game, both in terms of how it played out and what we all thought it meant at the time.

The 2007 season was the definition of "up and down," with early losses to South Florida and Miss State, but wins over #3 Florida (at the Swamp) and Alabama (in Tuscaloosa). At the end of the regular season, old OC Al Borges was out and new OC Tony Franklin was in, bringing with him his fast-paced Spread attack.

Surprising nearly everyone, Auburn entered their bowl game in the Georgia Dome having already installed much of Franklin's offense—and it seemed pretty darned effective against Clemson throughout the game. During the fourth quarter, Franklin even went so far as to steal a page from Steve Spurrier's manual and swap his quarterbacks in and out every play; senior Brandon Cox would come in and throw short passes, and then freshman Kodi Burns would come in and run the ball. For a while the game looked to be in hand, but some timely plays by Clemson, including a long CJ Spiller run, brought the Other Tigers back and sent the game to overtime. Clemson managed a field goal, and then the Tigers drove into scoring position. Kodi's run up the middle, spinning and

72

breaking loose into the end zone, sent the Tigers home with the win. The domination over Clemson continued for yet another year.

7. Ohio State, Hall of Fame Bowl, 1989 season.

This game—the "Fame Game," as Tiger players called it—was both Auburn's last game of the 1980s and their first game of the 1990s, being played on January 1. This was fitting, for it ended up being a tough, hard-fought win over a solid foe.

We discuss this game in detail elsewhere in this book, but in brief: The Tigers appeared tight early on, and a massive hit delivered by the Buckeyes defense to Auburn running back Stacey Danley appeared to give the indication that the Tigers would struggle with this Big Ten foe. However, the shot on Danley actually seemed to wake the Auburn team up—from that moment on, they mostly dominated, and quarterback Reggie Slack (in his final Auburn appearance) led the Tigers to a 31-14 win over John Cooper's Ohio State.

(Interestingly, the defensive backs coach on that Buckeyes team was Ron Zook, later head coach of Florida, and one defensive player was future Nebraska head coach Bo Pellini.)

6. Northwestern, Outback Bowl, 2009 season.

The game that would not end!

In Coach Gene Chizik's first year in control of the Tigers program, he led a 7-5 Auburn squad to a New Year's Day bowl (it helped that most of the SEC inexplicably finished with very similar and very mediocre conference records, so that bowl selections became as much a popularity contest as anything else). There they faced the passing attack of Mike Kafka, who proved able to repeatedly bring the Wildcats back each time Auburn took the lead.

After Northwestern tied the game late with a touchdown and two-point conversion, Demond Washington fumbled the kickoff return and Northwestern lined up to kick the game-winning field goal. They missed. It was their kicker's second miss (third if you include an earlier PAT). Into OT we went.

After Auburn went up 38-35, Northwestern appeared to have lost the game twice but on both occasions were somehow spared. First Kafka appeared to fumble the ball away, but replay gave it back to the Wildcats. Then they missed a field goal but Auburn was flagged for running into the kicker. Finally they attempted a fake field goal and were stopped just before the goal line.

This game doubtlessly instilled confidence and resilience in the players who would return for 2010: the game is never truly over until it really is over!

5. Nebraska, Cotton Bowl, 2006 season.

Not one of the more scintillating offensive performances in football history, this one carried all the earmarks of a latter-era Tommy Tuberville contest, with the defense standing strong and creating turnovers while the offense did just enough to eke out the win.

The 2006 Tigers came remarkably close to playing for the SEC and National Championships, rising as high as #3 in the Coaches' Poll prior to a loss to Arkansas (with a certain Gus Malzahn as the Hogs' OC). A later loss to Georgia meant the Tigers would not be contending for anything beyond a decent bowl game—so getting to face the vaunted Cornhuskers in Dallas seemed like a decent enough way to wrap up the year.

Coach Bill Callahan was still in the midst of attempting to turn Nebraska into a pro-style passing team, and it wasn't working out so well. Auburn had issues on offense—an offense that in Al Borges' third year continued to slide—and simply didn't seem capable of putting big points on the board. The two teams went to halftime tied at 14, but Auburn's two scoring drives together amounted to only 23 yards. Perhaps even more remarkably, both touchdowns were scored by fullback Carl Stewart. The only scoring in the entire second half was a third quarter field goal by John Vaughn in his final game for Auburn. The Tigers held on to win, 17-14.

Let's be honest, though—just about any win over Nebraska is a good win, and it will always feel nice to be able to look back on the Tigers' bowl records from years past and see a nice win over the Cornhuskers on there—all other circumstances aside.

4. Penn State, Capital One Bowl, 2002 season.

Carnell "Cadillac" Williams had suffered a season-ending leg injury at Gainesville earlier in the season, and the Tigers' offense looked to be headed south—until mighty Ronnie Brown stepped up and more than ably replaced Williams as the human dynamo in the Auburn backfield. As it turned out, Auburn would win the Iron Bowl in a huge upset and then actually head south—to Orlando for the Capital One Bowl against Penn State and Joe Paterno, who had crushed Auburn in the rain-soaked Outback Bowl following the 1995 season.

Getting healthy in time for the bowl game after suffering a few dings against Georgia and missing the Iron Bowl, Brown put on an MVP performance as the Tigers rushed for 200 yards and secured the 13-9 victory. Meanwhile, the Auburn defense held vaunted Nittany Lions running back Larry Johnson to only 72 yards on twenty carries. By winning this bowl game Auburn entered 2003 as a trendy pick to win the SEC and contend for the national title. Alas, 2003 is a whole other story...

3. Michigan, Sugar Bowl, 1983 season.

The wait between national championships would have—should have!—only been twenty-six years, not fifty-three, but for the prejudices and preconceptions of a group of AP writers who not only failed to move the Tigers to #1 after this game, but didn't even move them up from third to second.

Auburn entered this Sugar Bowl—its first in years—ranked third behind Nebraska and Texas. Powered by sophomore Bo Jackson and senior Lionel James, and with super fullback Tommie Agee and efficient option quarterback Randy Campbell sharing the wishbone backfield, the Tigers had roared through what was inarguably the toughest schedule in the country (and one of the toughest in football history), defeating Boomer Esiason's Maryland, Florida State, undefeated Georgia, and fifth-ranked Florida, among other foes. In fact, four of their final five opponents were ranked in the top ten, with Alabama the only exception down at #19. The only team to get the better of the Tigers in 1983 was a loaded Texas squad, who lined up to face Georgia in the Cotton Bowl earlier in the day on January 1.

For Auburn to have a chance at being voted National Champions, several rather unlikely things had to fall into place: Georgia had to upset Texas in Dallas; Miami had to upset the alleged "Team of the Century," Nebraska, in the Orange Bowl; and Auburn had to beat a Michigan team that had vowed the Tigers would not win the game running the football on them.

As it turned out, every one of those things happened, the night culminating with Al Del Greco nailing his third consecutive kick to lift Auburn to a 9-7 win over the Wolverines. Many Auburn fans went to bed that night believing they were unquestionably going to be ranked #1 the next day.

Of course, that didn't happen. In fact, they remained #3, with Nebraska falling to second and one-loss Miami, by virtue of their win over the Cornhuskers, leaping all the way from fifth to first. No matter that Miami had lost earlier in the year to Florida—a team Auburn had beaten. The Canes began their run of national titles and Auburn settled in for yet another round of "wait till next year."

Certainly the low-scoring nature of the Sugar Bowl contributed to the voters' snubbing of Auburn, despite the Tigers running for over three hundred yards against a stout Bo Schembechler defense. While the Tigers managed only three field goals in defeating Michigan, Miami threw the ball on Nebraska. And, as one reporter put it, for some reason, nobody remembered Miami losing to Florida but everyone remembered Auburn losing to Texas. If Auburn had won 35-7, would the Tigers have been crowned champions? We will never know...

2. Virginia Tech, Sugar Bowl, 2004 season.

The next best thing to a National Championship game, the Sugar Bowl following the 2004 season pitted undefeated and third-ranked Auburn against Virginia Tech, champions of the ACC.

The Tigers were not particularly thrilled to be playing in this game—a hard thing to imagine when considering we're talking about the Sugar Bowl. But the Auburn players and fans all believed the Tigers should have been in Miami, in place of Oklahoma, facing USC in the Orange Bowl. It must have been hard for the team to get up for this game, but they managed to fight and claw their way to a 16-13 victory.

This game is in some ways reminiscent of the game down below here at #1: In both cases, an undefeated season and at least the outside possibility of a national title were on the line. In both cases, Auburn looked throughout the game to be clearly the better team.

77

In both instances, the Tigers made key mistakes here and there, kept their own score lower than it should have been, and allowed a formidable but lesser team to hang around and stay in the game and mount a very late comeback. And in both games the Auburn defense played in stellar fashion—except for a lapse or two late in the game that nearly let the opponent grab the victory.

Auburn actually was shutting out the Hokies as late as the start of the fourth quarter, 16-0—but the score should have been much more in Auburn's favor. Two late long touchdown passes by Virginia Tech's Bryan Randall pulled the Hokies to within three points, but the Tigers held on for dear life and escaped with the win. Once again, as in 1983, the Tigers were competing with another pair of teams in another bowl for the right to claim the national title, and they had needed to win with "style points" in order to impress the voters. Once again, they failed to do so. At least this time, unlike in 1983, the Tigers did move up to second, ahead of the team that lost the other game.

Jason Campbell finished his Auburn career with the MVP award, having gone 11-16 for 189 yards, with one touchdown and one interception. Cadillac Williams and Ronnie Brown finished their spectacular Auburn careers with a combined 129 yards on the ground. Kicker John Vaughn was three-for-three and provided ten of the Tigers' points.

With USC vacating the 2004 National Title, there was some talk before the 2010 season of Auburn being retroactively awarded at least one of the championships—the Football Writers' Association of America's Grantland Rice Award. Ultimately, that group decided not to do so. Ironically, only a few months later, Auburn would be bringing home the Grantland Rice Trophy anyway:

1. Oregon; BCS National Championship Game, 2010 season.

There's probably little that can be said here that hasn't already been said—and recently. Just a couple of notes:

While the ultimate result of this game was an unquestionable win for Auburn, bringing all the hardware (BCS crystal ball, Grantland Rice, AP, etc.) home to the Plains... the fact is that this was not one of the better games Auburn played that season. It may in fact have been Cam Newton's worst game as a Tiger. It is, of course, an enormous credit to Cam to point out that what may have been his worst performance was still far superior to what most other quarterbacks could have accomplished in that setting.

The Tigers inexplicably struggled on offense for much of the game. Cam threw an interception—his first in seven games—and fumbled late in the contest, giving Oregon the chance to drive for the winning score, which they proceeded to do. Cam and a wide-open Darvin Adams failed to hook up on a long bomb that would have been an easy touchdown in any other game of the season. Cam's too-short pass to an equally wide-open Eric Smith on fourth and goal resulted in a turnover on downs rather than a score. And on and on. Only freshman running back Mike Dyer looked like he had come to play his best game for the offense, and he delivered when the game was on the line, winning the MVP trophy as a result.

The difference, of course, was the defense, and they simply must be mentioned here. After mostly improving all season long, week to week, they absolutely dominated the Ducks in Glendale. Nick Fairley unleashed every form of SEC mayhem imaginable upon Darron Thomas and LaMichael James and their poor, victimized offensive line.

Even so, as we watch this game over and over (and surely will continue to do so forever—Van has it on his iPhone and every other device capable of showing it), we can't help but think two things, every time: "If only we'd put together another performance like we did against Carolina in Atlanta a few weeks earlier," and, "So what— we won anyway! National Champs at last!!"

The Rise and Fall of the Bowden Empire

Part 1: The Rise

The first clue that the Terry Bowden Era at Auburn would be a bumpy one was right there for everyone to see, right at the beginning, but we either missed it or didn't grasp its larger cosmic significance at the time: The first poster distributed to fans after his hiring, laying out the 1993 schedule on top of a color photo of a hunkered down Bowden in sweats, revealed that a pencil had been jammed squarely into one of his eyes.

Of course, there wasn't actually a pencil in his eye, but it certainly looked that way. Bowden was shown in profile, with said pencil in all likelihood tucked behind his other ear. All we could see in the photo, however, was his face—and that pencil, lined up squarely with his eye. It was pretty disturbing, once you "saw" it.

And indeed his tenure was a bumpy one—one that at first took us to new heights, and one that later made us feel as if someone had just jammed a pencil right into our collective Auburn Family eye.

81

The year was 1992 and, for a variety of reasons—choose whichever you prefer, or come up with your own—the glorious Pat Dye era at Auburn had just ended. Probation, poor health, a downturn in fortunes on the field in his last three seasons, various allegations of wrongdoing—all were being talked about at the time. In any case, however, Dye stepped down after the 1992 Iron Bowl, and Auburn needed a new head coach. Someone with the stature to continue Auburn's decade-long resurgence and prominence in college football, and perhaps even to finally get to that mountaintop—the one place Pat Dye, for all of his accomplishments, was never quite able to get us—and win another national championship.

The president, athletic director, and trustees needed to make the right hire. They'd certainly done so the last time, in 1980, after the firing of Doug Barfield, when (after a brief and unsuccessful flirtation with Vince Dooley) they'd gone all the way out to Wyoming and brought back a former Bear Bryant assistant who'd been an All-America lineman at Georgia. This time, after the obligatory mentions of then-vogue names like Ken Hatfield and Fisher DeBerry, they looked to another famous coaching family tree, and word came down that Auburn had hired a Bowden.

What? Bobby Bowden was leaving Florida State to coach at Auburn? Really??

Um, no.

Well then, you mean his eldest son, Tommy, who had been an offensive assistant for Dye at Auburn as well as coaching for Bill Curry at Alabama and Kentucky. (He had also coached James Brooks during a one-year stop as running backs coach at Auburn, back in 1980.)

Um, no.

The Bowden we had hired was one Terry Bowden, the youngest son of Bobby and little brother of Tommy. The head coach at Samford.

Oookay...

By all accounts (and by "all accounts," we mean Terry himself said so later—and Terry did indeed love to say things, especially about himself), the youngest Coach Bowden gave "the interview of a lifetime" before being selected to be Auburn's new coach. He stressed his law degree and his abilities as a public speaker (again, he did indeed love to speak. And speak.) In terms of coaching, he promised to combine a "Bobby Bowden offense" with a "Pat Dye defense"—certainly an approach that had great appeal to Auburn officials and fans, and particularly those who had regularly derided Pat Dye's offensive philosophy as "up the middle, up the middle, up the middle, punt." In order to provide the "defense" half of this equation, he retained Wayne Hall as defensive coordinator—a move that would yield dividends early on, but would later result in severe friction within the coaching staff. He also retained longtime Auburn linebackers coach Joe Whitt, about whom one might possibly be reminded of the old line, "Knows where the bodies are buried."

Terry Bowden arrived on campus at the end of the 1992 season, and was immediately known to all and sundry as "Terry" rather than "Coach Bowden." (One tries and fails to imagine the general Auburn Family regularly referring to Coach Dye as "Pat.") He'd known success at Samford in lower-division football, and his infectious enthusiasm and energy provided a strong contrast to Dye's more laid back approach. Clearly the players responded to this—at least, at first.

Scarcely had Bowden and his staff settled in before the NCAA announced the penalties Auburn would be saddled with as a result of infractions committed during Dye's final years. The severity of the sanctions was shocking and quite surprising to Bowden, as much as to anyone: Auburn would suffer scholarship reductions—a punishment that generally hurts any team's competitiveness severely, over time—as well as a one-year ban from television appearances. Worst of all, as it would turn out, the Tigers would be ineligible for postseason play for the next two seasons, 1993 and 1994. Because the new SEC Championship Game was considered a post-season event, the Tigers would not be allowed to participate in it. Of course, at the time, few considered this much of a penalty; how could a team that had won a combined ten games over the previous two seasons, under the illustrious Pat Dye and some of the same assistant coaches, possibly turn around and actually win the SEC West the following year—particularly with the psychological ramifications of "nothing to play for" hanging over everyone's heads?

Of course, if you're reading this, you probably already know what happened next: Buoyed by Bowden's relentless optimism and "AttitUde" slogan, Auburn went 11-0, winning every regular-season game on their schedule and becoming the only major college program that year to still be undefeated at the end of the season.

The season started fairly slow, with a narrow win over Ole Miss and a mere 35-7 victory over Bowden's old team, Samford. Then the Tigers traveled to Baton Rouge to clash with LSU, and we got our first hints that this team could be very special. In this game, senior quarterback (and Auburn's first four-year starter at that position) Stan White looked perhaps sharper than he had in his previous three seasons in leading the (good) Tigers to victory, and in the process broke Pat Sullivan's career passing record. (Eventually Stan would compile over 8,000 yards passing.) Auburn won the game, 34-10, but of course with no television coverage, nobody saw it outside of Tiger Stadium itself. (Van was there that night and still remembers being impressed with the efficiency and creativity of the offense.)

A come-from-behind win at home against Southern Miss and a very, very narrow escape at Vanderbilt (including a goal-line stand by the defense) had the Tigers at 5-0, and a win over Miss State the following week put the Tigers at an impressive and improbable 6-0, just past the midpoint of the season. The AP had taken notice and ranked Auburn 19th in the country, but of course everyone knew the streak, or "The Streak," with capital letters, as it was soon to be called, was about to end. After all, Week Seven's opponent was the University of Florida, coached by Steve Spurrier. And in three tries, the mighty Coach Dye himself had never been able to get a win over the Ball Coach (and had suffered a massive 48-7 humiliation in their very first encounter in the Swamp in 1990). What hope did a mere "Terry" have?

That, as they say, is why they play the game—for the 1993 Auburn-Florida contest turned out to be one of the greatest, most exciting games in Auburn history.

Florida rocketed out to a 10-0 lead and was threatening to go up, 17-0, when Auburn's Calvin Jackson intercepted a pass from future Heisman winner Danny Wuerffel and returned it almost a hundred yards for a touchdown. The score was suddenly 10-7 instead of 17-0, and this seemed to wake the Auburn players up. They went on to outscore the Gators the rest of the way, despite Wuerffel accounting for almost 400 yards passing and running back Errict Rhett adding nearly another 200 on the ground for Florida.

Four sacks (one by rarely-used future superstar crime novelist Ace Atkins, who made the cover of *Sports Illustrated* for it) and another interception of Wuerffel later, Auburn kicker Scott Etheridge nailed a 41-yard kick to give the Tigers the huge, staggering, totally unexpected 38-35 win. Jordan-Hare Stadium was a madhouse. A clearly shell-shocked Terry Bowden blurted to reporters, "I wouldn't have thought we could get into a scoring contest with Florida and win." But they had. Auburn was 7-0. The Streak was officially born. Talk began to turn to the idea of a national championship while unable to play in the post-season.

Four teams remained on the schedule, though—four and no more. No opponent in Birmingham (this was the year before the SEC moved the title game to Atlanta) and no bowl game. But one of those remaining teams was the defending national champion, Alabama—and if all Auburn could look forward to in "bowl" terms was the Iron Bowl, that would have to do.

The rest of that season was just as memorable, and for a variety of reasons. After a week off, the Tigers traveled to Little Rock and played the Razorbacks in the aftermath of a huge snowstorm. Auburn equipment managers were scouring every available source in the hours before kickoff to secure as much appropriately-colored warm-weather gear as could be had in a hurry. On the sidelines, a bundled-up Terry Bowden resembled nothing so much as an orange and blue snowman. Snowplows scraped incredibly thick layers of ice and snow off the field just before kickoff. Tiger fullback Reid McMillon, who had never enjoyed tremendous success before, had a big game; word afterward was that he normally tended to "overheat" during games, but playing in the icebox of a still-frozen War Memorial Stadium suited him just perfectly. Now a top ten team in the AP, Auburn won by ten, 31-21.

New Mexico State players the following week claimed that Auburn was running "a high school offense," but the Tigers didn't let that hinder them—they crushed the Aggies, 55-14. Two games remained now—two more opportunities to lose and end The Streak, or to achieve immortality. Two old friends—our two most bitter rivals: Georgia and Alabama.

Auburn fans were feeling the excitement of glory just around the corner as they traveled to Athens on November 13. Van had t-shirts printed up that read "10-0 AND ONE TO GO," but kept them hidden in a sack until the outcome was assured. The game was another exciting one, with lots of fireworks. Georgia was not a bad team but had managed to lose enough games that there would be no postseason for them, either—so this game represented a sort of bowl for them, too.

Auburn pulled away at the end, winning 42-28. Van handed out his t-shirts to the crowd of friends around him, much to the consternation of Bulldog Nation. The Tigers headed home with "one to go," but what a "one" it was: Alabama, the defending champs, in Auburn for only the second time ever.

Another instant classic.

All of the tickets to see the game in person at Jordan-Hare were long gone, of course—but the NCAA allowed it to be broadcast via closed circuit on the big screen in Tuscaloosa—and the entire ticket allotment for that stadium was sold out, as well, making it the first game in history to sell out two entire stadiums at once. Additionally, a service was set up to allow fans to call in to a special number on their phones and listen to the audio play-by-play—but so many attempted to call in that the telephone interchange actually melted. (John was one of many victims of this situation, as he sat frustrated in his apartment in northern Virginia, getting nothing but static on the line.)

The game was just as bizarre. Gene Stallings' Alabama led early, scoring two touchdowns and shocking the Tiger faithful. Auburn fought and scratched and clawed their way back into it, by way of a field goal and a safety to make the score an odd 14-5, Alabama's way.

Then came one of those plays that will never be forgotten by any who witnessed it.

Auburn's stalwart QB, Stan White, playing in his final college game, went down with a leg injury—with Auburn facing fourth down deep in Alabama territory. On came sophomore backup Patrick Nix, who proceeded to loft a pass to the great Tiger receiver, Frank Sanders. Sanders beat his man (Alabama's All-American DB, Antonio Langham, had mysteriously crossed to the other side of the field just before the snap, leaving Sanders in single coverage), grabbed the ball out of the air, spun around, and dived into the end zone for the touchdown—as Jim Fyffe went nuts in the play-by-play booth.

After the PAT, the Tigers trailed by only two—but momentum now was clearly with them.

A field goal a short time later put Auburn ahead for the first time, and then a totally unexpected blast up the middle by running back James Bostic—never what you'd have called a "speed threat"—that went seventy yards for a touchdown pretty much sealed the deal. Auburn had won, 22-14. The house was defended again. (Say what you will of Terry Bowden, but he never lost to Alabama in Jordan-Hare in three games there.) The Tigers were 11-0, best in the SEC, and had done everything possible to stake their claim to a national title.

There would be no national championship for the Tigers, of course. While several ranking services and organizations did name Auburn the national champions, the major ones turned elsewhere. The Tigers ended up fourth in the AP, who selected Terry's father's team, one-loss Florida State, as its champion. Auburn was not even eligible to be ranked by the Coaches' Poll. Bowden did win the "Bear Bryant" Award as coach of the year, ironically enough—a distinction shared by every Auburn head coach to have led the Tigers since the Bear's death.

The second-ever SEC Championship Game, which would have featured Auburn, instead saw two teams the Tigers had already beaten play one another: Alabama and Florida, in a rematch of the previous year's game. The Tigers had to sit at home, with only their "11-0 Best in the SEC" rings to console them.

Despite all of this, the 1993 season remains one of the greatest achievements in Auburn football history, and the accomplishments of that team and those coaches in those very particular circumstances—coaching change, turmoil, probation, and "nothing to play for"—should never, ever be overlooked. They did everything asked of them that year—everything they could do—and they shocked the world.

Searching for some way of motivating the team to play hard again the next season, when in all likelihood they faced the same scenario over again, Auburn coaches and fans latched onto the speculation of a few journalists who had been sufficiently impressed with Auburn's 1993 achievements to make the following pronouncement: "If they (Auburn) run the table again in 1994, you have to give it (a national championship) to them." In other words, while 11-0 in one season was not deemed sufficient to deserve a national title, going 22-0 across two full seasons, while on probation, just might be enough to swing some AP votes Auburn's way. Terry called this "AUdacity," and another t-shirt slogan was born.

With that in mind, the Tigers launched into the 1994 campaign right where they had left off in December of the previous year—by beating everyone in front of them, often in wildly improbable fashion, and slowly but steadily closing in on another undefeated season.

There were two key moments in the 1994 season that signaled the Tigers were legitimate threats to actually "run the table" twice-over: the LSU game on September 17 and the Florida game on October 15.

The events that transpired when the two Tiger teams clashed in Jordan-Hare—and when the space-time continuum itself seemingly warped beyond recognition—have been discussed often and at length before, including by your two intrepid Wishbone columnists. In brief: Auburn's offense was utterly inept against a ferocious LSU defense. Neither starting quarterback Patrick Nix nor super sub Dameyune Craig could get anything going. The defense, however, managed to keep the orange and blue Tigers in the game, running back an early fumble and then—staggeringly—returning three fourth-quarter interceptions for touchdowns. Even in the bizarre history of Auburn-LSU football, this game stands out as extra-super-bizarre. But hey, the Streak was alive, and the Tigers moved on.

Bowden billed the Florida game of 1994 as Auburn's "Super Bowl," and the Tiger players responded to the hype by coming out firing on all cylinders. Florida was ranked #1 in the country in the polls, the game was being played at the Swamp in Gainesville, and the Gators were out for revenge after the upset of the previous year. Oh, and Florida was a 17-point favorite. None of that mattered. Auburn went toe-to-toe with the Gators for sixty minutes and, with the game on the line, found victory. Patrick Nix engineered a quick and efficient drive in the closing moments that culminated with a fade pass to his favorite target, Frank Sanders, in the end zone. Auburn 36, Florida 33. The Streak had reached eighteen games and it rolled on, apparently unstoppable.

Three games later, however, it would stop—and not with a bang, but with a whimper. And the Fall of the Bowden Empire would begin.

Part 2: The Fall

With Auburn's miraculous victory over #1-ranked Florida in Gainesville in 1994, the Streak stood at a preposterous eighteen wins in a row. It seemed there was no stopping it—that it would never, ever end.

And then, three games later, it ended—and in unexpected and improbable fashion.

With two games remaining in the '94 season, Auburn faced the Georgia Bulldogs in Jordan-Hare Stadium. Prior to the game, Dawg coach Ray Goff said, "You don't just win all the time." Sooner or later, he was implying, the odds catch up to everyone. Sure enough, the odds caught up to Auburn that night against Georgia.

With the game tied at 23, the Tigers had one last opportunity to salvage the win. At every other moment over the past two seasons, when this sort of occasion arose, the Tigers always—*always*—closed the deal.

Not this time. Matt Hawkins shanked the field goal. Terry Bowden and the rest of the Auburn Family looked on in disbelief. The game was over and Georgia had, as they said, "won a 23-23 tie." Auburn still hadn't lost, it was true—but this more than *felt* like a loss, and the win streak had ended at 20.

The Iron Bowl in Birmingham a week later, against fourth-ranked and undefeated Alabama, felt like an anticlimax. Everyone knew the outside shot at a national title for "running the table twice" was now gone. At least three other teams were undefeated at that moment in time, including Nebraska and Penn State, and the one point in Auburn's favor in an argument with any of them—nothing but wins over two full seasons—was now out the window.

Alabama employed an option-based, grind-it-out attack that took advantage of Auburn's relative defensive weaknesses by simply avoiding the Tigers secondary and attacking at the line of scrimmage. This approach also kept Auburn's potent offense off the field for long stretches of the game.

The Tide roared out to a 21-0 lead before halftime and the situation looked dire. Auburn fought back in the second half with two drives that culminated with short quarterback sneaks for touchdowns. Now trailing only 21-14 and getting the ball back one last time, deep in their own territory, the Tigers began what could have been at least a game-tying drive. They moved the ball to near midfield and faced a fourth down situation, and they turned to what had worked so well for two seasons: throwing it to Frank Sanders.

Sanders caught the pass in the middle of the field but was immediately knocked backwards and down. The initial contact appeared to have come across the first down line—it should have been a successful conversion. However, the referees marked the ball further back toward the original line of scrimmage, and the measurement showed the play to have come up inches short. Alabama was given the ball and ran the clock out. The season was over at 9-1-1, and Auburn had suffered its first loss in football since Pat Dye's final Iron Bowl in that same stadium two years earlier.

Terry Bowden's record at that point was a sparkling, stunning 20-1-1. However, his record over the most recent two games was 0-1-1, and some fans and supporters who had always been a bit "iffy" on him were already sharpening their knives.

The 1995 and 1996 seasons would do little to placate those individuals.

Over those two campaigns, and despite now actually being able to challenge for post-season play, Auburn settled into the more expected role of also-ran in the SEC.

Picked to finish second in the country by *Sports Illustrated* and led by senior quarterback Patrick Nix and senior running back Stephen Davis, Auburn's 1995 squad looked good on paper, and rang up big wins against outmanned early foes, but then fell in tough contests to LSU, Florida, and Arkansas. Wins over Georgia and Alabama at the end of the season offered some degree of solace, but then a 43-14 shellacking by Penn State in the Outback Bowl brought emotions crashing down again. An 8-4 record was disappointing after fans had experienced the Streak over the past two seasons—and Bowden's post-Streak record now stood at a remarkably average 8-5-1.

Things only got worse in 1996. New starting quarterback Dameyune Craig offered a jolt of electricity to the offense, and the replacement of seemingly disinterested defensive coordinator Wayne Hall with legendary Bill "Brother" Oliver promised a renewed emphasis on strong defense. Unfortunately, the running game dropped off a cliff with the departure of guys like Stephen Davis, Joe Frazier, and Fred Beasley. A one-dimensional offense and a so-so defense yielded exactly what one might expect: another 8-win season with losses to the big boys from Florida, LSU, Georgia and Alabama, and the narrowest of wins over Army (!!) in the dreaded Independence (or, as fans derided it, Weedeater) Bowl in Shreveport.

Thus the pressure was on, and in a big way, when the 1997 season dawned for the Tigers. Terry Bowden had gone from 20-0 in his first twenty games to 16-9-1 in all contests since then, and Auburn had only managed a 9-7 mark in the conference over those past two seasons. Dameuyne Craig, however, was now a senior, and he had a nice squadron of receivers to throw to. If any sort of running

93

game could be generated at all, the Tigers had a shot at big things in 1997. Everyone was watching.

As it turned out, 1997 was not a bad year at all for the Auburn Tigers—good enough to provide Bowden a small measure of job security, at least for another year, but coming up just short of real glory. A come-from-behind win on the road against LSU proved that the team possessed real grit, and a big road win at Virginia to start the season looked great on television. Victories over Alabama and Georgia are always welcome, and the Tigers accomplished those two things in '97; unfortunately, the win at home in the Iron Bowl was seen by many as being far closer than it should have been— another perceived negative for Bowden. That Tide team would end the year with only four wins, yet it took a near-miraculous Alabama fumble and last-second field goal for Auburn to pull out the 17-15 victory.

Despite a competitive loss to Florida and an ugly shutout by Mississippi State—both in Jordan-Hare—the Tigers managed a 6-2 mark in the conference—a better record than they had achieved since 1994, and enough to get them into the SEC Championship Game for the first time.

There they faced the Tennessee Volunteers and their senior quarterback, Peyton Manning.

The Tigers and Vols had not met on the field since the year before the SEC split into two divisions, the annual AU-UT rivalry being one of the first victims of that new arrangement, as it placed Auburn in the West and Tennessee in the East. Auburn's last win over the Vols had been a 38-6 blowout back in 1988, with UT winning two subsequent match-ups in Knoxville and the 1990 clash in Jordan-Hare ending in a tie.

Tennessee, ranked third, was favored over an Auburn team that had not resided in the upper echelons of the AP poll since the loss to Florida back in October. Without a running game to speak of, it seemed unlikely that the Tigers could keep the game competitive. Somehow, they did.

Auburn actually led for much of the game. Capitalizing on key Tennessee mistakes and turnovers, the Tigers pulled in front, 13-7, after one quarter and 20-10 at the half, with key plays including a 51-yard strike from Dameyune Craig to Tyrone Goodson and a 24-yard fumble return by Tigers DB Brad Ware. Jaret Holmes was accurate in field goals from 30 and 48 yards, as well.

In the second half, however, the Tigers missed out on numerous opportunities to put the game out of reach, and Manning rallied the Vols to the comeback win. Well into the fourth quarter, with Auburn clinging to a 29-23 lead, Manning connected with Marcus Nash for a 73-yard catch-and-run. The extra point put the Vols up for good, 30-29. Auburn was unable to mount a final scoring drive and the game ended with Tennessee running out the clock.

Auburn had lost in the conference title game—but at least we'd finally made it there. The consolation prize was a return visit to the Georgia Dome a few weeks later, where Craig finished his dazzling Auburn career with a 27-17 win over Clemson in the Chick-fil-a Peach Bowl. The 1997 squad ended up with a record of 10-3, giving Terry Bowden his second and last double-digit-win season.

It was his last because he would no longer be Auburn's coach after six games of the 1998 season.

Trouble had been brewing almost from the time he was hired. Many Auburn fans and alumni hadn't liked Bowden at the time of his hire and hadn't much warmed to him after that, despite that gaudy, twenty-win streak to start his tenure. He did a remarkable job coaching the existing Auburn team in 1993-94, but his recruiting efforts were never able to match that performance. The Tigers lost out on many of the more desirable high school players and began to settle for individuals of questionable character, several of whom went on to get themselves in serious trouble because of their behavior.

With his talkative nature and animated personality, Bowden was the antithesis of what Tigers fans had grown used to in their previous coach, Pat Dye: a slow-talkin' good ole boy who espoused the virtues of the running game and a "hard-nosed defense." In short, "Buster Brown" Bowden (as his future defensive coordinator, Bill "Brother" Oliver, had dubbed him years earlier) simply rubbed much of the Auburn Family the wrong way, and by this point some of the actions he'd taken during his tenure—things the fans could overlook in a big winner—began to irk them all the more. There was the changing of the block letters "AUBURN" and "TIGERS" in the end zone to a sort of baseball jersey scripting; there were the orange drop shadows behind the white numbers on the home jerseys; there were the black-and-white murals added to the stadium exterior that year, no fewer than three of which featured Bowden himself prominently. Even the moment when Georgia's mascot, Uga, famously attacked receiver Robert Baker on the sidelines seemed somehow attributable to Bowden's mismanagement. Knives were being sharpened, Bowden's days on the Plains were numbered, and the disastrous start of the 1998 season provided the opportunity and the justification to jettison him.

A horrific 19-0 shutout at the hands of Virginia in Jordan-Hare started the season off with a thud. The situation improved momentarily when the Tigers returned the favor to Ole Miss in Oxford the next week, winning 17-0. This would be Terry Bowden's last win as Auburn coach, however—and ironically, coming against the man who would have his job a year later, Tommy Tuberville.

Things then spiraled out of control. Four straight losses—to LSU and Tennessee at home, and then to Mississippi State and Florida on the road—left the Tigers sitting at 1-5, with Arkansas, Georgia, and Alabama still ahead on the schedule. To make matters worse, the offense in particular seemed not only inept but unconcerned at times, with new starting quarterback Ben Leard laughing on the sidelines after throwing yet another pick-six (something that happened with shocking regularity during this woeful stretch of games). The Tennessee game was actually winnable right down to the very last moment for Auburn; a startling fact, given that the very powerful '98 Vols team would go on to finish the season undefeated and would be crowned national champs. The Tigers, however, could not get out of their own way against UT, throwing (yet another) interception that was returned for a score (this one a shovel pass, no less!) and then failing to complete a pass into the end zone at the end of the fourth quarter that could have sent the game into overtime.

After a 24-3 drubbing by Florida at the Swamp, Bowden had a meeting with the higher-ups. Some later claimed he chose that occasion to quit. He claimed he was fired. The composite picture that emerged was that Bowden asked if he could save his job at the end of the season and, being told "no," replied that he would just as soon end his tenure now.

One way or another, Bowden was out and Brother Oliver was the interim head coach. The Tigers under his guidance would win that weekend against Louisiana Tech and (narrowly!) on November 7 against Daunte Culpepper's Central Florida, but lose everything else and finish at 3-8—the worst record in modern Auburn history. At the end of the season, Oliver was cut loose as well (despite his vigorous protests).

While supposedly prohibited by the agreement he signed with Auburn from discussing the program with the media, Bowden could never keep his mouth shut for long, and eventually rumor and innuendo emerged, allegedly from him, indicating that various money-related improprieties had been happening in the AU Athletic Department for years. Bowden, so the story went, had disliked the bad things he saw happening and had ordered them stopped for the future, but perhaps had not done as much as he could have in the present. These sorts of questions would linger on into the regime of the coach that followed him, Tommy Tuberville (particularly as they related to super-trustee Bobby Lowder), clouding his tenure with the Tigers as well.

As of December 1998, the Terry Bowden era had officially ended, barely six years after it had begun with so many victories and such promise. Bowden's final record as Auburn's head coach was remarkably good: 47-17-1 in sixty-five games. When setting aside those first twenty wins during "the Streak," however, Bowden's final forty-five games resulted in a record of just 27-17-1.

It wasn't all bad, though. Despite the ugliness of his final season on the Plains, Terry Bowden's tenure as head coach left Auburn fans plenty to look back on with fondness and excitement. An SEC Western Division title—Auburn's first official one—and the Tigers' first berth in the SEC Championship Game, as well as a 2-1 record in bowl games, are all positives. Two shocking wins over Florida, the entire career of Dameyune Craig, and that miraculous win against LSU in 1994—who could ever forget those? And the home field successfully defended three times in a row in the Iron Bowl—that's an accomplishment any Auburn coach could be more than proud of.

Above all else, there was the Streak—that epic, two-year ride—during which Bowden motivated the players, revamped the offense, and forged twenty straight wins even as the program suffered the sanctions of probation.

The Terry Bowden era was not in retrospect a truly great one, but it was a very, very good one in a number of ways. We didn't exactly climb to the mountaintop, and we did sort of end up stuck deep in the valley, but along the way, Bowden gave us all one heck of a ride.

7

The Top Ten Auburn Games
That Never Happened

We turn now to ten Auburn football games that never actually took place.

Yes, you read that correctly. These are games that could've been, and maybe *should've* been, but never actually *were*. They are, in short, *phantom* games—games that for one reason or another never quite came together.

This is not, however, some silly collection of fantasy games—of games we might have liked to have seen, like Auburn vs. Miami in a make-believe BCS title game in January of 1984. No, these are games that actually could have happened if things had worked out slightly differently.

We don't make any attempt to rank these—they're pretty much in random order—though the last one down below here may have been the most consequential, believe it or not.

So let's get going:

The 1986-'87 Orange Bowl

After two somewhat disappointing efforts in 1984 and 1985 (and nothing makes Auburn seasons more disappointing than losing Iron Bowls that should never have been lost), Auburn rebounded in 1986 by unveiling a high-flying (for its day) aerial attack in place of the old "Bo left/right/middle" approach. QB Jeff Burger aired it out to receivers like Trey Gainous and Lawyer Tillman while the ground game scarcely lost a step in the capable hands (and feet) of Bo's so-called "nuclear sub," Brent Fullwood.

Only two narrow, frustrating and heartbreaking losses kept the Tigers from racking up a perfect regular season in 1986: Kerwin Bell somehow hobbled into the end zone to bring the Gators back for a miraculous 18-17 win in Gainesville, and the referees called back a late Fullwood touchdown run that would have beaten Georgia. (For more on the "Wet Dawg" game, see "Auburn-Georgia: The Past is Prologue.")

After the famous "Reverse to Victory" win over Alabama, the Tigers found themselves at 4-2 in the SEC and out of the running for the Sugar Bowl—but at 9-2 overall and in prime position for a New Year's Day bowl. Pat Dye quickly accepted a bid to play Southern Cal in the Citrus Bowl—only to have the Orange Bowl come along afterward and ask Auburn to participate in their game instead. Dye stuck to his word and Auburn went on to defeat Southern Cal in Orlando, 16-7, while Arkansas accepted an at-large bid to play Big Eight champs Oklahoma in the Orange Bowl.

Could the Tigers have fared better than the Razorbacks, who gave up 42 points to the Sooners and managed only a single TD as the clock expired? We will never know—but Auburn vs. Oklahoma in the 1986/87 Orange Bowl remains one of the greatest games Auburn never played.

The 1988-'89 Sugar Bowl vs. Notre Dame

This one is a simple case of the "if onlys."

If only Auburn had kept LSU from scoring that last-minute touchdown and making an ugly, 6-0 win into a hideous, 7-6 "Earthquake" loss, the Tigers would have likely finished the 1988 season undefeated and would have been sitting there in New Orleans on January 2, awaiting a matchup with the top-ranked Notre Dame Fighting Irish—and with the national championship on the line.

Instead, that Lou Holtz-coached and Tony Rice-led Notre Dame squad went on to play and defeat a sub-par West Virginia team for the title, while a disappointed Auburn fell to surging Florida State in a mostly meaningless Sugar Bowl, 13-7.

At least one Auburn player would later say that the LSU "Earthquake Game" was what galvanized the Tigers to play so well the rest of the way—so perhaps Auburn needed that loss in order to end up SEC Champions and get to New Orleans. Then again, maybe a narrow win in Baton Rouge would have done the trick just as well—and led what was arguably one of the finest Tigers squads in history to the brink of a national championship.

And the Tigers would have won that game with the Irish. Their offense wasn't bad, with Reggie Slack giving to James Joseph and Stacey Danley out of the backfield and throwing to a bevy of talented receivers such as Lawyer Tillman, Freddie Weygand, Duke Donaldson, and Alexander Wright, not to mention tight end Walter Reeves.* Meanwhile, Auburn's 1988 defense was one of the greatest in school history, allowing just over seven points per game. They allowed a mere seventy-nine points over the *entire regular season*. Didn't the 2010 National Champion Tigers' defense allow that many points to Arkansas alone?

The 1993 SEC Championship Game

Everyone knows the deal here, right? Auburn finished the 1993 season at 11-0 in Terry Bowden's first campaign on the Plains, but had been ruled ineligible by the NCAA for any post-season play—including the conference championship game. Thus Auburn stayed home and watched the team they had just beaten, Western Division runners-up Alabama, play and lose to the Florida Gators—a team the Tigers had already beaten once (38-35, in Auburn), and would beat again when they played one another the following year (36-33, in Gainesville). Had the Tigers been allowed to play in the postseason and had they defeated the Gators again, Terry Bowden might well have faced his father, Bobby Bowden, for the first time that season—in the Sugar Bowl, with the National Championship on the line.

The 1986 Florida State Game

Auburn played Florida State in Jordan-Hare in 1983, 1985, 1987, and 1990, and in Tallahassee in 1984 and 1989, along with a Sugar Bowl meeting after the 1988 season. Auburn won this epic mini-series with a record of four wins and three losses, and each of the games was memorable in one way or another.

The 1984 game was a track meet--the two teams scored back and forth until time expired with Auburn up, 42-41, and FSU on the Tigers goal line. The 1985 edition looked to be a repeat until Auburn pulled away late, in a fashion very reminiscent of the 2010 Arkansas game, and won 59-27. FSU returned the favor with a blowout win of its own in 1987. Auburn's wins in 1983 and 1990** were by very narrow margins, as were Florida State's 1988 and 1989 wins.

The only year between 1983 and 1990 in which the two didn't meet was 1986. What might have happened in a hypothetical Tigers-Seminoles clash that season?

That year was a rebound season for the Tigers, who had come off a thrashing at the hands of Texas A&M in the Cotton Bowl to finish the year (and Bo Jackson's career) at 8-4. For 1986, Coach Pat Dye put Pat Sullivan in charge of quarterbacks, and the result was a very decent passing game led by junior QB Jeff Burger. As has been mentioned elsewhere in this column, the Tigers ended up at 10-2 and very narrowly missed out on a Sugar Bowl berth.

With Mickey Andrews in charge of the defense, the Seminoles would at last have a unit on that side of the ball to rival or surpass their fantastic offensive prowess—setting the stage for the epic run of success the program enjoyed between 1987 and 2000. But in 1986 things hadn't quite jelled yet, and the Seminoles finished at 7-4-1. They lost on the road at Nebraska, Michigan, and Miami, and at home to Florida; their tie came against North Carolina at home in the third game. None of their wins, against the likes of Wichita State, Southern Miss, and Louisville, appears all that impressive.

Given this evidence, one must assume the Tigers would have gotten the better of the 'Noles that year--perhaps by a wide margin. One imagines Burger throwing for a lot of yards and Brent Fullwood and Tommie Agee running for even more. Of course, we can never know for certain, and the series did have the propensity for producing eye-popping outcomes in both directions. But it would have been nice

to deliver one more solid beat-down to the up-and-coming 'Noles, and to extend the Tigers' winning margin in the modern series to more than one game. The thinking here is that this would have happened.

The 1999 Florida State Game

With the dismissal/resignation of Terry Bowden partway through the 1998 season, Auburn lost all incentive to begin the following year's campaign against Bowden's dad and his pre-season #1-ranked Florida State team. New head coach Tommy Tuberville, seeing the rather shoddy state of the squad he had inherited, either asked for or went along with the AU Athletic Department's decision to buy Auburn's way out of that opening game. The contract had stipulated that either team could pay a lump sum up front and cancel the game, and that's what Auburn did.

The elder Bowden at first publicly supported the decision, commenting at the time that it didn't make sense to him to still play the game, since the only reason he had even considered putting Auburn back on the schedule again (after a run of six regular-season games and a bowl in the 1980s, with AU winning four of them) was the novelty of having father coach against son. But, predictably, as the jackals of the media descended to pick Auburn and Tuberville apart as "War Chickens," Bobby B began to change his tune and to decry the Tigers for opting out of the game.

Choosing not to play a powerhouse out-of-conference team seemed like a wise strategic move prior to the season, because it gave Auburn a greater shot at making a bowl game. Florida State went on to win its second national championship that season, while Auburn barely survived its opening game with the team that replaced the Seminoles on the schedule: Appalachian State. Clearly a victory for the Tigers in that game was extremely unlikely, to put it mildly. And there's no question Bowden would have had every incentive on a personal level to pour it on and truly let Auburn have it in the game. Could Auburn have won? You can never say never, of course, but let's be realistic. Meanwhile, one more win that season and Auburn would have made a bowl game. It very nearly worked out, too—only extremely narrow last-second losses to Ole Miss and Miss State kept them out.

So—War Chicken? Not so fast. Perhaps the powers-that-were in the AD's office knew what they were doing, after all.

The 2001 LSU Game—in September

Yes, Auburn did play LSU in 2001—on December 1, *two weeks after* the Iron Bowl! In fact, it amounted to a de facto SEC Western Division Championship Game, since the winner would advance to Atlanta to play Tennessee. But the game was not originally scheduled for that date, or even that month. It was originally to have happened in mid-September, and was derailed by the terrorist attacks on New York City and Washington, DC of September 11.

Auburn lost a tough, 27-14 contest to the Bayou Bengals in December—but what would have happened if the two teams had met on the original date of September 15?

An Auburn victory certainly wouldn't have been assured, but beating them then would have been more likely than beating them at the end of the season. After all, Nick Saban's Tigers started the year with a mere 2-2 record and didn't hit their stride until the second half of the campaign, finishing with six straight wins. If you were going to catch the Bayou Bengals that year, you needed to catch them early—and Auburn didn't get that opportunity.

Also, remember, the 2001 Iron Bowl was one of the worst ever for Auburn; the Tigers managed to give up thirty-one points and score only seven in their second consecutive loss to Alabama in Jordan-Hare Stadium. Even with a week off, the demoralizing effects of that game had to linger into the LSU contest. With a win over LSU in September, the Iron Bowl loss wouldn't have affected the Tigers' fate—and they'd have had their rematch in Atlanta with the Vols three years earlier than it ultimately came.

Could they have beaten a UT team potentially headed for a national championship matchup that year? Of course they could have. After all—LSU did!

The 1993-'94 Sugar Bowl or Citrus Bowl

If not for the NCAA's postseason ban, there's no way of knowing to which bowl game the 1993 Auburn Tigers would have been invited, simply because they first would have had to face Florida in a rematch in Atlanta in the SEC Championship Game. If they had managed to beat the Gators a second time that season, they'd have found themselves with a 12-0 record and surely holding down a spot in the Sugar Bowl with perhaps one-loss Florida State opposite them and the national title on the line. Say the Tigers couldn't have won that game and you basically admit you did not follow them at all that season; they always, always found a way to get the job done. If, however, their famous "Streak" had ended under the Dome and they'd lost to the Gators, they'd still have been 11-1 and wouldn't have fallen too far—probably to the Citrus Bowl, in place of Tennessee, although they might have been chosen as an at-large team in place of Miami for the Fiesta Bowl against Arizona. That could have been interesting.

But of course we shall never know.

The 1994-'95 Peach Bowl

For the 1994 season, unlike the previous year, the options a bowl-bound Auburn team would have faced at 9-1-1 were a bit more restricted. The likelihood, as we see it, is for the Tigers to have landed in the Peach Bowl (in place of 8-4 Mississippi State) against a 9-3 North Carolina State. You'd think they would have had a better option than that, but digging through the bowl matchups from that season doesn't really produce a lot of better options. In this day and age of a gazillion different bowls and the seventh-best SEC team still landing in a decent postseason berth, we sometimes forget just how crummy the bowl options for second-tier and even lower-first-tier SEC programs used to be, only a short time ago. Remember—even at 9-2 and with an equal share of the SEC title, the 1989 Auburn team managed only the Hall of Fame Bowl. Maybe the 1994 Tigers could have replaced Tennessee in the Gator Bowl against Virginia Tech? It would've beaten staying at home for the holidays!

The 2003 Georgia Tech Game in the Georgia Dome

Auburn played Georgia Tech in 2003 for the first time since their ongoing series ended with the 1987 matchup. The Yellowjackets defeated the Tigers, 17-3, in a season in which the Tigers mostly struggled on offense with a coordinator-by-committee approach that attempted unsuccessfully to replicate the strategies and the successes of Bobby Petrino the previous season.

The game was not originally to have been played at Grant Field, however. That stadium was under renovation at the time, and the plan was to have been for the Tigers and Yellowjackets to meet in the Georgia Dome, with a 50/50 ticket split, followed by a home-and-home arrangement for 2004 and 2005. Tech changed the deal so that they could open the season with Auburn in their expanded facility in 2003, and the 2004 game was dropped entirely. The 2005 game was a home matchup for the Tigers.

Aside from the disappointment of fans who had hoped to watch the two teams face off before an evenly-divided Georgia Dome crowd in 2003, one other thing perhaps merits a moment's thought: The Yellowjackets defeated the Tigers in both actual contests—in 2003 and again in 2005. And 2004 was Auburn's perfect season. What would have happened if the Tigers had faced Tech that year?

Auburn fans doubtlessly scoff at this; the 2004 Tiger team was a juggernaut, well-coached and hungry. And yet, and yet, and yet... you never know. And, because of the change to the agreement, we never will.

The 2004 Bowling Green Game

We saved this one for last, and we did so for a reason.

The fact that Auburn did not get to play Bowling Green—a team originally on the schedule but later swiped by another program—doesn't seem on the surface to be that big a deal. One would be forgiven for thinking it to be probably the least significant of the ten on this list. But Bowling Green's decision to back out of playing this game is far more meaningful to Tigers history than you may realize. And the story gets even stranger than that.

Everyone remembers 2004. Auburn went undefeated but finished third in the BCS rankings after the conference title games were played, and thus were left out of the national championship game in favor of Southern Cal and Oklahoma. One major reason often cited for Auburn being ranked below the Sooners was Auburn's strength of out-of-conference schedule compared with OU's. In particular, people point to the fact that Auburn played the "lowly" Citadel.

But why was the Citadel on Auburn's schedule?

They weren't supposed to be!

The Citadel was a last-minute replacement—Coach Tuberville had to call half the programs in the country to find someone able to juggle their schedule to fit Auburn onto it—after one of Auburn's original non-conference opponents, Bowling Green, was paid by a third party to drop Auburn and play them instead. The third party offered more money than the deal with Auburn had called for, and represented arguably a slightly "bigger name" opponent. So Bowling Green bought out the game.

It's true that in some years there wouldn't have been a lot of difference between the Citadel and Bowling Green. But this particular squad was very good and relatively highly-regarded. They were a Division I team, as well, while the Citadel was I-AA. And the head coach was none other than Urban Meyer! Thus the Falcons boosted their new opponent's strength of schedule and hurt Auburn's when they took the money and ran.

We told you at the start of this that the story got even stranger. Here, friends, is the kicker: What team paid Bowling Green to drop Auburn and play them instead?

Why, Oklahoma, of course.

The Oklahoma that snuck into the BCS title game just ahead of Auburn—mainly due to an ever-so-slightly higher strength of schedule.

* Here's a little bonus trivia: In the Pat Dye Era, Auburn played in three Sugar Bowls: the games following the 1983, 1987, and 1988 seasons. In those games combined, Auburn scored two touchdowns. One was a pass from Jeff Burger to Lawyer Tillman; the other was a pass from Reggie Slack to Walter Reeves. Auburn did not score a rushing touchdown in three Sugar Bowls coached by Pat Dye.

** The 1990 win over FSU at Jordan-Hare was the scene of an infamous "giant group hug" immediately after the game, in which both of your intrepid Wishbone columnists were caught up in a massive and emotional melee in the stands and ended up actually falling two rows down before the scrum broke apart. This was followed by a lengthy rendition of the Seminole war chant by the Auburn student section, directed at the visiting fans as they filed out of the stadium. Van confesses that he was shamefully joining in the arm-chopping and chanting while John was telling everyone to cut out the foolishness.

The AUdacity of Hope:
1994 and the Streak

They called it "the Streak."

In 1993, his first season on the Plains, Head Coach Terry Bowden had guided the Auburn Tigers to a perfect 11-0 regular season record, capped by a stirring, come-from-behind victory over Alabama at Jordan-Hare Stadium.

The sanctions of NCAA probation, however, prevented that squad from playing in the post-season and from appearing on television. There would be no SEC Championship Game appearance and no bowl game for the Tigers in 1993—or the following year. Perhaps as importantly for Auburn's final ranking, there would be no chance to impress the various poll voters with televised victories. With the win over Alabama, the 1993 season simply...ended. In the final AP poll, the undefeated Tigers were ranked fourth, while one-loss Florida State, coached by Terry Bowden's dad, claimed the title.

During the off-season, the one constant in the media seemed to be that while Auburn could not legitimately lay claim to a national title with "only" eleven victories, the voters could not deny them one the following year if they "ran the table again" and pushed their overall record under Terry Bowden to 22-0, even with no bowl eligibility. In effect, commentators were predicting that pollsters would award Auburn one championship for both seasons combined.

There were reasons for Tigers fans to feel encouraged as the 1994 season rolled around. The television ban had ended with the conclusion of the 1993 season, so viewers (and poll voters) around the country would actually have the opportunity to watch the team perform this time around. Commentators had intimated throughout the '93 season that the more unlikely Auburn wins were accomplished via "smoke and mirrors," so the Auburn players and coaches had to relish the chance to show the viewing public that they were winning not through gimmickry but thanks to hard work, tough play, and innovative schemes. Hopes were high going into the 1993 campaign that maybe—just maybe—the Tigers could accomplish the improbable one more time. It was no accident that the theme of the season, as selected by Bowden, was "AUdacity"— representing the audacity to think that they actually could go undefeated in back-to-back seasons and claim a share of the national championship.

The task would be all the more difficult because Auburn's first-ever four year starter at quarterback, Stan White, had completed his eligibility the previous season. This time around, the Tigers would be led by junior Patrick Nix, with sophomore (and future star) Dameyune Craig serving as the backup and occasional goal-line quarterback. Gone also was starting running back James Bostic, a bruiser who had always been able to scratch and claw his way for critical yardage.

The Tigers were not entirely devoid of talent in the backfield, however. Two future NFL fixtures, Stephen Davis and Fred Beasley, carried the ball, with hard-nosed blocking back Joe Frazier clearing the way. The receiving corps included the stalwart Frank Sanders along with dependable Thomas Bailey and up-and-coming stars Willie Gosha and Tyrone Goodson. Andy Fuller provided solid play at tight end, and the offensive line featured stars Willie Anderson and Victor Riley along with center Shannon Robique.

The special teams were in good hands (and feet). Kicker Matt Hawkins proved serviceable throughout his career, while in Terry Daniel the Tigers had one of the finest punters ever to play for Auburn. His booming punts traveled so far, Mississippi State's Jackie Sherrill actually demanded that the referee inspect a ball he had kicked to determine if it had been secretly filled with helium!

The defense was something of a mixed bag. Willie Whitehead, Gary Walker and Mike Pelton anchored a tough line, but the linebackers didn't exactly strike fear in the hearts of opponents. Marcellus Mostella and Jason Miska fought hard on every play but this unit wasn't quite All-SEC caliber. The defensive backfield, however, was a different story. The Tigers enjoyed stellar play from corners and safeties such as Brian Robinson, Ken Alvis, Chris Shelling and Fred Smith, and the two biggest wins of the season—LSU and Florida—had their fingerprints all over them.

Terry Bowden's coaching staff featured an array of soon-to-be big names, as well. Future Tulane and Clemson head coach Tommy Bowden served as offensive coordinator. Wayne Hall, mastermind of Pat Dye's great defenses of the late 1980s, remained as defensive coordinator. Future Florida State head coach Jimbo Fisher tutored the quarterbacks while Rick Trickett coached the offensive line, alongside recruiting superstar Rodney Garner.

This was the squad, these were the coaches, who faced the seemingly impossible task of running the table in back-to-back seasons. Given all that was stacked against them, however, they almost made it. They came so very close. Along the way, they thrilled us and shocked us with shootouts and great escapes, and in the process produced some of the most memorable Auburn football games ever played.

Coming into the 1994 season, Auburn was ranked 12th in the AP Poll. Early wins against Ole Miss and Northeast Louisiana increased the "Streak" total to thirteen games as the Tigers welcomed LSU to town on September 17. What followed over the next few hours will never be forgotten by those who witnessed it.

Auburn's offense proved wholly ineffectual against a stout LSU defense. When Patrick Nix couldn't move the ball, Dameyune Craig was sent in at quarterback, to equally futile results. LSU, meanwhile, was able to maintain a healthy lead throughout most of the contest. The only score generated by the Auburn offense, and the only score the offense would create the entire game, as it turned out, was a 40 yard field goal early in the second quarter. Every other point Auburn would need to win the game was scored by the defense.

Late in the second quarter, Auburn's Chris Shelling fell on an LSU fumble in the end zone. Missing the extra point, the Tigers in blue found themselves ahead, 9-7. Auburn would not lead again until the very end.

Soon after the fourth quarter began, LSU kicked a field goal to increase their lead to 23-9. Auburn showed virtually no signs of life at this point, and any sensible fan of the blue-clad Tigers could be forgiven for writing the game off as a loss, and the Streak as done at thirteen. Dreams of a repeat undefeated season and an outside shot at the national championship seemed to evaporate into the humid east Alabama afternoon heat.

Then came one of the more shocking turns of events in college football history.

Attempting to convert a fourth down, LSU's quarterback, Jamie Howard, threw downfield—into the arms of Auburn defensive back Ken Alvis, who returned the interception forty-two yards for a touchdown. A few plays later, it was Fred Smith's turn to pick Howard off and take it to the house. LSU managed a field goal to push back out to a 26-23 lead, but then Coach Curly Hallman inexplicably called for another Howard pass on third down. This one was snagged by Brian Robinson, who took it in for the decisive score. The game ended with Chris Shelling grabbing his second of the game, this time in the Auburn end zone, to fend off a late LSU comeback attempt.

Auburn had pulled out the miraculous 30-26 win. LSU was defeated and demoralized. The Streak lived on.

It must be noted that none of the scores on the three fourth quarter interceptions came easy; Auburn's DBs had to fight their way tooth and nail into the end zone every single time. Given the utter futility of the offense that day, one can only speculate as to what might have happened if Nix or Craig had been called upon to punch it in for a score if the defense had failed to take it to the end zone on any one of those plays.

Easy wins the following weeks against East Tennessee State, Kentucky, and Miss State set the table for Auburn to travel to Gainesville and face the #1 ranked Florida Gators. Terry Bowden preached to his players that, given that Auburn could not play in a bowl game this season, this was their "Super Bowl." The Streak stood at seventeen. The Gators were eighteen-point favorites. Hardly anyone gave the Tigers a chance.

Four quarters later, Auburn had proven everyone wrong. They scratched and clawed and held the mighty Gators to only thirty-three points. The secondary once again came through, repeatedly intercepting starting senior quarterback Terry Dean and forcing

Coach Steve Spurrier to switch to sophomore (and future Heisman Trophy winner) Danny Wuerffel, who scored three touchdowns to help the Gators take the lead late. The Auburn secondary stepped up once again and got the ball back for Patrick Nix, who promptly drove the Tigers down the field for a last-minute score, hitting Frank Sanders with a fade pass in the left corner of the end zone. Auburn had won, 36-33, and Tigers had defied the words scrawled on the huge sign someone had hung over the railing of the Swamp that stated, "The Streak Stops Here!" It did not; now it stood at an impressive eighteen in a row since Terry Bowden had become head coach.

Stephen Davis bulldozed the Hogs from Arkansas the following week, muscling Auburn to a 31-14 win. East Carolina put up only a token struggle for Homecoming, and the Tigers found themselves ranked #3 in the AP Poll, with the Streak standing at twenty games. Running the table again and laying claim to at least a share of the national championship no longer seemed quite so far-fetched, quite so AUdacious. Maybe, just maybe, this team was special enough to get it done.

Alas, the Bulldogs of Georgia, as they had so many times before, had something to say about that. Coach Ray Goff, in fact, had a very specific comment that he directed toward Terry Bowden: "You don't just win all the time," he was quoted as uttering during game week. His words would prove prophetic, to the disappointment of Tigers fans everywhere.

Not a particularly impressive squad, finishing the season with a record of 6-4-1, the Bulldogs had even lost to Vanderbilt in Athens a few weeks earlier. Nevertheless, as is their wont, they saved perhaps their best shot for Auburn. And it was a painful one.

Auburn got the ball back in the final seconds with Georgia having pulled into a tie at 23-23. Patrick Nix led the team into field goal range and Matt Hawkins came out to attempt the game winner. Alas, the kick went wide and the game ended in a draw. (This was two seasons before overtime came to NCAA football.)

For Georgia, this was a moral victory. For Auburn, it was a crushing disappointment. After the game, Terry Bowden recounted to the media that he had been very surprised that Hawkins had missed the kick; given the experiences of the previous twenty games, he'd all but taken it for granted. "No! We make those kicks," he recalled saying at the time. The headline of the Columbus, Georgia paper the next day summed it up: "UGA Beats Auburn, 23-23."

The winning streak was over, as was any realistic chance of a national championship. All that remained was a trip to Birmingham for the only "bowl" the Tigers would be able to participate in that year: the Iron Bowl. What followed was one last incredibly memorable contest; one more courageous rally by the offense; and one more disappointment in a season that had gone so right for so long, only to tumble off the tracks at the very end.

Both teams entered the Iron Bowl undefeated for the first time since the 1971 contest. Only Auburn's draw with Georgia marred either team's record; the Streak now stood at twenty-one games unbeaten, the entire tenure to date of Coach Terry Bowden. The game was played in venerable Legion Field in Birmingham, before an overwhelmingly pro-Crimson Tide crowd.

Alabama seemed to surprise Auburn's defense by running an option-based attack at the Tigers in the first quarter, and quickly reeled off three shocking touchdowns to take a 21-0 lead early on. At that point, the Tigers found their footing on defense and Alabama would not score again. Unfortunately, there was simply not enough time left for the offense to catch up.

Auburn capped off two long scoring drives with short goal-line plunges by the quarterback to pull within 21-14 late. Getting the ball back with the clock winding down in the fourth quarter, Patrick Nix attempted to do what he had been so successful at doing all season long: leading the team to a game-winning (or at least game-tying) score at the end. Operating from deep in their own end of the field, Nix passed to Fred Beasley out of the backfield for critical first downs and moved the ball out to near midfield. There the Tigers bogged down and faced a monumental fourth down situation. On the play that followed, Frank Sanders caught Nix's pass and appeared to have moved beyond the first down marker before being tackled slightly behind it. The referee marked the ball short of Sanders' point of advance and the measurement determined that the Tigers had failed to convert. Alabama got the ball back and ran out the clock.

With that, the 1994 season was over, as was the Streak. Terry Bowden had suffered his first loss as the Tigers coach; his record at Auburn following the Streak would be only 27-18-1. Dreams of a national title had evaporated; what was worse, the amazing undefeated run had been snapped by hated Alabama.

In retrospect, however, the accomplishments of the 1994 Auburn Tigers should not be undervalued. Their win against Florida was one of the greatest underdog victories in Auburn history, and the improbable and AUdacious win over LSU should always be seen as among the most astonishing comebacks in the annals college football.

They didn't take home any trophies in 1994, but they gave Auburn fans everywhere a roller-coaster ride of epic proportions, ignored the sanctions of probation to stretch the Streak out to a remarkable twenty wins in a row, and showed the world that you can never, ever count out the Auburn Tigers.

The Rise and Fall... and Rise and Fall...
of Tommy Tuberville

Part 1: The First Rise, 1999-2000

A more complete biography of Tommy Tuberville, coach at Ole Miss, Auburn, Texas Tech and Cincinnati, among other stops, is surely coming someday. That is not our purpose here.

Here we simply wish to look back over a tumultuous decade during which Auburn's head football coach was Thomas Hawley Tuberville—a decade that began with five wins and ended with five wins, but in between saw Auburn beat Alabama six times in a row, win five bowl games and five SEC Western Division titles, win 85 games overall, and very nearly climb to the top of the college football world.

Of course, it was also a decade during which Tuberville's Auburn teams went from mediocre to good to disappointing to excellent (peaking with the undefeated season of 2004) to very good to "slow slide back downhill" (reaching the nadir with the disastrous 2008 campaign).

Our story begins with the fallout from another infamous season. The 1998 campaign had been an unmitigated disaster for Auburn. But at last it was over, and a new year was beginning. That new year would bring with it a new coach, a new staff, and a steady improvement in Auburn's fortunes—though it didn't quite look like it at first...

1999.

Terry Bowden had taken the hint that his days on the Plains were at an end, and he hit the road midway through that '98 campaign. Defensive Coordinator Bill "Brother" Oliver took over as interim head coach for the remainder of the season and clearly had designs on keeping the job permanently. The Auburn athletics administration, on the other hand, didn't have much interest in Oliver as head coach. From the beginning, it seemed they knew the candidate they wanted (and by "they," we pretty much mean super-trustee Bobby Lowder).

They wanted Tommy Tuberville.

A former defensive coordinator at Miami (Florida) and Texas A&M, Tuberville had guided Ole Miss through a particularly rough stretch of NCAA probation (including severe scholarship restrictions) that he had inherited from the previous regime. During that time, he'd managed a decent winning percentage—higher than anyone probably had a right to achieve at Ole Miss under those conditions—and had even pulled a couple of upsets over rival LSU. He claimed to love Ole Miss to the point that he would have to be "carried out in a pine box." It seems as though, when a football coach makes a remark like that, they're on the next train out of town. Indeed, Tuberville was trading blue and red for blue and orange before the year was over.

Oliver was still in the mix, however. Tuberville supposedly had a few private conversations with him about the possibility of his remaining as defensive coordinator, but nothing came of it. Ultimately, Tuberville decided to promote his defensive backs coach from Ole Miss, John Lovett, to be Auburn's new defensive coordinator. Lovett would survive three seasons on the Plains before becoming (along with Noel Mazzone) the first of several assistants to be cut loose as Tuberville repeatedly shook up his staff.

The Tuberville Era got off to a rough start due to two off-the-field situations that became black eyes for the Tigers in the media. One was Tuberville's revocation of athletic scholarships for five players left over from the Terry Bowden regime. While no one argued that the players didn't really merit football scholarships (Bowden had tacked them on to a very poor recruiting class to fill out the numbers and save face as his ship was sinking), many objected to the taking away of scholarships from players that had not otherwise done anything wrong. The Athletics Department responded to the outcry by finding the five players jobs within the department where they could earn their money.

The other firestorm erupted after Tuberville exercised Auburn's option to cancel the game with Florida State that had been scheduled by Terry Bowden as the season opener. By paying FSU a six-figure fee, Auburn was free to schedule a lesser opponent, and they did so by lining up Appalachian State. Tuberville had at least two reasons for doing this: one, a look at the schedule revealed that Auburn had a very real chance at making a bowl game appearance in his first year on the job—the first year after a catastrophic 3-8 campaign. The Tigers had to play their SEC foes but there was no rule that said they had to play FSU—the #1 ranked team in the country at that point, and destined to go on and win the National Championship that year. By replacing the Seminoles with a more beatable out-of-conference opponent, Tuberville hoped to get the

Tigers to a bowl game. His other reason was even simpler: Auburn had only scheduled the game (and Bobby Bowden at FSU had only agreed to it) because it would have been the first time in NCAA history that a son's team played against his father's team. Bobby Bowden had no other interest in playing Auburn; the Tigers had, after all, gotten the better of FSU from 1983-1990, with Pat Dye's squads winning four out of seven contests. Bowden quickly and happily agreed to the cancellation. Only later, when reporters and commentators began to use the cancellation as an excuse to criticize Auburn and Tuberville, did Bobby Bowden reverse his position and begin to decry Auburn's decision to cancel the game.

As it turned out, and as discussed elsewhere in this book, the Tigers did win the replacement game over App State, but they still fell short of the six wins necessary to qualify for a bowl game.

In retrospect, the 1999 team did have an opportunity to forge a decent season, given their mostly strong defensive play (particularly on the line) and a few astonishing wins over better-regarded teams. But painfully narrow losses in key games knocked them out of contention for a bowl game and a winning record.

The big wins were remarkable. After uncomfortably squeaking past App State and Idaho by a touchdown each to start the season, Auburn traveled to Baton Rouge to take on Gerry DiNardo's LSU. They proceeded to utterly dismantle the Bayou Bengals and to cost DiNardo his job, just as they had done to Curly Hallman five years earlier with the "Interception Game." Auburn throttled LSU, 41-7, beginning the game with a fake field goal run by Damon Duval and never looking back.

(This one became known afterward as the "Cigar Game," thanks to Tuberville handing out victory cigars to the players in the locker room—a custom long-practiced by Pat Dye's teams in the Eighties. Why LSU took such exception to it here, we may never know—but they certainly did, and have complained about it ever since. They pretty much despised Tuberville from then on.)

Later in the season, the Tigers would similarly crush Georgia in Athens, racing out to a score of 38-0 early in the third quarter on the strength of native son Ben Leard's passing, before the Dawgs salvaged some late points to make it look more respectable, at 38-21. Receiver Ronney Daniels, an older guy who had come back to football after a minor league baseball stint, dominated Georgia with big catches and runs.

As it turned out, a young high school quarterback from Mississippi was in attendance at both of those games. He was considering both LSU and Georgia, came to see them play Auburn—and was treated to the sight of UGA and LSU fans streaming from the stadium early as Auburn put the hammer down on them. Soon afterward, he committed to the Tigers. His name was Jason Campbell, and he would be a very critical pickup for Tuberville and his staff on the march to national title contention.

The games that cost Auburn a chance at a 7-4 record and a decent bowl game were the contests with the two Mississippi schools. Both were in Jordan-Hare and in both cases Auburn was in position late to win the game. In both cases, things fell apart and the Tigers lost.

Ole Miss was a particularly painful game for Tigers fans and for Tuberville because that was the team and the college he had just left at the end of the previous season. The Rebels fans were breathing fire and out for blood against him and his new team, and they got it. Auburn drove down the field late and lined up to kick the game-winning field goal, but missed. The game went to overtime, and Ole Miss won, 24-17. It marked Auburn's first loss to Ole Miss since Pat Dye's final season, seven years earlier.

Despite the lack of recent historical connections, the Mississippi State game was just as agonizing on the field—and of course the Bulldogs' coach was one Jackie Sherrill, who had cultivated a very visible and seemingly mutual animosity with Tuberville. Auburn led the game at one point, 16-3, while State was trying to run the ball. Finally Sherrill gave up and started calling pass plays, Auburn's secondary couldn't quite cope, and the Dogs were able to score two late touchdowns to win, 18-16.

Of course, the Iron Bowl eternally offers the possibility of sweet redemption to even the most wretched of its participants in a given year, and 1999 would be no different. Auburn limped in at 5-5 but with no running game to speak of. (The Tigers had at one point turned to miniscule wide receiver Clifton Davis to try to provide some speed in the backfield; all that it accomplished was to nearly get Davis killed.) Alabama came in at 8-2 and on their way to the SEC Championship Game, but at that point they still had never achieved victory in Jordan-Hare Stadium. Could the Tigers somehow dig down deep and throw a stumbling block in the Tide's path and protect the house?

No. They lost, 28-17, and the stranglehold over the Tide in our own stadium had finally ended. Dye had beaten Bama there in the First Time Ever game; Terry beat them there three more times. Now Tuberville was 0-1.

The effort was good. Auburn's strong defensive line kept the Tide (and super RB Shaun Alexander) in check most of the night, but with no running game, the Tigers simply couldn't control the ball or the clock and eventually they crumbled.

Offensive coordinator Noel Mazzone came up with an innovative approach to this game on offense that did find success briefly: He positioned four receivers on one side of the formation in a diamond shape (led by then-receiver, later DB Travaris Robinson) and none on the other side. Star receiver Ronney Daniels started out at the single back spot. Before the snap, Daniels would motion out to the opposite side of the formation as a lone receiver there. Bama had to know the motion was coming every single play; otherwise, the formation would've been illegal, with only six men on the line. Nonetheless, it helped the Tigers roll down the field, as it forced the defense to choose between trying to cover all four guys on one side and doubling Daniels on the other. It was a clever approach—one we've never seen used anywhere else, possibly because no team since then has ever been as utterly bereft of running backs as this one was. Could it have worked for a full sixty minutes, though? Probably not. Turnovers and penalties brought the drives to a halt in key moments, and the Tide eventually pulled away late.

So Tuberville's inaugural campaign was over at 5-6, and the problems were glaringly obvious. At season's end, Auburn's leading rusher had been fullback—yes, we said *fullback*—Heath Evans, with a whopping 357 yards. Clearly Auburn had a need, glaring and desperate, for a running back that could move the chains and score some points. Auburn coaches were recruiting (and would ultimately get) future star RB Ronnie Brown, but Brown wasn't quite ready for the spotlight in his freshman year, and ended up redshirting. So, if Brown couldn't carry the load in 2000, where on earth could Auburn turn for such a game-changing player? And without a dependable running back, could the Tigers even win five games again in 2000?

That most pressing question had to be answered, and answered in a hurry, as the 2000 season loomed ahead.

2000.

With Tommy Tuberville's inaugural season in the books at a disappointing 5-6, the Tigers faced another daunting challenge the next year if they couldn't find a running back able to survive the rough and tumble world of SEC football. But, on such short notice, where could they ever find such a back?

As it turned out, he was on the same JUCO team as a quarterback the coaches were recruiting. Daniel Cobb may not have ever become a great Auburn QB, but he did introduce Tuberville's staff to one Rudi Johnson.

Problem solved.

The 2000 season was a breath of fresh air for the Tigers after the angst and misery of the previous two years. It began with a breakout performance by the rugged Johnson at running back against Wyoming. Johnson proved to have the ability to get stronger as the game wore on, such that while he was often not that impressive early, by the fourth quarter he was dragging defenders along for the ride as he rang up yet another first down. And, as Cam Newton demonstrated in 2010, having a player who can be counted on to convert short 3rd down runs on a consistent basis is utterly invaluable.

The first half of the season went by in a flash, with a big road win against Ole Miss in Tuberville's first return to Oxford since leaving the team at the end of '98, and a huge home win against LSU—34-17—in Nick Saban's first coaching matchup against Auburn.

The season hit a pothole in the middle, with the Tigers experiencing their first loss in a trip to Starkville. Jackie Sherrill continued to torment Tuberville, shutting down Rudi Johnson and squeezing out a narrow, 17-10 defeat for Auburn. The next week, in Gainesville, Florida carpet-bombed the Tigers, 38-7. From 5-0 to 5-2, just like that—and with Arkansas, Georgia and Alabama still to play.

The Tigers regrouped upon their return from Florida, however. They got past a troublesome bunch from Louisiana Tech (who would give them even bigger fits the next season) and then won a grind-it-out game over Houston Nutt's Arkansas, 21-19, breaking a two-year slide against the Hogs. (The next two seasons, Arkansas would exact all the revenge they could ever want.) Next the Tigers faced Georgia at home, and a rather strange phenomenon confronted them: the home team in the series had not won since 1991, when the Bulldogs won in Athens. The game went to overtime but eventually, behind strong running from Rudi Johnson, Auburn prevailed, 29-26.

The Iron Bowl a week later would be the first played in Tuscaloosa in nearly a century, with the game in Alabama's home years finally moving away from Birmingham's Legion Field. Many fans on both sides of the divide were shocked to learn that Alabama had never beaten Auburn in Bryant-Denny Stadium, losing twice to the Tigers in the late 1800s and once again in 1901. Auburn extended the streak into the 2000s, continuing to hold the Tide scoreless (they had not scored a point in any of those previous games in Tuscaloosa, either) in a steady drizzle and riding three Damon Duval field goals to victory, 9-0. It was Auburn's first shutout of the Tide since 1987 and meant that new Alabama coach Dennis Franchione began his tenure in T-Town with a loss to the Tigers.

At 9-2, Auburn had clinched its second SEC Western Division title in only Tuberville's second season, and would face Florida in a rematch of the October 14 game, this time in Atlanta.

It wasn't pretty. Again the opponents were able to limit Rudi Johnson's running and Ronney Daniels's receiving, and the Tigers struggled to put points on the board. While the defense managed to hold the Gators to "only" 28 points, the offense could only manage two field goals.

Now 9-3, the Tigers nonetheless were offered a spot in the Citrus Bowl in Orlando on New Year's Day, where they would face the

Michigan Wolverines. A more diversified attack, including throwing the ball to players like Markeith Cooper in the slot, kept Auburn in the game, but the defense was generally unable to slow down Michigan's powerful running attack, and the Tigers fell, 31-28.

With the end of the season, hope sprung anew for Tigers fans everywhere. The year hadn't ended well, with two losses, but getting back to Atlanta and playing on New Year's Day represented a big turnaround from the dregs of 3-8 just two years before. As the new millennium dawned, the future looked bright indeed.

Little did anyone suspect then that, the following year, the Tigers would effectively play only half a season, and the real grumbling about Tuberville would begin.

Part Two: The First Fall, 2001-2003

2001:

New players burst onto the scene for Auburn in 2001, some destined to make a huge impact on the program for years to come, others...not so much.

Jason Campbell had signed with Auburn and then redshirted the 2000 season, as had Ronnie Brown. Now they would be joined by true freshman Carnell "Cadillac" Williams. Cadillac's recruitment was a thing of legend: Reportedly leaning at first toward Alabama, he had changed his mind and decided that Tennessee represented his best opportunity as a player. Tuberville would have none of it. He and several assistant coaches descended on the Williams household all at once, making their best pitch to lure the young running back to the Plains. It worked. When signing day came, Cadillac unzipped his jacket to reveal an Auburn jersey underneath.

Williams immediately impressed his new teammates with his work ethic. They jumped him early, calling him "Yugo" as if to take him down a peg because of his fancy nickname. He responded by working hard and earning lots of playing time by the end of his freshman season.

Unfortunately, reality intruded into the '01 season very quickly. After early wins over Ball State and Ole Miss, Auburn prepared to travel to Baton Rouge for a game with LSU. That game would have taken place on September 15. But on Tuesday of that week came the terrorist attacks forever after known as "9/11." All games for that Saturday were postponed to later in the season.

A week later, with the country still deeply in shock, the Tigers faced a flight to New York for a game with Syracuse at the Carrier Dome. One can only imagine the mind-set of young men boarding a plane for New York, less than two weeks removed from seeing jumbo jets fly into the World Trade Center towers. The Tigers held their own for a while—and Jason Campbell even rushed for a long touchdown—but unblockable defensive end Dwight Freeney seemed to spend the entire game living in the Tigers' backfield, and eventually Auburn fell to the Orangemen, 31-14.

The next three weeks can rightly be summarized as the "Damon Duval Show." Never before or since has one kicker delivered victory against three straight opponents in consecutive games. First came Vanderbilt, a team that has tended to give the Tigers a much closer contest in Nashville than in Jordan-Hare. Indeed, this time victory seemed in their grasp—but they attempted a fake field goal late, which was snuffed out by the Tigers. Moments later, it was Auburn winning the game by riding Duval's leg to a 24-21 triumph.

The next week, Auburn welcomed nemesis Jackie Sherrill's Mississippi State to the Plains—a Miss State to whom Auburn had now, unthinkably, lost four consecutive games. The Bulldogs made this one close, too, but Duval once again proved the difference as his late field goal pushed the Tigers to victory, 16-14.

The trifecta was accomplished the next weekend, with Steve Spurrier bringing what would turn out to be his final Florida squad to Auburn. The Gators were undefeated and ranked #1 in the country, and they had crushed the Tigers every season since Terry Bowden's big "Super Bowl" win in the Swamp in 1994, even winning twice over Auburn the previous year. There was nothing to indicate this game would be any different—but it was.

Switching between Campbell and Daniel Cobb at quarterback, and making do with a patchwork linebacking corps due to injury, the Tigers scratched and clawed and kept the game close all the way to the end, deadlocked at 20-20—whereupon Damon Duval was asked to do it again. The forecast had called for rain for most of the game, but it had miraculously stayed away—until just before the final play, Duval's field goal attempt. As the Tigers lined up for the kick, the winds began to swirl and heavy rain blew into the stadium. Duval got the kick away, and everyone watching on television or from the north end of the stadium could see that it was going to go horribly wide right. Except—it didn't. Duval's kicks always tended to curve out and back in, and in some cases that phenomenon had caused him to miss, as the ball crossed all the way back across and beyond the face of the goalposts before reaching them. This time, a combination of Duval's curveball and the storm blowing in caused the ball to hook back in—right down the middle, dead center. The Tigers had knocked off top-ranked Florida and Duval had won his third game in a row with a last-second kick.

At that point, however, the 2001 season was essentially done. It was as if the Tigers decided to take most of the rest of the year off. A week later, on October 20, they defeated Louisiana Tech 48-41, but it would require overtime to finish off the directional Bulldogs. Once again victory came on the final play of the game, but for once it wasn't Duval who got it done but troubled receiver Deandre Green catching the winning score.

Remarkably, the Tigers would win only one more game that season—over Georgia in Athens on November 10, thanks to a rugged, 41-carry performance by Cadillac Williams. (After the game, Tuberville famously admonished first-year UGA coach Mark Richt that you can't win in the SEC without emphasizing the run game.)

Even more astonishingly, in a year when the SEC West teams knocked each other off, the Tigers would still finish the season with a share of the Division title, despite (eventually) losing five games.

One of those losses, of course, was perhaps the most infamous Iron Bowl loss of Tuberville's career: an "out of nowhere" crushing by Dennis Franchione's Tide squad, 31-7. It had begun promisingly enough, with Cadillac Williams moving the ball against the Tide's strong defense—but then he'd gone down under a pile, and suffered a broken collarbone. With him out of the game and out for the season, the Tigers couldn't get anything going on offense the rest of the way.

How could it happen? Auburn fans searched for answers. Some pointed to a Halloween frat-party photo that had made the rounds the week before the game, showing several white Auburn students in blackface and others dressed as the KKK. This, they claimed, had angered some players to the point that they simply allowed the Tide to win. Others rejected this as preposterous, but the bad feelings remained, hanging like a cloud over Jordan-Hare. Grumblings about Tuberville grew louder as the season spiraled downward.

One way or another, the Iron Bowl was done, and for most of Auburn history, that would also mean the regular season was done, as well. Alas, not so this year—one opportunity for redemption remained: LSU.

That game with LSU—a de facto divisional championship game—marked yet another in a long line of oddities in the Auburn-LSU series. You know about the "Earthquake Game" and the "Barn Burner" and the "Cigar Game" and the "Interception Game." This one was the "9/11 Game," originally scheduled for September 15. For the first time since the Iron Bowl rivalry was renewed in 1948, the final game of Auburn's season was with someone other than the Crimson Tide. The atmosphere surrounding this contest was perhaps even more intense than that on the field of play; there were scuffles among fans before and especially after the game, and a minivan painted in Auburn colors was vandalized and set on fire. Attendees on both sides complained for days afterward of shoddy treatment by the other side, and at one point the university presidents even got involved. The Auburn-LSU rivalry was reaching a new—and distasteful—level of intensity.

As for the game itself, a 27-14 defeat kept Auburn out of a second consecutive Championship Game, sending an LSU squad with the same 5-3 conference mark as Auburn to Atlanta instead.

Coda to the 2001 season was a berth in the Peach Bowl in the Georgia Dome in Atlanta against North Carolina. The Tigers hadn't faced the Tarheels since a 20-10 win in 1988, and this time the Heels would get the upper hand. Carolina's fierce defensive line, led by Julius Peppers, gave Auburn's offense fits all game long. The Tigers fought back late to pull within six, but couldn't close the deal and lost, 16-10.

A season that had begun with such promise and that had seen the heights of 6-1 had ended at 7-5. Even a share of the Western Division title didn't mean much, since the Tigers had been denied the trip to the Championship Game thanks to the LSU tiebreaker.

Pressure ramped up on Tuberville in the offseason, and he responded with the first of his trademark moves: cutting loose the offensive and defensive coordinators.

The 2002 season would begin with two new faces on the sideline—faces that would become very, very familiar to Auburn fans and college football fans everywhere in the years to come.

2002.

Gene Chizik and Bobby Petrino. Perhaps you've heard of them.

Those were the two new faces on the Auburn sideline as the 2002 season began.

Tuberville had dismissed John Lovett and Noel Mazzone and, in their place, brought in Chizik from a successful stint as DC at Central Florida and Petrino from the NFL's Jacksonville Jaguars. Petrino wanted to get into college coaching and jumped at the chance to take the reins on an offense with players like Jason Campbell and Carnell Williams. Chizik wanted to be a head coach and moving from Orlando to Auburn was a nice step in his path; little could we have guessed then where that path would eventually lead both him and the Auburn Family.

The season opened with a very big, very splashy start: at the Coliseum in Los Angeles, facing Southern Cal, on what amounted to a college version of "Monday Night Football." (The NFL season would not begin for another week, so ABC televised this game in that time slot.) The Trojans had been down for a while, but with Coach Pete Carroll in his second season there and rejuvenated quarterback Carson Palmer leading the offense, they were getting back to their historical ways of dominating the (then-) Pac-10 and beyond.

The game was close to the bitter end, with Carnell Williams ripping through the USC defense early (before leg cramps slowed him later on). But with the game tied at 17 deep in the fourth quarter, the Trojans regained the ball and used a short passing game to methodically march down the field, chewing up the clock. They scored to go up 24-17 as time was nearly gone, and that would be that.

The Tigers, still adjusting to Petrino's more pro-oriented schemes, reeled off four wins in a row after their return from California. One was a 42-14 crushing of Mississippi State in Starkville—the first of five consecutive epic beatdowns of the Bulldogs by Auburn. The other of note was Auburn's first-ever win against Syracuse, who visited Jordan-Hare on September 28. The Orangemen were not having a very good season, but they held their own against Auburn the entire way, eventually forcing three overtimes before succumbing to a Cadillac Williams winning touchdown. Regardless of the record of Syracuse, this was a particularly satisfying win for those who still remembered the 1987-'88 Sugar Bowl and all that went with it, and had waited patiently to exact some revenge.

(This was also the game where, afterward, a New York columnist wrote a piece extolling the virtues of football and football culture in Auburn, Alabama—an article that would make the rounds of delighted Auburn fans' email inboxes for years to come.)

The next two weeks would bring the season to what seemed at the time a crashing halt.

First came Arkansas, which essentially locked up its place in that year's SEC Championship Game by crushing the Tigers in Jordan-Hare, 38-17. They'd beaten Auburn pretty handily in Arkansas in 1999 and 2001, but most Tigers fans thought, "It can't happen here!" It did. Auburn's defense had no answer for Fred Talley and the rest of the Razorback rushing attack, falling 38-17. Auburn would go on to again finish in a tie for the Western Division title, but the loss to Arkansas kept the Tigers out of Atlanta. The Hawg Hex, as we have written about extensively elsewhere, was in full effect.

The next week the Tigers visited Florida in Gainesville for their one and only clash with a Ron Zook-coached Gators team. Things did not go as planned.

The Gators raced out to a 23-7 lead by the fourth quarter; it could have been worse, but Auburn's defense held them to three field goals from inside the ten yard line. Even more catastrophically, Cadillac Williams suffered a broken leg in the second quarter that would rule him out for the rest of the season. (This injury meant he would miss the LSU game again; believe it or not, he would not face the Bayou Bengals as a player for the first time in his career until his junior season.) Things looked dark indeed for Auburn—until a certain number 23 chose this moment to make his explosive entrance into Auburn history.

Ronnie Brown took over this game, scoring all three touchdowns for the Tigers. With Jason Campbell stepping in at quarterback in the fourth quarter, the offense reeled off sixteen straight points and tied the game at 23-23. Damon Duval lined up late to do again what he had done to the Gators the year before in Auburn: beat them on a last-second kick. This time, however, the kick was blocked. In overtime the Gators scored a touchdown and then stopped Jason Campbell on fourth down to win, 30-23.

One weapon from the Auburn arsenal was out, but another one had been discovered in Brown. He would score two rushing touchdowns the following week as Auburn shocked Nick Saban's LSU in Jordan-Hare, 31-7. The Tigers held LSU to only 79 yards of passing offense while racing out to a 17-0 lead at the half and 31-0 in the fourth before LSU tacked on a late score to avoid the whitewashing. Jason Campbell quarterbacked the entire game for

Auburn and while going only 7-11 passing for 105 yards, he rushed for 37 and had Ronnie Brown and Tre Smith behind him to account for a combined 175 more.

The next week at Ole Miss became the Ronnie Brown show, as he carried the Tigers to a 31-24 win. Cadillac might have been in the repair shop but the "Hummer" was just getting revved up.

After a routine pasting of Louisiana-Monroe, Auburn welcomed the fourth-ranked, one-loss Georgia Bulldogs to Jordan-Hare the next Saturday for what would become one of the legendary games—and most painful defeats—in series history.

Despite the Bulldogs being strong favorites, having lost only to nemesis Florida, Auburn led the entire game until the very end. Ronnie Brown led the way with 103 yards of rushing as the Tigers held a 14-3 halftime advantage. Unfortunately for the Tigers, Brown injured his ankle in the second half and was mostly ineffective afterward. A late third down conversion that would have kept the Bulldogs off the field the rest of the way was stopped as Brown simply couldn't surge forward on his bad wheel. Finally Georgia got the ball back in the waning moments and faced a fourth down at the Auburn 19 yard line. Not just the game itself but also the participants in the SEC Championship Game—both of them—hung in the balance.

Then came 70-X-Takeoff, with David Green hitting a leaping Michael Johnson in the Tiger end zone for the game-winner.

Just like that, Auburn was out of the SEC Championship Game (though they still tied for the Western Division) and Arkansas was in. Just like that, Florida was out of the title game as well, and Georgia was in. This is, as far as we can determine, the only time in twenty-plus years of SEC Championship Games that one single play in one game has changed both divisions' representatives.

Just as bad, Auburn now faced the prospect of literally limping into Tuscaloosa for the Iron Bowl with both Ronnie Brown and Cadillac Williams out with injuries. To make matters worse, rugged blocking fullback Brandon Johnson was also on the shelf. Auburn fans watched the date in T-Town approach and wondered what in the world the Tigers would do for a rushing attack.

As it turned out, they did quite well, despite the ninth-ranked Crimson Tide being heavy favorites.

Third-string back Tre Smith stepped in for Brown, with the tight ends serving to block. The relatively diminutive Smith rang the Tide up for a stunning 126 yards on 25 carries, while big tight end Robert Johnson caught two touchdown passes from Jason Campbell. The defense locked down Alabama and their feared "smoke draw" play, allowing only one touchdown as the game wound down to a 17-7 Auburn victory. This actually marked the first time Alabama had ever come away with *any* points against Auburn in Tuscaloosa in *three centuries* of games there—something Tuberville almost gleefully pointed out after the game, saying, "They did finally score on us." It was this sort of thing—sort of a "Steve Spurrier Lite" approach—that made Tide fans really despise Tuberville. That and the fact that he regularly beat their teams.

Auburn would not be going to Atlanta but they did earn a berth in Orlando's New Year's Day bowl—now renamed the Capital One Bowl—for the second time in three years. This time the opponent was Penn State. Having had time to heal, Ronnie Brown exploded on the Nittany Lions for 184 yards, leading the Tigers to a 13-9 victory and MVP status while far outshining Penn State's more heralded running back, Larry Johnson, in the process.

The 2002 season was over with a pair of big wins. Ronnie Brown had been a revelation when he had burst onto the scene like a supernova following Cadillac Williams's injury against Florida.

During the offseason, monstrous running back (and future New York Giant) Brandon Jacobs announced that he was transferring from his junior college to Auburn. And of course Tre Smith, the hero of the Iron Bowl, was only a sophomore. Talk of the "Four Horsemen" buzzed around campus and across the Auburn Family. Added to that, a more mature and consistent Jason Campbell at quarterback, a strong defense, and a squadron of very talented young receivers such as Ben Obomanu and Devin Aromashodu, who had come on in a big way during the year, seemed to indicate that 2003 was going to be a very big year for Auburn. A very, *very* big year. Maybe a *national championship* year.

Or so we all thought.

2003:

The 2003 season would turn out to be one of the most disappointing, based on pre-season expectations, in Auburn history. Remarkably, given the amount of talent on the team and the sense before the season started of just how far this team could go, they would be the only squad from 2000 through 2005 to fail to win even a share of the SEC Western Division.

The first sign of impending disaster came at the end of the 2002 season when, even before the bowl game, Offensive Coordinator Bobby Petrino accepted the head coaching job at Louisville, after only one year with the Tigers. Not wanting to disrupt an offensive system that had only been in place a few short months, Tuberville opted to stick with the same playbook and simply hand the OC reins over to offensive line coach Hugh Nall, along with newly hired QB coach Steve Ensminger. This "Nallsminger" approach (as some critics dubbed it) would prove to be a catastrophically bad decision; Nall never liked the Petrino offense, didn't particularly want to coach it, and simply was not nearly as effective as Petrino at operating it. He and running backs coach Eddie Gran didn't seem comfortable with having more than one of the Tigers' four superstar backs in the game at a time, so at any given moment three of the team's best offensive players were sitting on the bench. Bulldozer Brandon Jacobs barely saw the field, and Williams seemed to have the coaches' favor over Brown for long stretches. The result was a self-limiting offense that could not move the ball, could not convert first downs, and would not even score a touchdown until September 13.

Disaster struck in the opening game. Auburn had barely fallen short against Southern Cal in Los Angeles the previous year, but the Tigers had basically their entire team back and were facing the Trojans at home this time. Before the game, there was some talk of "USC can't play in heat and humidity like this." At Tuberville's instructions, for maximum visual impact on television, the fans mostly wore orange. The stage was set for what should have been a monumental victory.

There was one other factor at work that could have motivated the Tigers to play well. During the off-season, the team's longtime play-by-play announcer, Jim Fyffe, had passed away—a tragedy that affected many Auburn fans deeply. In an attempt to honor Fyffe, the Auburn cheerleaders during pre-game festivities instructed the crowd that after Auburn scored its first touchdown, one side of the stadium would yell "Touchdown" and the other side would yell "Auburn," in a re-creation of Fyffe's signature call. Some immediately considered this a jinx, but much more would be involved in the unfortunate nature of how this game played out than mere bad luck.

As it turned out, all the orange in the stands didn't help, the "home climate advantage" proved to be a myth, and Jim Fyffe would sadly never be honored by that particular cheer. Without Petrino calling the plays, the offense could do nothing, and the Tigers fell, 23-0, to the eventual national co-champions. There would be no more talk of special new touchdown celebrations—though the "all-orange" concept would survive into the regime that followed.

The week after the stunning shutout by USC, Auburn traveled to Grant Field to face Georgia Tech for the first time in nearly two decades, and managed only a field goal in a 17-3 loss. Just as had happened in 1984, a potential national championship season had seen the Tigers start 0-2. This time, after two weeks of play, they had managed a grand total of only three points. The Four Horsemen of the AUpocalypse had yet to even make it out of the stable.

Against Vanderbilt they finally scored a touchdown—in the third game of the season, a potential national championship season!—and won, but it was too little, too late. They managed tough wins over Tennessee, Arkansas (on the road) and Miss State before falling in a big way to LSU in Baton Rouge, 31-7, in what some fans dubbed "Black Saturday." The LSU defense never allowed the Tiger run game to get going, bottling up Williams and Brown all night, and the passing game was hopeless. A heartbreaking loss to Ole Miss at home (when star receiver Ben Obomanu dropped the potential game-winning pass in the Rebels' end zone) and then a crushing defeat on the road at Georgia (the first Auburn game Van ever left at halftime, out of sheer disgust) meant that this supposed squad of limitless potential had become, astonishingly, a 6-5 team—the first of Tuberville's teams since his opening campaign in 1999 to fail to win even a share of the Western title—with only the Iron Bowl left to play.

Auburn President William Walker and Athletics Director David Housel, as we all later discovered, chose that moment to board a private plane and fly to Louisville for a secret meeting with Bobby Petrino, to discuss the possibility of the former Auburn OC taking over as the Tigers' new head coach the following year.

142

Tuberville knew some of what was happening. He felt he was essentially coaching for his job against Alabama on November 22.

Coach Nall was given free rein for this game to run the offense the way he wanted to, rather than trying to copy Petrino's approach. This plan worked to a degree, and Auburn took the lead on the very first play from scrimmage when Cadillac Williams "went crazy" (in the words of new play-by-play radio announcer Rod Bramblett) and dashed eighty yards for the opening score. Later in the first quarter, a catch and long run by Obomanu (plus 2-point conversion by Campbell) and a John Vaughn field goal put the Tigers ahead by the unusual score of 18-2.

The Tigers held on for a 28-23 victory, amassing an impressive 519 yards of total offense in the process. It was Auburn's first win over Alabama in Jordan-Hare in six years (since 1997). Nonetheless, an emotional Tuberville afterward was uncertain if he had just coached his final Auburn game. What he (and Walker and Housel) hadn't counted on was a certain airplane flight becoming public, after someone spotted the plane on the runway and jotted down its tail numbers.

Auburn earned a bid to the Music City Bowl in Nashville and beat Wisconsin there, 28-14, but questions still floated in the air: What would become of Tuberville now?

As details of Walker's and Housel's trip to Louisville emerged, the Auburn Family chose to close ranks and rally behind Tuberville and to largely condemn the president and AD for the surreptitious nature of their visit with Petrino. Despite the disappointment of the 2003 season, Tigers supporters reminded themselves that Tuberville had beaten Alabama three out of five times, had won a share of the Western Division of the conference three times, and had gotten the Tigers to Atlanta in his second season. Many also saw the main issue of the 2003 squad—lack of real focus on offense—as a

143

correctible problem, not requiring the replacement of the head coach.

Walker and Housel backed down and Tuberville reaffirmed his commitment to the Auburn program.

On Friday, January 16, President William Walker resigned under pressure. He was replaced by Ed Richardson as interim president. Many speculated that this would be "it" for Housel, as well, as Walker had steadfastly supported Housel staying on in his job.

Richardson quickly placed well-respected Senior Associate Athletics Director Hal Baird in charge of the day-to-day operation of the Athletics Department, changing his title to Athletics Assistant to the President. (Baird had retired as Auburn's baseball coach in 2000.)

On February 13, after interviewing multiple candidates, Tuberville hired Al Borges away from the University of Indiana to be the new offensive coordinator. Borges was seen by many as a surprise choice (and he and Tuberville were quickly ridiculed by Paul Finebaum on his radio show when the hire was announced), but Borges had led a prolific UCLA offense a couple of years earlier, and impressed Tuberville with his ideas about making adjustments at halftime. (Other candidates, including those who advocated a "spread" offensive attack, Tuberville later reported, had mostly insisted a team should "keep on doing what you do," even when trailing at the half, while Borges had offered innovative and creative suggestions.)

A month later, with the essentials of his job now in Baird's hands, Housel announced he would retire in January of 2005. During that final year of Housel's tenure, Baird (who repeatedly asserted that he had no interest in a permanent AD position at Auburn) served as point man on the replacing of the men's head basketball coach, women's head basketball coach, head baseball coach, and ultimately the search for a new AD that would take the place of both himself and Housel. This process concluded on December 22 with the hiring of Jay Jacobs as the new Athletics Director.

Thus the disastrous season of 2003 was in the rear view mirror at last, and Auburn was making wholesale changes throughout the following year that would leave the Athletics Department looking very different. One face that remained the same, however, was that of the head football coach. Tommy Tuberville remained, as did his stalwart defensive coordinator, Gene Chizik, now entering his third year on the Plains. As they welcomed Al Borges into the fold and prepared for the upcoming season, the Auburn Family hoped the bad times were over and maybe a little better future lay ahead.

No one, however, could have dreamed just how much better the 2004 season would be, and just how close it would come to confirming Tuberville's bold prediction: "We will win a national championship at Auburn University."

The 2004 team would certainly do everything in their power to make that statement a reality.

Part Three: The Second Rise, 2004-2006

2004:

The new season began with, for some, an odd mixture of hope and cynicism, excitement and resignation that perhaps Auburn football could never be better than an occasional contender in the SEC West. Tommy Tuberville was still well-liked by much of the Auburn Family, and their outpouring of support on his behalf at the end of the 2003 season had literally saved his job and ended those of his two bosses, the university's president and athletics director. Most fans simply didn't blame or condemn him for everything that had gone wrong, and believed he was still the man to get things going in the right direction again. When he selected Al Borges to be the new offensive coordinator, Auburn fans held their collective breath, tried to ignore the derision coming from supporters of the team across the state, and waited to see what would happen.

And, *oh my,* but something happened.

Borges had promised from the get-go that he intended to have Carnell Williams and Ronnie Brown on the field at the same time. Why keep at least one of your best players on the bench at all times? (It probably helped the team that Brandon Jacobs, the huge running back, had opted to transfer again—this time to Southern Illinois—easing up the logjam in the backfield somewhat. He would go on to make a mark in the NFL with the New York Giants.) Taking advantage of Brown's skills as a receiver, Borges employed him on short and intermediate passing routes out of the backfield while utilizing Williams's quickness as a runner. Additionally, Borges introduced a variety of motion plays into the offense, giving opposing defenses something else to have to think about before the ball was snapped. Finally, Borges encouraged Jason Campbell to get the ball downfield to his talented group of receivers, creating a deep-passing game Auburn really hadn't possessed to that degree since possibly the days of Pat Sullivan.

Wins against Louisiana-Monroe and at Miss State to start the year didn't tell observers much, but at least this team, unlike its previous incarnation, appeared capable of sticking the ball in the end zone. The real test—and in many ways the game of the year—came in week three, against Nick Saban and (as fate would have it, his last squad at) LSU. The fifth-ranked Bayou Bengals were coming off winning a share of the national title in 2003. They had crushed Auburn on "Black Saturday" in Baton Rouge. Now they were

VAN ALLEN PLEXICO & JOHN RINGER

coming into Jordan-Hare, and the Tiger offense would be called upon both to score more than the seven they'd managed the previous year (they did, barely) and to keep the ball out of LSU's hands so the enemy Tigers couldn't score 31 again.

Both missions were accomplished. The teams traded early scores, then went through the entire middle section of the game scoreless. Finally the good Tigers found themselves down 9-3 late in the fourth quarter (LSU having missed an extra point after their lone touchdown). On fourth down, Jason Campbell scrambled and found receiver Courtney Taylor for the first down. A couple of plays later, he found Taylor again in the end zone. With the game now tied, 9-9, John Vaughn actually missed the EP. A penalty against LSU allowed him to retry the kick, however, and (as Nick Saban melted down on the sideline) Auburn prevailed, 10-9.

While Auburn hadn't scored many points, the adjustments by Borges were obvious. His motion before the snap and schemes for Campbell to roll away from pressure afterward kept the ball in Auburn's hands longer, and kept the LSU offense off the field. Gene Chizik's defense had come through in a big way, limiting LSU to only two scores. With that mega-game out of the way and the defending champs beaten, 2004 suddenly held a lot more promise than anyone might have suspected just a week earlier.

Two weeks later, Auburn traveled to Knoxville, where they hadn't won since 1983—twenty-one years! The tenth-ranked Volunteers had two highly-touted freshman quarterbacks to throw at Auburn. The Tigers responded by devouring both of them. Ronnie Brown's epic touchdown run, plowing through the Tennessee defense and dragging them along with him into the checkerboard end zone, became the iconic image of this 34-10 Beatdown in the Big House.

The Tigers went on to mangle Arkansas on October 16, by a score of 38-20, in a game that was never that close. Interestingly, the 20

147

points scored by the Razorbacks were by far the most points allowed by the Tigers defense in the regular season. In fact, they did not give up a rushing touchdown until the Kentucky game on October 23. Gene Chizik's reputation was rising fast.

After a thrashing of Ole Miss, Auburn faced the highest-ranked foe left on their schedule, the #8 Georgia Bulldogs. Losses to the Dawgs the previous two years were large in the minds of the Auburn players, but equally important was the need to score a resounding win in a nationally televised game. For even though Auburn was undefeated and had beaten two top-ten teams already, they had begun the year (due to the woeful underperformance of the previous squad) ranked only 17th (and had actually dropped to 18 in the AP Poll after week one). They reached third in the rankings after the Arkansas win, but ahead of them all season long were USC and Oklahoma, also undefeated. Those two teams had begun the year 1-2, and showed no signs of dropping for as long as they kept winning. Under the BCS arrangement, if Auburn finished the year still ranked third, they would have no recourse and would be on the outside looking in when the national title matchup was announced.

The Tigers did everything humanly possible against Georgia, shutting the Dawgs out for almost the entire game while scoring 24 points in a variety of creative ways, including Cadillac Williams throwing a halfback pass for a score. The 24-6 win was not enough to lift the Tigers over the top two teams, nor would the win in Tuscaloosa against Alabama the following weekend, nor the 38-28 victory in the SEC Championship Game in a rematch against Tennessee (the only other team to have beaten Georgia, thus allowing them to sneak into Atlanta ahead of the Dawgs).

Those last two games were noteworthy for a couple of reasons. Against Alabama, the Tigers actually trailed at the half, 6-0, when it seemed nothing would go right for them. (They even missed a field goal just before halftime that would have at least gotten them on the board against the Tide.) In the second half, MVP-to-be Jason Campbell uncorked deep passes to his receivers and the Tigers pulled out the 21-13 comeback. Against Tennessee in the Dome, the Tigers looked to have things well in hand until two late Gerald Riggs runs pulled the score closer, at 31-28. Campbell answered with another long pass to Ben Obomanu, and the Tigers had won their first SEC Championship since 1989.

Unfortunately, that wouldn't be enough. USC and Oklahoma won the rest of their games and went off to play one another in the Orange Bowl for the national championship. Third ranked Auburn was assigned to the Sugar Bowl to play ACC champ Virginia Tech. In most seasons, an SEC Championship and a trip to the Sugar Bowl would seem like astounding accomplishments, to be reveled in at the time and celebrated forever after. In 2004, however, it all felt like a consolation prize. The Tigers could have easily checked out and sleepwalked through the game, but they didn't—despite how rankled most of them felt about being there. They bested the Hokies, 16-13, for their first Sugar Bowl win since 1983. They ended the season at #2 after Oklahoma was blown out by USC, a clear indication that it should have been the Tigers facing the Trojans in the big game all along.

So 2004 was in the books—a bittersweet year by any estimation. Tuberville had survived the palace coup and had prospered, and of course success is the best revenge. His team had faced four top-ten-ranked opponents and had beaten them all, along with nine other foes. (Tennessee the second time around would probably have made for a fifth top-ten foe, except that their loss to Auburn the first time had dropped them in the polls.) They had ended the year as SEC Champs, Sugar Bowl Champs, undefeated and second-ranked in the country. And yet not only did they not have the big prize to show for it all, they weren't even permitted by the existing system to play for it. Tuberville lobbied extensively beforehand, on ESPN and in other places, for the SEC Champs to get a shot, perhaps through some sort of "plus one" arrangement, and Auburn's players had even said they would be willing to face USC "in the parking lot" for the national title. Of course none of that was going to happen. Auburn would be denied simply because of basic mathematics: Three teams cannot play one game for a title. Somebody had to be left out, and the team that had the steepest hill to climb, starting at the lowest position of the three, was the one.

Two years later, the SEC would begin an epic run of consecutive BCS National Championships (including one by Auburn, finally) that had many around the country looking back at this 2004 squad and admitting, finally, that maybe they should have been the ones to play USC. When, years later, the Trojans were forced to vacate the 2004 title, a push was made to have the BCS and/or the Grantland Rice Trophy organization recognize Auburn as the true champions for that season. Ultimately, however, this was not done, and today the official records show that nobody won the 2004 national championship. Auburn fans are mostly divided on the issue, with some wishing to claim this title (along with 1983 and several more) and others not wishing to seem too much like Alabama and claim everything that might remotely qualify as a title.

All in all, it's hard to imagine an SEC team in the Modern Era finishing at 14-0, with multiple wins against top ten-ranked teams and a victory in the Dome in Atlanta, and not even getting the opportunity to play for the national title. This 2004 Auburn team remains one of only six SEC squads since the expansion and division of the conference in 1992 to finish the year unbeaten and untied. Fully *half* of those teams (1993, 2004 and 2010) were Auburn Tigers teams. It's truly an astonishing accomplishment, trophies or not.

2005.

With the end of the 2004 season, the stellar backfield of Jason Campbell, Ronnie Brown, and Cadillac Williams all moved on to the NFL, taking DB Carlos Rogers with them. Brown became the second pick in the draft, Williams the fifth, and Rogers the ninth. Campbell went to the Redskins late, making all four of them first-round selections by the pros. How far they had come from the dog days of 2003.

Auburn fans celebrated that fact but also gazed upon the remains of the team they had left behind and wondered what the Tigers would really be capable of in 2005, having lost so much firepower. Running back (and snowboarder) Tre Smith was entering his senior season and had earned the opportunity to finally become the Tigers' featured back, but few truly expected that he could hold up in that role across an entire season; he wasn't a big guy by any means. Auburn had brought in a much sturdier back—Kenny Irons—as a transfer from South Carolina, but the coaches were not entirely pleased with his grasp of the offense and particularly the blocking assignments early on. And so, in the first game of 2005, at home against Georgia Tech, Smith was given the start and much of the playing time.

That decision likely cost Auburn the win, as Smith was largely ineffective against the stout Yellowjackets defensive front. Tech prevailed, 23-14.

Just like that, the win streak begun against Alabama at the end of the 2003 season was over. It had lasted sixteen games, four short of the mighty run by Terry Bowden's first two squads in 1993-94. And Auburn had gone from 13-0 to 0-1.

The Tigers regrouped, leaned more heavily on Kenny Irons and on the passing of new quarterback Brandon Cox, and began to win.

Cox is an interesting story in his own right. He guided the Tigers to a 29-9 record as the starter, and is (as of 2013) still the most recent Auburn quarterback to be the regular starter for more than one season for the Tigers. He was a member of the Tigers squad in 2002 and was still throwing passes for Auburn when the clock struck midnight to usher in January 1, 2008—quite a long stretch of time to be a college player. And yet he very nearly wasn't a Tiger at all, and for more than one reason.

Cox had first signed with Auburn out of high school way back after the 2001 season, at the same time the Tigers had acquired that great receiving class that included Ben Obomanu, Devin Aromashodu, Courtney Taylor (who took a redshirt that first year), and Anthony Mix. As the top QB in the South, he (along with Aromashodu) had reportedly leaned toward Florida—until Steve Spurrier announced he was leaving Gainesville to try his hand coaching in the NFL. He reported to campus in mid-'02, but once there he suffered from a flare-up of myasthenia gravis (a condition he'd been first diagnosed with during tenth grade) and chose to leave Auburn to get his health issues under control and (reportedly) to deal with family and personal issues.

He returned to campus the following year, 2003, and promptly redshirted, then backed up Jason Campbell in 2004. That left him three years of eligibility remaining; he would turn 22 years old midway through his first season as a starter.

Five straight wins followed the opening loss to Tech. One was a big win on the road against Arkansas, in which Kenny Irons rushed for 182 yards; another was an epic beatdown of Steve Spurrier's South Carolina team, 48-7—the same score Spurrier's first Florida team had hung on Pat Dye's 1990 Tigers.

Then came one of the most disappointing and inexplicable losses in recent years: LSU.

As usual, the game was memorable in a weird way. LSU was ranked #7, while Auburn had climbed back to #16—the same ranking they had begun the year with. In a hard-fought, low-scoring struggle in Tiger Stadium, Auburn's normally reliable kicker, John Vaughn, missed five field goals, including one that would have won the game in regulation and one that would have sent it into a second overtime. Instead, LSU prevailed, 20-17, despite a 218-yard rushing performance from Irons.

The Tigers closed out the season with four big wins, taking down Ole Miss, Kentucky, Georgia and Alabama. The last two deserve a bit more discussion.

Georgia was ranked ninth in the country and on their way to the SEC Championship Game. The game was at Sanford Stadium in Athens, where the Tigers hadn't won since 2001. It was a wild one, with the scoring spread out evenly by both teams across the length of the game, and eight lead changes before it was done. It came down to Auburn facing a fourth and ten at its own 34. The situation appeared dire, but then Brandon Cox hit Devin Aromashodu running in the open, and "Ace" took the ball all the way down to the Georgia goal line before fumbling it into the end zone, where Courtney Taylor, who had been trailing the play, managed to recover it. By rule (because it had been fourth down) the ball was placed on the three, where it had been fumbled—a catastrophe for Georgia, because this meant that Auburn could run the ball, run the clock, and score at the last second, rather than giving it back to the Dawgs with time still left. Indeed, John Vaughn came through with the short kick as time expired, and the Tigers had the 31-30 victory.

A week later, the Tigers welcomed eighth-ranked Alabama to Jordan-Hare for another memorable contest. The Tigers raced out to three touchdowns in the first quarter, sacked Brodie Croyle eleven times, and held on to win, 28-18. It marked four straight Iron Bowl wins for Tuberville and Auburn. Kenny Irons went over a hundred yards rushing for the sixth straight game and the Tigers had defeated a top ten team for the sixth time in their last seven tries. Read that last part again, because it's a remarkable statistic: Auburn had beaten a top ten team for the sixth time out of seven tries. Tuberville's teams could be infuriating in their occasional losses to lesser teams, but they could almost always be counted on to give the best opponents their best—and often to win.

The season ended in Orlando with yet another visit to the Capital One Bowl. Unfortunately, the Tigers did not bring their "A" game this time, while foe Wisconsin was all fired up over the impending retirement, after the game, of their longtime coach, Barry Alvarez. Playing Auburn in a bowl game for the second time in three seasons, the Badgers gave the Tigers fits and won the game, 24-10. This was Tuberville's first bowl loss since the 2001 Peach; he would not lose another as Auburn's coach.

The 2005 season was over and the team had finished only 9-3, but that record is a bit deceptive. This was a very good team. The loss to Georgia Tech happened at the very start of the year, as the team was transitioning from the Campbell/Williams/Brown era to something else, and still finding itself. The LSU loss was practically an Act of God—though that sort of thing seems typical of Auburn-LSU games. And the bowl loss resulted from a combination of factors including the opponent being fired up to send their longtime coach out on a high note. Each game easily could have turned out differently, and indeed at the end of the year many observers were calling this team "the best in the SEC."

2006.

The following season marked an important transitional moment for the Auburn program. While Brandon Cox was still around (and would be for one more year), by 2006 he had lost not only his rushing attack, as Kenny Irons moved on, but also most of his squadron of top-flight receivers, such as Devin Aromashodu, Ben Obomanu, and Anthony Mix. Only the ageless Courtney Taylor remained, having redshirted in 2002 while the rest of his recruiting class of wideouts—one of the best in Auburn history—played.

The team also lost its defensive coordinator for the second straight year. Gene Chizik had accepted the same position at Texas under Mack Brown following the undefeated 2004 campaign (and went on to coach the defense of an undefeated Longhorn squad that next year). His replacement for 2005, David Gibbs, never quite caught on and accepted a job with the Kansas City Chiefs after one season on the Plains. Tuberville looked around and found the perfect replacement that off-season: Will Muschamp.

Muschamp had been a player at Georgia and an assistant under Nick Saban at LSU. He'd followed Saban to the Miami Dolphins in 2005 but jumped at the chance to come back to the college game and accepted the DC role at Auburn. In both of his two seasons on the Plains, his defenses ranked in the top ten nationally, leading the SEC in scoring defense in 2007.

It was a good thing the Tigers had such good defenses those two years, because Al Borges' offense was growing increasingly anemic. Gone were the reliable rushing attack and the reliable receiving corps. The 2006 Tigers won a couple of monumental games— beating eventual #3 LSU and eventual national champion Florida— but also managed to lose to Arkansas (with Gus Malzahn running the offense) and Georgia. Those two losses kept the Tigers—who had climbed all the way up to #3 in the AP Poll before the Arkansas game on October 7—out of the SEC Championship Game yet again. They still might have reached that game, and possibly been in position for the national championship game, but for the catastrophic loss at home to Georgia on November 11.

Four games merit greater detail during the regular season. First came #7 LSU on September 16. In a tough defensive struggle for the ages, the Tigers held on for a 7-3 win (controversial due to various late penalty calls that were arguable either way), gaining some revenge for the "Field Goal Game" of the year before.

Two weeks later, Auburn visited South Carolina and actually managed to control the football for every single second of the third quarter. The Tigers received the second half kickoff, drove down the field, scored a touchdown, onside kicked, recovered the ball, and did it all again. When Steve Spurrier's team touched the ball in the second half for the very first time, it was already the fourth quarter and they had, astonishingly, gone from a touchdown ahead to a touchdown behind. Even more amazingly, the Gamecocks then proceeded to control the ball for almost the entire fourth quarter, but came up short, falling to Auburn, 24-17.

Against Florida on October 14 in Jordan-Hare, the Tigers faced the team that had slipped into their #3 spot in the AP Poll after their upset by Arkansas. All they did was to pull off the first of their two wins against Urban Meyer and Tim Tebow—and in improbable fashion, ringing up 27 points without the offense ever scoring a touchdown. (Shades of 1994 LSU!) It was a wild and wacky affair, giving us the "Pontiac Game-Changing Performance of the Year" as Tre Smith ran back a blocked field goal just after halftime to give Auburn the lead at 18-17. A field goal and then a last-second fumble return by Patrick Lee made the final score 27-17 Auburn.

The 2006 Iron Bowl was not a particularly memorable affair, with that Tide team finishing the season at 6-6 and 2-6 in the SEC. It would be Mike Shula's last year as Alabama coach. It also marked five straight wins by Tuberville's Tigers in the series, a prospect most Tide fans found not just distasteful but unthinkable.

One item of note about this game stands out, however: Two of Auburn's touchdowns came after the defense forced turnovers deep in Alabama territory. The offense was becoming increasingly limited and seemed capable of scoring only when good starting field position was gift-wrapped for them by the defense. The brilliance of Al Borges' offensive attack in 2004 and 2005 had given way to a far less productive unit by the end of 2006, and 2007's offense would prove even more limited. Change was again in the air.

The bowl game only reaffirmed this situation. The Tigers faced Nebraska in the Cotton Bowl on January 1, and again couldn't put together much in the way of long scoring drives, finishing with only 178 yards of offense. Fortunately, again, they didn't have to, as the defense and special teams provided great starting position and held the opponent in check all game long. The total yards of Auburn's two touchdown drives? A whopping 23 yards. Nevertheless, the Tigers had won, 17-14, with the stalwart Courtney Taylor the offensive MVP in his final game. Most Tigers fans were happy about it, noting that any win over Nebraska is an occasion worth celebrating and remembering.

Part Four: The Second Fall, 2007-2008

2007:

The 2007 senior class would prove to be the winningest in Auburn football history, compiling 50 victories in their time with the Tigers (if you count redshirt seniors and go back to include 2003, or averaging ten wins a year). And yet as the 2007 season wore on, it became increasingly obvious that changes were needed, and changes were on the way. Those changes would ultimately prove to be much more dramatic than anyone could have guessed as the smoke cleared from the win over Nebraska in the Cotton Bowl to end the 2006 season.

Brandon Cox was back for one more campaign; he'd been on campus since Jason Campbell and Carnell Williams were sophomores. For this last season he would be joined in the backfield by Brad Lester (a talented running back who never quite achieved the levels of greatness the Auburn Family had hoped he would), Ben Tate (who had arrived from Maryland the previous year), and freshman Mario Fannin.

Al Borges remained the OC and Will Muschamp the DC; like Cox, both would be gone by the end of the year.

The season got off to a rocky start as Auburn trailed visiting Kansas State 13-9 deep in the fourth quarter of the opener. Cox threw a touchdown with two minutes left to put Auburn ahead, and then Antonio Coleman ran back a fumble to ice the game, 23-13. Tigers fans could breathe a sigh of relief, but it was obvious there were problems.

Those problems were exposed a week later as Auburn took on South Florida for the first time. Five turnovers allowed the Bulls to take the game into overtime, where they prevailed, 26-23, thanks to a 14-yard touchdown pass that trumped Auburn's field goal.

Five more turnovers doomed Auburn to another loss the next week, against Mississippi State. By the time the Tigers traveled to Gainesville on September 29, their record was only 2-2 and few held out much hope for a win. The #3 Gators were hungry for revenge after Auburn's big win over them the previous year on the Plains, and Tim Tebow was in the midst of a Heisman-winning campaign. To everyone's surprise, the Tigers led at the half, 14-0, and 17-3 after three quarters. The Gators rallied to tie the score at 17-17 late, but Wes Byrum kicked a 43-yard field goal to win it as time expired. Actually, he kicked it twice, as Urban Meyer called for a timeout just before the ball was snapped; Byrum didn't see the signal in time and went ahead and made the kick. Forced to re-try after the timeout, he hit it a second time, then ran past the Florida bench doing the Gator chomp.

Two weeks later, Byrum again provided the game-winner, nailing a twenty yard kick with less than a minute remaining to give the Tigers a 9-7 win over Arkansas in Fayetteville.

A week later, Auburn traveled to Baton Rouge for yet another memorable tussle with the future national champion Bayou Bengals.

This game marked Les Miles' third contest against Auburn; his record stood at 1-1 after the first two. This time around, Auburn held its own against fifth-ranked LSU most of the way, leading 17-7 at halftime and 24-23 late. Unfortunately, LSU was able to drive down to the Auburn 22 yard line with mere seconds to go. Les Miles, in one of the first games that would contribute to his reputation for erratic decisions and bizarre clock management, opted to eschew the field goal attempt and instead to have the QB throw the ball into the end zone. Miraculously, Demetrius Byrd caught it for the winning touchdown with one second remaining on the clock. LSU had won, 30-24, in another heartbreaker for the good Tigers in Baton Rouge.

Auburn's record at this point was 5-3, but two wins the following two weeks over Tennessee Tech and Ole Miss pumped it up to 7-3. Then came one of the more disappointing performances in modern Auburn history: The Tigers seemingly rolled over for Georgia, losing 45-20. They would limp into the Iron Bowl at 7-4 but with hopes of delivering a sixth straight win in the series, this time over new Tide head coach Nick Saban.

The game was low-scoring and not particularly pretty, but the Tigers managed the big win in Tuscaloosa, 17-10, as Auburn defensive coordinator Will Muschamp coached against his old boss and held Saban's bunch to only ten points. The streak was up to six now, and Tuberville's position on the Plains seemed about as secure as it could be.

The Tigers were invited to the newly-dubbed Chick-Fil-A Bowl (formerly the Peach Bowl) in the Georgia Dome in Atlanta, where their opponent would be the same one they had faced there after the 1997 season.

That brings us to a very peculiar historical fact: The bowl in Atlanta served as the final bowl game for all four of Auburn's previous head coaches in the Modern Era. Pat Dye beat Indiana there in 1990; Terry Bowden beat Clemson there in 1997; Tommy Tuberville beat Clemson again there in 2007; and Gene Chizik beat Virginia there in 2011. The rule seems to be, if you're Auburn's coach, don't win your bowl game in Atlanta or your days are numbered!

Between the Alabama game and the bowl, there had been one shakeup on the coaching staff. Al Borges had met with Tuberville to discuss the direction of the offense, and he later reported that it quickly became clear to him during the conversation that he would not be returning as offensive coordinator the following year. He went ahead and left at that point, and Tuberville quickly hired "spread" guru Tony Franklin as his successor.

Franklin had developed a reputation as an offensive genius while at Kentucky, coaching under Hal Mumme and alongside Mike Leach in that school's famous "basketball on grass" passing attack. He'd helped develop Tim Couch, Dusty Bonner, and Jared Lorenzen as Wildcat quarterbacks (as in the team "Wildcats," not the wildcat position/approach), each leading the SEC in passing and each accounting for upwards of a zillion yards through the air in Lexington.

Tuberville and Franklin assured the media that they would be sticking with the existing plays and game plans for the bowl, before Franklin would implement his own system for the following year. This turned out to be false. Franklin installed quite a bit of his spread system during the eight days of bowl practice, and Auburn ran it exclusively against Clemson.

During the season, Brandon Cox had experienced injuries and difficulties and had been replaced on occasion by freshman Kodi Burns. For the bowl game, Franklin took a page from Steve Spurrier's occasional approach and simply swapped quarterbacks every play, with Cox in when there was more need for a pass and Burns in when the opportunity to run presented itself. The approach paid dividends; in overtime the Tigers from Auburn defeated those from Clemson, 23-20, with Burns running in the winning score. The stalwart Brandon Cox, meanwhile, wrapped up his lengthy Auburn career with the win, his eligibility expiring at last as 2008 dawned.

With the season over, Will Muschamp turned down the offer of a raise at Auburn to accept the same job at Texas—just as Gene Chizik had done three years earlier. (Chizik had become head coach at Iowa State, beginning his infamous 5-19 run that would eventually see him back on the Plains.) Tuberville quickly hired Paul Rhoads, who had made a splash as defensive coordinator at Pitt that year.

At first glance, with the 2008 season fast approaching, it looked as if all was well at Auburn. Tony Franklin had seemingly proven himself and his system—with only a few days of practice time—in the Chick-Fil-A Bowl, and Rhoads seemed like a good, solid fit for the defense. But there were problems beneath the surface. Kodi Burns was not developing as a reliable SEC quarterback, and there didn't seem to be anyone else to turn to behind him on the depth chart. Mario Fannin had shoulder issues and fumbled a lot, and Ben Tate couldn't carry the load by himself. Franklin was not working well with the other, more established Auburn coaches—a situation that would only fester as the months went by and as Auburn began to lose games in 2008. The defense wasn't quite clicking with Rhoads in charge the way it had with Muschamp. Recruiting was sliding.

As the new season rolled around, trouble was brewing on the Plains—though few understood just how much trouble, or how quickly it would blow up in our faces.

2008:

The first sign that things were going terribly wrong for the Tigers probably came in week three, against Mississippi State. The result was a game that quickly became one of the great punch lines in modern SEC history: Auburn won but did so by the baseball-looking score of 3-2. The Tigers held the Bulldogs to only 116 yards of total offense that day, but managed only 315 themselves, and only scored on a Wes Byrum field goal in the second quarter.

Transfer Chris Todd, who had followed Franklin from Troy to Auburn, had taken over the bulk of the quarterbacking duties despite a notably weak arm. He completed 14 of 26 passes but for only 159 yards, with a 5.9 average.

The next week, Auburn faced sixth-ranked LSU and lost in another squeaker, giving Tigers fans hopes that maybe things weren't quite so bad—after all, they'd once again hung close with LSU, and nearly won. An ugly win over Tennessee the following week didn't really impress anyone, but it was a win over the Vols, and it stopped the bleeding momentarily.

The next week, the bleeding became a tidal wave.

Auburn traveled to Nashville to face Vanderbilt, a team the Tigers had not lost to since sometime in the Polk administration. (Well, Eisenhower, actually. Certainly not in the lifetimes of your intrepid Wishbone columnists.) Auburn played decently enough early on, taking a 13-0 lead in the first quarter. A missed Wes Byrum extra point might not have seemed important at the time, but it would loom quite large later.

After the first quarter, the wheels came off. The Tigers managed only four yards rushing in the second half. You read that correctly: *Four yards*. And to a defense that had been considered the weakest against the run in the SEC, to that point in the season. Vandy scored twice, made both extra points, and that was the ballgame: 14-13, Commodores.

Six weeks into the season, and with a supposed genius as OC, Auburn ranked 104th in the nation in total offense.

Upon returning to the Plains, Tuberville met with Franklin and laid down the law: he had to work more effectively with the coaches and he had to be more hands-on with the players, who clearly were not absorbing the new system, six-plus weeks into the season. Franklin responded by marching out onto the practice field and attempting to take all the offensive coaching into his own hands in very demonstrative fashion. Tuberville had had enough at that point and, on Wednesday, dismissed Franklin.

Handing the reins over to Steve Ensminger, the former co-coordinator (along with Hugh Nall) from the 2003 season, didn't help. The bleeding only grew worse. Players checked out. Some told reporters that the team was no longer a team; divisions were growing and chemistry was long gone. The Tigers dropped games against a weak Arkansas squad in their first year under our old friend Bobby Petrino, at West Virginia as running back Noel Devine ran wild in the second half, and even at Ole Miss, 17-7. Only a 37-20 win over Tennessee-Martin on November 8 provided a victory the rest of the way—the first since they'd beaten Tennessee back in September.

Most humiliating of all was the absolute shellacking by Alabama in Bryant-Denny on November 29. As the Tide took advantage of an Auburn team by then in utter disarray, Saban urged his players to pour it on, shouting profanities about how much he hated Auburn. The final score of 36-0 served as a kind of death knell for this lost season, and as a precursor for the major changes about to happen. In simple terms, the Tuberville Era was at an end.

The Monday after the Iron Bowl, Tuberville met with AD Jay Jacobs and occasionally with Auburn President Jay Gogue. The meetings dragged out over three days, with Jacobs and Gogue asking Tuberville to draw up a detailed, written plan for how he would make the Tigers competitive again. That plan never materialized. On Wednesday, Tuberville resigned.

Jacobs later claimed he was "shocked" by the resignation and asked Tuberville, who had received a contract extension through 2013 just a year earlier, to stay on. Tuberville refused, saying it would be best for both parties—Auburn University and Tuberville— for him to step down. Jacobs and Gogue decided to give Tuberville the $5.1 million payment he would have received had he been forced to resign, even though they were under no obligation to do so, given the circumstances. In part this was because Tuberville was not leaving to accept a job at another institution; he intended to remain in Auburn with his family "for about a year" before getting back into the coaching arena elsewhere. "It was the right thing to do," Jacobs told reporters later, in regard to the payment.

Tuberville was as good as his word. He remained in Auburn for the 2009 season, doing occasional commentary for ESPN, then accepted the head coaching position at Texas Tech, following their dismissal of Mike Leach. (Many observers questioned how happy he was there, in desert west Texas, and indeed in 2012 he moved on again, to Cincinnati.)

Tuberville's exit happened so quickly, much of the Auburn Family was stunned. The Tuberville Era had lasted ten years, with so many highs and just a few lows along the way. And now it was over.

Those that had never liked him, or that had turned against him recently, had lots to say—and not just against the head coach. His assistants—dubbed by critics the "barbecue boys" for their laid-back demeanor and perceived lack of intensity in recruiting—were taking things too easy, some complained.

They had plenty of criticisms for Tuberville himself, of course. He was too conservative, they said. (This about a guy once known far and wide as the "Riverboat Gambler.") Maybe if he'd run the scores up a little bit, back in 2004, they argued, Auburn would've gotten to play for the national title. He'd survived as long as he had by chucking his assistant coaches over the side whenever he got in trouble. He'd ceded control of the state, in recruiting and otherwise, to Nick Saban, they claimed, in effect unconditionally surrendering to Alabama. He didn't want to do what was necessary to compete with Saban. He was content for Auburn to be second-best in the state.

Was any of this true? It's all debatable, of course. Everything depends upon one's perspective. It was true that the program had been declining ever since the end of the 2006 season, with the roots of that decline probably stretching back earlier than that. The big-name recruits like Campbell and Williams weren't coming to Auburn anymore, and the top players in the state each year were nearly always choosing to go to Tuscaloosa. Saban's constructing of a national champion powerhouse across the state would've required Tuberville to dig down deep and re-energize and reinvigorate the Auburn program just to keep up. That was clearly something Tuberville no longer had the desire to do.

And so he chose the other option: He stepped down.

For a decade he was the face of Auburn football to the state and to the nation. He survived a palace coup that ultimately cost his own university president and athletics director their jobs. He beat the Tide six straight times and seven out of ten. He exited the Plains with a lifetime 4-3 record against Nick Saban. He won the SEC Western Division five times (in his first seven seasons), took the Tigers to two conference championship games, won one of them plus a Sugar Bowl, won five bowls in all, and won everything it was possible for Auburn to win in 2004. And he left, more or less, on his own terms.

Members of the Auburn Family have every right to be critical of the man for some of the decisions he made and actions he took during that tumultuous ten years. But they have to respect him. They *have* to. He more than earned that much.

For a decade he gave his all for Auburn University and for the Auburn Family. We are, all of us, richer for the experience.

10

The Top Ten Games in Jordan-Hare Stadium, 2001-2012

Here we present our evaluation of the best games Auburn has played in the friendly confines of Jordan-Hare Stadium in the Twenty-First Century—in the years since 2000. These games were all coached either by Tommy Tuberville or Gene Chizik. As with the earlier list, our criteria include both "spectacular game action" and "larger importance" of the game to its season and to Auburn history.

Honorable Mentions go to several games from the past decade that were memorable for one reason or another, but didn't quite make the top ten. These include:

Syracuse, 2002. The Tigers at last exacted a measure of revenge on an Orangemen program that had given us nothing but sour grapes (which we then gave back to them—literally) after our 1987-'88 Sugar Bowl draw and then had beaten us in the Carrier Dome a couple of weeks after 9/11 the previous season. Though the game was entirely too close, given the poor quality of the 2002 Orangemen team (it went to three overtimes before Cadillac

Williams settled it with a short TD run), any victory over Syracuse after a fifteen year wait was pretty sweet.

LSU, 2002. Nick Saban's team had beaten us in Baton Rouge the year before and had knocked us out of the SEC Championship Game in the process. The 2002 game was expected to be another LSU victory. Certainly nobody saw an epic, 31-7 beatdown coming, but Auburn delivered it, courtesy in part of the running of Ronnie Brown and very strong defensive play.

Alabama, 2003. "Go Crazy, Cadillac!" This game, a 28-23 Auburn win, probably saved Tommy Tuberville's job for another five years (coming at the end of the disappointing season soon to be better remembered for "JetGate" than anything else). It featured Carnell Williams carrying the ball the distance on the first play of the game, and a long catch and run by Ben Obomanu later on.

Alabama, 2007. Not a particularly memorable game except that it was the sixth and last win in Auburn's (and Tuberville's) epic "Streak" of victories over Alabama. Of note: it was also Nick Saban's first season as Alabama coach, and after this game, Auburn's (and Tuberville's) record against Saban stood at 4-2.

10. South Carolina, 2010.

In hindsight, and especially after the way the rematch in the SEC Championship Game turned out, this game didn't seem particularly momentous. At the time, however, it was very big—one of the games Van had expected that we would lose, before we knew what kind of a season 2010 was going to turn out to be—and when all was said and done, the positive but very narrow outcome was absolutely critical to everything that followed.

What happened was that Steve Spurrier brought the Gamecocks into Jordan-Hare for the fourth game of the season—a nighttime game on ESPN—never having beaten Auburn since joining the SEC. And, in what would turn out to be the most important match-up between the two teams up to that point in history, Carolina very nearly won.

Auburn had struggled mightily the week before, just squeezing past Clemson in OT when Clemson's kicker missed a potentially game-tying field goal re-kick. Auburn had even dropped from 16 to 17 in the AP rankings after that contest. During the game, the Auburn offensive line had at first been pushed around, then was challenged at halftime by the coaches, and then came out ready to rock in the second half. Auburn finished that game with momentum, but Carolina looked very good and their freshman sensation running back, Marcus Lattimore, was expected to slice and dice the relatively mediocre Auburn defense. Certainly Lattimore, who had very nearly signed to play with Auburn the year before, would outrush his freshman star counterpart at Auburn, Mike Dyer—or so the experts believed.

As it turned out, that would not be the case. Dyer gained 100 yards on 23 carries, compared to Lattimore's anemic 14 for 33.

But as good a game as Dyer had, it scarcely compared to the offensive explosion exhibited that night by one Cameron Newton.

Cam ran for three touchdowns, including his first really famous long-range score, ending it with a Superman-style leap from the vicinity of the five or six yard line into the end zone. He also threw for a pair of TDs. By game's end, Newton had piled up 334 yards of total offense. The rest of the SEC, and the country, were now watching.

Despite their futility at rushing, the Gamecocks did manage to throw the ball pretty well, with Stephen Garcia throwing eight passes to Alshon Jeffery for 192 yards and two touchdowns. Two

169

costly fumbles by Garcia, however, led to the ever-trigger-happy Spurrier pulling him in favor of backup Connor Shaw—only to see Shaw toss interceptions on both of his drives. The second pick-off came in the end zone as Carolina was driving for a potential game-tying score.

While Carolina had led, 20-14, at the half, Auburn's defense picked it up when it had to—something they'd continue to do all season long—and limited the Gamecocks to only seven points in the second half, along with creating those critical turnovers.

When the clock hit 0:00 and everyone in orange and blue could breathe again, the Tigers had recorded a 35-27 victory, stood undefeated at 4-0, still had never lost to Carolina in conference play, and had sent a warning shot across the bow of the SEC in general. Additionally, Auburn had notched its 700th win in program history, and the country was now giving its full attention to this team and its astonishing quarterback.

9. Alabama, 2005.

The 2005 Iron Bowl was what we refer to, in technical terms, as a *weird game*.

Auburn led 21-0 before the first quarter was over. The Tiger defense (led by Stanley McClover) sacked Alabama QB Brodie Croyle five times in that quarter alone and held the Tide to minus-17 yards of offense. By the time the game was finished, Croyle would be sacked eleven times, with seven different Tiger defenders recording at least half a sack.

And yet Auburn scored only once more after that torrid first quarter.

Even stranger: None of Auburn's four scoring drives covered more than 61 yards. (The four drives were for 40, 31, 55, and 61 yards, respectively.)

So, you might be saying, we can assume that Alabama turned the ball over a lot, giving Auburn short fields to work with. Right?

Wrong. Alabama did not fumble and did not throw an interception in the entire game.

Ah, then—one might reasonably conclude that the Auburn punt-return and kick-return teams had an epic night.

Wrong again. Auburn's kick return yardage was 17 yards, and their punt return yardage was minus-4.

It was just defense. Over and over, defense. Here's the stat that somewhat answers the issue: Alabama's Jeremy Schatz punted ten times for an average of 37 yards. When you're punting from your own goal line after giving up more and more sacks, the other team's return squad doesn't have to be great to give the offense good field position. They just have to catch the ball and hold on to it.

Auburn didn't score again after the 2:07 mark of the second quarter, but that was the Tuberville way: Grab a modest lead, if you can, and cling to it.

Alabama scored in every quarter after the first, but it wasn't enough to make up for that onslaught by the Tigers at the beginning. Auburn had the 28-18 win and a new catchphrase to boot: *Honk if you sacked Brodie!*

8. Florida, 2006

The 2006 Auburn Tigers were a team in contention for the National Championship for much of the season, and were ranked third in the country when they took on Arkansas on October 7, the week before the Florida game. Unfortunately, as we have documented extensively before, the Hawg Hex struck with full force. The Arkansas offense, masterminded by future Auburn offensive coordinator and later head coach Gus Malzahn, threw everything but the kitchen sink at the Tigers and won, 27-10.

Falling to tenth in the rankings, Auburn wasted little time getting back on track. The Florida Gators—a team Auburn had not played since the infamous overtime loss in Gainesville four years previously*—were coming to down the very next Saturday, having just moved up into the #3 spot in the coaches' poll the Tigers had vacated the week before. (They were second in the AP rankings.) ESPN GameDay was on hand, and both Lee Corso and Kirk Herbstreit picked Florida to win.

The loss to Arkansas seemed to have exposed the Tigers as somewhat overrated, perhaps—while Kenny Irons was having a fine season at running back, Brandon Cox's passing numbers had fallen off, in part due to his top receivers (that magical freshman group of 2002) having departed following the 2005 season, with the exception of the redshirted Courtney Taylor. Indeed, the 2006 Tigers struggled for most of the season to put points on the board, and the Florida game would prove to be only one of numerous examples where it fell to the defense and special teams to either put the offense in an easy position to score, or to actually score the points themselves. In fact, Auburn's offense failed to record a single touchdown in this game—and yet, much like the Tigers in that wild and wooly 1994 LSU game, the other two components of the team picked up the slack, and Auburn would go on to win by ten.

Despite a lack of offensive fireworks by the home team, the game turned out to be extremely exciting and entertaining. The defense was able to hold Florida scoreless in the second half, after the Gators had led 17-11 at the break. John Vaughn nailed four field goals and the defense notched a safety. Reserve running back Tre Smith (who must have been on his ninth year of eligibility at that point) ran back a blocked punt for a score in what would later be named the "Pontiac Game-Changing Play of the Year." Finally, Patrick Lee returned a fumble for a Tiger touchdown on the game's last play, resulting in a 27-17 win.

This game would turn out to be Florida's only loss of the year and the Gators would go on to claim the National Championship. The Tigers fought their way back into national contention beginning with this win, but a crippling loss to Georgia in November spelled an end to any hopes of a title for this squad. Even so, the Tigers ended the year 11-2, with a gritty win over Nebraska in the Cotton Bowl—and the Florida game was the crown jewel in the 2006 campaign.

*As of this writing, that 2002 overtime loss to Ron Zook's Gators remains Auburn's only loss to Florida in this current century—and millennium.

7. Florida, 2001.

There was little reason to suspect, beforehand, that the 2001 Auburn Tigers would stand a chance against mighty Florida when they met in Jordan-Hare on October 13. Unranked Auburn came into the game with a record of four wins and a loss. They had barely eked out victories against the likes of Ole Miss, Miss State, and Vanderbilt (with Damon Duval hitting game-winning kicks against the Dogs and Commodores). The Gators, meanwhile, were undefeated, ranked #1 in the country, and were staggering 21-point favorites.

But this was Auburn-Florida, where things rarely seem to go as scripted.

In a back-and-forth affair, and with the bad weather the meteorologists had predicted always looming on the horizon but not quite arriving, the two teams found themselves locked up at 20-20 in the fourth quarter. Florida had dominated statistically to that point, but Auburn's defense (using players from deep down the depth chart, due to injury) scrapped and clawed and managed to minimize the Gators' scoring chances. Florida quarterback Rex Grossman, who had beaten Auburn twice in the previous season (once in Gainesville and again in Atlanta), was picked off on four occasions, while the Gator running game was utterly shut down.

Auburn's offense, meanwhile, was now being led by quarterback Daniel Cobb, in place of freshman Jason Campbell. Cobb managed the game well and did just enough to keep the Tigers in it.

As the game's final moments ticked down, Auburn reached Florida's 27 yard line and sent Damon Duval out to attempt the game-winner. Just as Duval was lining up to kick, the long-expected wind and rain struck, sweeping from left to right across the stadium and the field. Duval lofted a long curveball of a kick, which looked hopelessly off-target to the right at first, but somehow swung back around—into the oncoming weather front!—and passed perfectly between the uprights.

The top-ranked Gators had been humbled and knocked from their perch in Steve Spurrier's final season. The Ol' Ball Coach afterward noted that his wins against the Tigers were usually blowouts, while Auburn's wins over his Gators tended to be last-second field goal affairs. Very true, coach. But a win was a win, and the Tigers happily took it.

6. West Virginia, 2009.

The box score for the 2009 Auburn-West Virginia game states the following, rather nonchalantly: "Weather: Light rain."

"Light rain?!"

Well, sort of.

In actuality, the game was preceded by an absolute deluge—enough to cause kickoff to be pushed back an hour. During the game and for days afterward, ESPN announcers and others would marvel at how well-constructed the drainage system beneath Pat Dye Field was, noting the efficiency with which it had handled the sudden flood and carried the water off the grass surface rapidly and with no damage to the turf.

They noted one other thing of interest, too: The Auburn fans—and particularly the students—remained in the stands. They sat or stood there beneath a torrent strong enough to make one consider building a large animal-carrying boat and they didn't flinch and they didn't run away. They simply stood there and waited. And when the weather cleared a bit and the game was allowed to begin, the players coming back onto the field saw that. They saw it and they acknowledged it.

What followed was the game that would do as much as any to define the early Gene Chizik Era at Auburn—the game that, probably more than any other, laid the foundations for the run to the BCS National Championship the following year.

Auburn had faced the Mountaineers in Morgantown the previous season, with running back Noel Devine eventually running the already-disintegrating Tiger team to death. This time around, in Jordan-Hare, things got off to a bad start for the men in orange and blue. Devine punched in a short TD and then broke off a 71-yard run to put WVU up 14-0 with less than five minutes gone in the game. Many Tigers fans surely couldn't help but think, "Here we go again."

But this time the Tigers hung around. A long Wes Byrum field goal and a short pass from Chris Todd to Darvin Adams pulled Auburn to within four. But then Jarrett Brown drove WVU seventy-four yards for another TD and it was 21-10, bad guys—and we weren't even out of the first quarter!

In the second quarter the Tigers duplicated their first quarter feats exactly, as Byrum and Adams scored ten more and pulled Auburn to within only a point at the half.

The third quarter went back and forth, as Devine scored again (the PAT was missed) and then Mario Fannin took a pass 82 yards for a score. A WVU field goal just before the end of the quarter pushed the 'Eers out to a three-point lead, at 30-27.

In the final frame, the Auburn defense made its presence known at last. They shut West Virginia down and out, turned the ball over on the Mountaineers' 19 yard line, and then after the offense scored from there, ran back an interception for the TD that sealed the deal. Auburn had won, 41-30—won by double-digits, despite giving up over 500 yards of offense. It was remarkable.

What mattered here wasn't just the win—though it was a good, out-of-conference win against a quality opponent, providing a bit of revenge for one of the many disappointing defeats of the horrendous 2008 season. What really mattered, and what would continue to matter for months afterward, was that the Auburn Family had come together to support this team, despite the horrible weather conditions and the Tigers falling behind by double-digits early and the game not ending until 11:21 Central time. That quality—that "All In" mind-set of the Auburn faithful—would carry the team and its supporters on a magical mystery tour that wouldn't end until a certain contest in Glendale, some sixteen months later.

Many today would argue that what flowered into glory in the dry Arizona desert began with faith and dedication forged in the pouring rain.

5. Georgia, 2010.

As big as this game was in the 2010 campaign—an Auburn victory would mean an SEC West title and a trip to Atlanta, regardless of what happened against Alabama in Tuscaloosa a week later—it was perhaps even more important from a psychological standpoint.

Two days before the game with Chattanooga, the weekend previous, the first allegations about Cecil Newton and improprieties in his dealings with representatives from Mississippi State first emerged. Cam's response to critics who questioned if he would be able to focus on that game was to simply throw for a career-high 317 yards and four touchdowns (and run for a fifth) against the Mocs—all in the first half.

But with a week for the charges and insinuations to sink in and stew, it was the Georgia game that was to prove the true test of just how resilient Newton could be.

A lot was on the line. Auburn was undefeated in the conference and overall, but the SEC Western Division title was still up for grabs. If the Tigers beat Georgia, they would win the West and go to the SEC Championship Game in Atlanta regardless of what happened against Alabama in Tuscaloosa a week later. Some commentators even argued that a win against Georgia and a win in Atlanta would be enough to get the Tigers to the BCS National Championship Game in Arizona even if they were to lose to the Tide.

But for any of that to be the case, Auburn first had to beat Georgia—and for a time, that didn't look like a done deal.

Prior to kickoff, very real questions hung in the air as to whether Newton would be the starter at quarterback—or if he would be allowed to play at all. Visions of Barrett Trotter attempting to step in as the starter in a major SEC clash for the first time in his career and lead the Tigers to victory floated through the heads of many Auburn faithful as kickoff neared. With all due respect to the good Mr. Trotter, it wasn't an entirely pretty picture to imagine.

As it turned out, Newton did get the start—the crowd went wild at that announcement, proving they were thoroughly taking his side in the matter and providing him and the rest of the team with much-needed energy—and he did play the entire game.

The Bulldogs came into the game with a record of only 5-5, but were playing much better with the return from suspension of their star receiver, A. J. Green. Indeed, in the first quarter alone, Green scored two touchdowns and helped pace Georgia to a 21-7 lead. (Auburn had scored first on an astonishing run by Newton, in which he plowed along the right sideline and dragged half the Bulldog secondary into the end zone with him. Instant replay was needed to show that he had, indeed, crossed the goal line with the ball.)

In the second quarter, Auburn scored twice (with touchdowns by Onterio McCalebb and Philip Lutzenkirchen) while the defense clamped down and blanked the Dawgs, sending the game to halftime tied, 21-21.

The third quarter saw Georgia attempt to keep pace with the Auburn offense, tying the game at 28-all after Auburn had finally taken the lead on another short McCalebb run. But after McCalebb added his third short rushing TD of the game, Georgia could respond only with a field goal and, to borrow a tennis metaphor, the Bulldogs' serve had been broken. They'd had their chance to score and had settled for three points. Auburn led, 35-31, as the third quarter ended.

In the fourth the Tigers pulled away at last. Another Lutzenkirchen touchdown and then a short run by Newton put Auburn up for good, 49-31. Auburn remained undefeated and now the SEC Western Division title was theirs. A trip to Atlanta beckoned. A jubilant Newton raced around the stadium, high-fiving everyone within reach, as fans exulted. Georgia fans whined, as they are wont to do—mostly about the play of Nick Fairley.

Questions about Cam's eligibility remained to be answered, of course, and the whole mess wouldn't ultimately be sorted out until a year later, when the NCAA concluded its investigation of the matter for good, finding no wrongdoing by Auburn or by Newton. But Cam's performance against Georgia that day—his accomplishments on the field, with his team, and the sheer spirit of joy and confidence as he played and celebrated—went a long, long way toward clearing the air and blowing away some of the black clouds that had hung over the program for the previous nine days. It was a spiritual as well as a football victory—and a critical one in both respects.

4. Arkansas, 2010.

A couple of other games in 2010 were perhaps bigger or more consequential or more memorable, but no game all year was as "don't blink your eyes" *exciting* as this one.

Points? You want points, you say? This game gave you *108* of them!

It is somewhat astonishing to state that in a contest where the Auburn defense allowed the opposing team to score 43 points, roll up 566 total yards, and let the opponent's *backup* QB complete fifteen of his first seventeen passes, the Tigers would go on to win by 22 points. But there it is.

179

The game was a track meet—an offensive explosion (and the highest-scoring non-overtime SEC game in history) to put even those mid-1990s games with Steve Spurrier's Florida to shame.

Auburn had been unsuccessful against Bobby Petrino's Razorbacks in two previous attempts, with the final squad of his former head coach, Tommy Tuberville, falling to them in 2008 and the first squad of Gene Chizik doing the same the next year. This game would be different, however—oh, would it *ever* be different.

Unlike several of the other close contests of the 2010 season, the Tigers didn't fall far behind early in this one and have to claw their way back. They led most of the way, and only seemed in real danger when backup Tyler Wilson replaced an injured Ryan Mallett at quarterback in the second quarter and started carving up the Auburn secondary.

The real fireworks for Auburn came in the fourth quarter. With 14:09 to go, Arkansas had taken its first lead in a while, going up 43-37 on a Greg Childs touchdown reception from Tyler. What followed had to be seen to be believed, and resembled nothing so much as the final frame of the 1985 Florida State game where, as the *Birmingham News* headline at the time put it, after a fourth quarter scoring explosion by the Tigers, "The Dam Breaks and Auburn Wins by 32."

The Hogs had taken the lead, but they would not score again. Unfortunately for them, the same could hardly be said for the Tigers.

Emory Blake started the festivities off with a fifteen-yard scoring catch from Cam Newton, capping off a nice drive and putting Auburn back ahead at 44-43. The Hogs were pushing to try to reclaim the lead when Zac Etheridge picked up a Broderick Green fumble and ran it back 47 yards for another score. Now it was 51-

43. (This was the moment later cited by Auburn players as the real turning point in the game, and there's little doubt that's true.)

On the first play of the next drive, Tyler Wilson threw an interception that was returned by Josh Bynes to the Hogs' seven yard line. You could just feel the Razorbacks starting to unravel now. Cam Newton took two plays to blast his way in for the score, and now it was 58-43.

This time it took Arkansas three plays to turn the ball over, with Wilson again throwing it to Josh Bynes at the 47. Again it took two plays to score, this time with runs by Mike Dyer. The second one sealed the deal, covering the final 38 yards to the end zone and sending Auburn on to victory at 65-43.

A victory over Arkansas is always extra-sweet, given the notorious Hawg Hex about which we have written extensively before. A victory over Bobby Petrino should be savored like fine wine. A win in a game where the opponent scores 43 points in your own stadium? That's something to be appreciated and cherished. And a win that keeps you at the top of the SEC West standings, undefeated, and on track for Atlanta (and beyond)? That, my Tiger friends, is simply priceless.

3. Georgia, 2004.

By this point, late in the 2004 season, third-ranked Auburn's ultimate goal was to somehow jump over Oklahoma or USC into one of the top two spots in the BCS rankings, in order to secure a place in the BCS National Championship Game. In order to do that, the Tigers had to look impressive in wins against quality opponents— and the Georgia Bulldogs were as good of an opponent as the Tigers were likely to face the rest of the way.

Ranked eighth in the country, the Bulldogs had lost only to Tennessee and were full of confidence as they entered Jordan-Hare for an afternoon game on CBS.

Auburn stood in their way, and fans were hoping to see the Tigers at their best on the field that day. They would not be disappointed.

An Auburn offense that had had such trouble scoring the previous season was now clicking on all cylinders, thanks to the efforts of rookie Offensive Coordinator Al Borges. The floral-shirted coach had found creative ways to involve both Carnell "Cadillac" Williams and Ronnie Brown in the offense simultaneously. With Jason Campbell blossoming as the true star quarterback Tigers fans had always hoped he would become, throwing to a bevy of great receivers such as Devin Aromashodu, Ben Obomanu, Courtney Taylor and Anthony Mix, Georgia had its hands (or paws) full trying to slow down the Auburn attack.

The first scoring drive for Auburn combined one long pass to Brown with numerous runs by Williams, culminating with a one-yard dash by Cadillac around right end to provide the Tigers the early 7-0 lead. Gene Chizik's defense clamped down hard on David Greene and company, and the Bulldogs could get nothing going for most of the game.

Early in the second quarter, the Bulldogs managed to block a Kody Bliss punt and set up shop deep in Auburn territory—only to have future first-round NFL draft pick Carlos Rogers make an amazing leap and grab, intercepting the Greene pass in the end zone.

The second Auburn scoring drive, later in the second quarter, was something of a mirror-image of the first. This time Campbell mostly threw the ball to Williams, while Brown did the damage on the ground. To cap it off, Williams actually threw a halfback pass over the head of Georgia's star safety to the waiting hands of Anthony

Mix, who scrambled into the end zone. Auburn's defense held the Dawgs to three and out on the next series, and Cadillac returned the punt to Georgia's 38. Tight end Cooper Wallace took a pass down to the Bulldog 16, but the Tigers were stopped cold after that and settled for a 32-yard John Vaughn field goal. The game went to halftime with Auburn ahead, 17-0.

Turnovers after long drives and strong defensive play by both teams kept the score the same well into the second half. As the third quarter wound down, however, a 42-yard punt return by Cadillac set the Tigers up at Georgia's thirty yard line, and Auburn would not squander this opportunity. Less than a minute into the fourth quarter, Campbell swung a pass out to Ronnie Brown, who took it fifteen yards for the score.

With just over two minutes to go in the game, the Bulldogs finally got on the board, as David Greene strung together a series of passes against essentially a "prevent" Auburn defense. The resulting touchdown catch by the Bulldogs was controversial but it survived replay, to the disappointment of Tigers fans who had been hoping for a complete shutout of Georgia in this one. (Certainly that might have helped Auburn's cause as it sought to climb above Oklahoma in the BCS rankings.) The two-point attempt by the Bulldogs failed, and the game ended with Auburn again deep in Georgia territory as time expired.

In a monumental SEC clash of grave importance to Auburn in its conference and national aspirations, the Tigers had come through like the champions they were destined to be, crushing a great Georgia team, 24-6. Though the game that follows it on this list is perhaps better remembered as the real lynchpin of the 2004 undefeated season, this victory over Georgia was probably the Tigers' best performance against a quality opponent that year, and was without question one of the finest performances in modern Auburn football history.

2. LSU, 2004.

The 2004 LSU game is such an easy contest to discuss. So many things concerning that game readily come to mind, even almost a decade later.

Auburn has gone undefeated three times in the past two decades (1993, 2004, 2010) and each one of those seasons seemed to come out of nowhere. (If you thought our national championship in 2010 was shocking—and *we* did—just wait till the day Auburn accomplishes it in a year when we're actually *expected* to do well!) Of the three, however, the one where an argument could be made that it sort of *should* have happened was probably Tommy Tuberville's 2004 squad. All the pieces were in place, from seniors at quarterback and running back, to probably our best squadron of receivers in many years, to a dominant defensive back and a powerful defense and kicking game. Gene Chizik had our defense clicking on all cylinders and new hire Al Borges certainly found ways to get production out of a talent-laden offensive unit that had been entirely stagnant the previous season under different coaching.

When the dust settled following the Tigers' win over Tennessee in the SEC Championship Game, however, USC and Oklahoma were also still undefeated and they were chosen to play one another for the BCS title, leaving Auburn, relegated to facing Virginia Tech in the Sugar Bowl. It was cold comfort, after the games had all been played, to see USC absolutely destroy Oklahoma and leave Auburn ranked second in the final polls—the place the Tigers should have been all along, but recognized by the voters one poll too late to matter.

Be that as it may, the 2004 season was one for the ages for Auburn, and should be remembered and celebrated for all the team accomplished on the field. And when we turn our attention to that season, and to the games played within Jordan-Hare Stadium (one of the main criteria for this list), a couple of games stand out as absolutely critical. One of them is elsewhere on this list; the other is the LSU game on September 18.

LSU's head coach that day was Nick Saban. Perhaps you've heard of him. His LSU squad had destroyed the good Tigers the previous year, in a game in Baton Rouge the Auburn faithful quickly dubbed "Black Saturday." (Van was at a resort in Jamaica that weekend, fearful he wouldn't be able to see the game. As it turned out, he did see it—and wished he hadn't.) That LSU team had gone on to claim the 2003 National Championship. When they walked into Jordan Hare in the fall of 2004, they had a swagger about them, and were to some degree intimidating. Auburn had experienced its ups and downs with LSU over the years since the conference split put the two of us in the same division and forced us to play annually. Games hadn't always gone the way they were expected— to say the least. But if 2004 was to be a big year for Auburn—a redemptive year—then the Bayou Bengals needed to be handled. The year before, despite having Jason Campbell and Cadillac Williams and Ronnie Brown on the squad, the offense had done little to nothing. This year, however, we had a new weapon—one with a big belly and a loud Hawaiian shirt, and a plan for how to use the other weapons on offense. Enter: Al Borges.

Borges employed multiple formations and lots of pre-snap motion to gain whatever advantage could be gained over LSU's huge, tough defensive line. It wasn't spectacularly effective, but it kept the Bayou Bengals slightly off-balance, and eventually it did produce just enough points.

At the beginning of the contest, it didn't look to be the defensive battle it would turn into. LSU drove down the field in fourteen plays and scored a touchdown on their opening possession but kicker Ryan Gaudet missed the extra point. Then Auburn's John Vaughn pulled the (good) Tigers to within three with a field goal near the end of the first quarter, concluding a matching fourteen-play drive on Auburn's first possession. Were we in store for a shootout? Seriously?!

LSU added a 42-yard FG early in the second quarter, taking the Bayou Bengals to a 9-3 lead...but that would be all she wrote until almost the last minute of the game. Now the expected defensive slugfest materialized, with both offenses grinding away fruitlessly like two European soccer teams stuck in a nil-nil draw.

The rest of the second quarter, all of the third, and most of the fourth would expire before Auburn finally put together a scoring drive that featured two absolutely clutch, critical plays—both involving passes from Jason Campbell to Courtney Taylor. The first was a fourth down conversion on a rollout pass to the right side of the field. Campbell avoided heavy pressure and got the ball downfield to a leaping Taylor, who just barely converted the down. After a couple of Carnell Williams runs to the outside were stuffed for no gain by the ferocious LSU defense, Campbell rocketed a pass to Taylor in the middle of the end zone with 1:14 left to tie the game at 9-9. Jordan-Hare erupted.

The drama was scarcely over. Super-reliable kicker John Vaughn inexplicably duplicated Gaudet's feat and missed the game-winning extra point! But—wait—hold the phone—there was a flag on the play! LSU violated the obscure and rarely-called "climbing on top of your teammate to try to block a kick" rule, and Auburn was allowed to re-try the kick. As Nick Saban melted down in a rage on the LSU sideline, Vaughn redeemed himself by booting the do-over (this one just barely making it between the uprights) to give Auburn the 10-9 victory. A Junior Rosegreen interception on LSU's final drive secured the win for the Tigers.

The rest of Auburn's season wouldn't really feature any more close contests—certainly nothing like this, where the Tigers had to come from behind in the final minutes. This game would be the pivotal moment—the defining moment—of the Undefeateds of 2004. And a monumental moment it was. The great 1988 squad had said their *loss* to LSU in Baton Rouge was the kick they needed to get their attention and to transform them into a championship squad. The 2004 team demonstrated that a narrow *win* over LSU could do the trick every bit as well.

1. LSU, 2010.

We all know that the 2010 Auburn Tigers were the ones to finally break the curse and secure a coveted crystal football for the Auburn Family. Unlike their forebears in 2004, who rarely won by less than double digits, it seemed as if this unit had to come from behind in frantic fashion nearly every week. But they did. They *always* did. *Every single time.*

We weren't always sure they would be able to—not even with those two human forces of nature, Cam Newton and Nick Fairley, acting like magic erasers and destroying the other team's offenses and defenses on a regular basis.

But there was one particular moment in the 2010 season when many of us—certainly we intrepid Wishbone columnists, at least—came to truly believe in this team. When we concluded that they really could beat *anybody* on a given day, and could quite possibly win it all. That moment for us was the LSU game.

LSU came into the 2010 contest undefeated and ranked sixth in the country. Auburn was also undefeated and ranked fifth. The game would turn out to be a classic, with both teams scrapping hard for the few points the two defenses would allow. Indeed, it had been obvious even before kickoff that this game would be the exact opposite of the Arkansas game the week before; it would be a low-scoring affair, pitting a great Auburn offense against a great LSU defense, and a mediocre LSU offense against a struggling-at-times Auburn defense.

The scoring was scarce but was spread fairly evenly across the four quarters. Each quarterback scored on a short run in the first half, both kickers made a field goal, and the game went to halftime tied at 10-10. The second half would be a bit more electric.

Auburn's first score of the second half was quite possibly the single most spectacular play of the year for the Tigers, and the one that most visibly defined Cam Newton's Heisman-winning season individually. Newton took the snap at midfield, faked a handoff, picked his way to the right through the line, put a hand down briefly to reverse his course, and then rambled in seeming slow-motion to about the fifteen—whereupon LSU's blazing defensive back, Patrick Peterson, caught up with him. In response, Cam actually seemed to find another gear and pulled away from Peterson just enough to cross the goal line as he was being tackled and hitting the ground. Newton's Superman-like efforts on the play electrified the crowd and put Auburn up by seven.

LSU retaliated early in the fourth quarter, using a trick play to score from 39 yards out on a halfback pass from Spencer Ware to Reuben Randle. Linebacker Josh Bynes saw it developing but couldn't disrupt the play in time. The game was once again tied—but would not remain so for much longer.

The final score, and yet another spectacular one, came on a simple give from Cam Newton to human rocket Onterio McCalebb. More often than not, when executing this famous "jet-sweep" play, Newton would keep the ball himself, as he had done on his previous score. This time, he allowed McCalebb to take it, and take it he did—zipping around the formation and then down the left sideline for seventy yards and the score in what seemed like the blink of an eye.

The Auburn defense, which for all its struggles at times actually did manage to hold opponents to an average of fewer than four points in the fourth quarter, stopped LSU with three minutes left. Victory was sealed. Auburn was still undefeated and Cam Newton had solidified himself as the Heisman front-runner.

Huge contests with Georgia (at home) and Alabama (on the road) still remained to be played, but this was the game where many members of the Auburn Family nodded their heads and said to themselves and their loved ones, "This team actually can go all the way." This was also the game where, afterward, Van went online and bought two tickets to the BCS Championship Game in Glendale, Arizona.

It was now clear to everyone: If we could win this one, we could win 'em all.

And we did.

11

Cam Newton and Auburn:
Justice at Last

In mid-October of 2011, approximately nine months after Auburn defeated the University of Oregon to win the BCS National Championship in Glendale, Arizona—and after dragging out a thorough investigation into the allegations surrounding Cam Newton as well as claims made by former players on the HBO network—the NCAA took the unprecedented step of publicly announcing that Auburn had been cleared of all charges, and that the investigations were over.

Coach Gene Chizik had openly pressed the NCAA to do this—to end the investigations, and to announce to the public that they were doing so—from the very beginning. He had even gone so far as to question an NCAA representative in front of the other conference coaches during the annual SEC meetings in Destin, Florida that offseason. Chizik's motivations were clear: He didn't believe Auburn had done anything wrong, and he felt some of the other conference coaches were using the investigation as a weapon in recruiting against the Tigers. Essentially he called the NCAA out, demanding that they put up or shut up.

In October, they shut up.

The relief felt by the Auburn Family was nearly overwhelming. While few within the Auburn circle itself had ever truly believed the Tiger coaches had done anything wrong, and while the support for Cam was rock-solid and unwavering, there still lingered within the hearts of many Auburn faithful the queasy feeling—the *fear*—that somehow, some way, the capricious NCAA could conclude that the Tigers should be stripped of their precious crystal football. Fans of many other programs across the conference and the country had taken the reporting of jumped-up bloggers and reporters with axes to grind at face value, or were simply too lazy to actually bother to read the details of the situation. For them, Auburn and Cam having done something illegal was taken pretty much as an article of faith. For them, the 2010 title already carried an asterisk with it. For them, it was only a matter of time before the 2010 title was inevitably stripped.

For them, that day in October of 2011 after the NCAA announced its findings (or lack thereof), your intrepid Wishbone columnists presented the following brief but passionate broadside:

Hey you—Mr. New York Times reporter.

Hey you—Mr. Talk Radio Show Host and guests with "inside" knowledge.

Hey you—Mr. ESPN college football "reporter."

Hey you—Mr. Bama fan conspiracy theorist message board poster.

This is for *you*.

192

Here are the colleges currently on NCAA probation. You may notice a certain school whose name has been dragged through the mud quite a bit over the past eleven months, yet whose name isn't on the list—and won't be. Here's the list:

- Alabama

- Boise State

- Central Florida

- Florida International

- Florida State

- Georgia Tech

- Memphis

- South Carolina

That's right—despite everything you've heard and been told just relentlessly ever since late last season, Auburn has been cleared. As surely every Auburn man, woman and child knows by now, the word came down from on high (ie the NCAA) on Wednesday that Auburn has been cleared of any violations in the Cam Newton investigation.

Understand this very clearly: The NCAA crawled all up inside Auburn's athletic department and lived there for a year and they couldn't find a single thing.

And they were looking *hard*. Oh, were they looking. After all the headlines and hoopla last fall about Cam... After the ocean of stories and columns and speeches on talk radio about how college football is corrupt and something must be done... After all that, the NCAA Enforcement staff got serious, and started hitting schools right and left. Georgia Tech? Who even knew they were under investigation? Yet they were nailed. LSU? Nailed. Ohio State - nailed and nailed and nailed again. Ouch. South Carolina? Nailed. Oregon? Under investigation. Boise State? Nailed (for stuff the *tennis team* did).

Oh, and Auburn? Surely they nailed us for something, right? There was so much *talk*—so much *smoke*! So...where's the fire?

Let's review the roll call of "bombs" that went dud in the last year, shall we?

- "The Bingo Trial and FBI Tapes." Result: Nothing. No mention of Auburn or even of college football.

- "NCAA Investigation of Cam including tax files and financial records from the Church." Result: Nothing.

- "The 'HBO Four' Allegations." Result: Nothing.

- "The bank" theories. Result: Nothing.

- The "Danny Sheridan/Auburn Bagman Allegation." Result: Nothing (other than Sheridan and radio host Paul Finebaum looking like bigger fools than normal).

- "Radio show claims it has tapes of Cam accepting benefits." Result: Nothing (and the person making the allegation got fired).

Notice a pattern?

Auburn was tried and declared guilty in the court of public opinion based on this evidence: Someone with connections to Mississippi State tried to offer his dad money to get Cam to go to MSU (or maybe his dad asked someone at Miss State about money). That's it. That's all there ever was. And many, many "journalists" in this country have dragged Auburn through the mud every day since the story first came out.

The argument usually went something like this: "If it happened with MSU, it must have happened with Auburn." In other words, the sum total of the "evidence" the accusers could present was "a feeling" or "my common sense just *tells* me..."

Auburn people like us aren't surprised that nothing was found on Cam. But we have to say we were surprised that the NCAA looked as hard as it could at Auburn and found *nothing. Nada. Zilch.* And they wanted to get Auburn so badly—after the embarrassing talk of corruption last fall, the NCAA wanted to nail Auburn as badly as any school they have ever investigated.

The chorus of "Cam and Auburn are guilty" was loud and long. We will not be satisfied if the NCAA announcement of exoneration is printed in the fine print at the bottom of a few websites and then goes away. This story needs to be told - a young man, his family and a university were tried in the media - unjustly. The desire to draw page views and readers led to piling on and some of the worst sports journalism in American history.

The NCAA must have come to recognize this. Their announcement on Wednesday, clearing Auburn of any wrongdoing in the matter, was virtually unprecedented. Usually they don't ever say they're done sniffing around. This time, not only did they announce it, they used the opportunity to denounce the so-called reporters and bloggers who have been throwing around unsupported allegations.

Auburn won the National Championship in 2010. And yet, the next morning, instead of being able to turn on the car radio and enjoy the talk about it, all we heard was, "Well, mark this one with an asterisk, because it's only a matter of time until the NCAA takes it away."

Wrong again, ESPN!

And Kirk Herbstreit helpfully informed us, via the Finebaum show on Wednesday, that Auburn fans could now celebrate their National Championship.

Well, gosh, Kirk—we appreciate you giving us the permission. But, to be honest, we have to tell you—you're just a wee bit late.

We've been celebrating the national title every day since January 10th, 2011!!

War Eagle!

12

The Top Ten Auburn Games
Not Played in Jordan-Hare Stadium

Here we examine the ten best games Auburn played during the Modern Era in stadiums other than their own Jordan-Hare Stadium. The list does not include bowl games, because they have their own list elsewhere in this book.

The methodology was thus: John chose the ten numbered games and offers commentary, and then Van followed up with more discussion of John's choice and (in some cases) suggestions of alternate games against that same opponent.

As could be expected, the 2010 season definitely caused us to rework this list pretty comprehensively. One could even argue that every away game from that season should be included, as each one of them led us closer toward the national title. That wouldn't make for a particularly interesting or entertaining list, though, so we're going to limit the 2010 games as best we can.

John adds: I ranked these purely on the basis of *"best* games" rather than *"most meaningful* games."

10. Georgia, Athens, 2005 season.

John: The improbable finish. Fourth and 11 at our 34. Brandon Cox to Devin Aromashodu for 63 yards—and then the ball is stripped and recovered in the end zone by Courtney Taylor. A gigantic play. Georgia went on to win the SEC Championship Game but experts were saying Auburn was probably the best team in the conference by the end of the year.

Van: I watched this game in a bar in Lawrenceville, Georgia, not an hour away from Athens, surrounded by Dawgs fans. When Brandon completed that fourth down pass and Devin raced the length of the field, I was the only person in the room jumping up and down and screaming—and the only one probably in immediate danger of being stabbed to death by a hundred steak knives, now that I think about it.

The really remarkable thing about how this game ended was that what could have been an absolutely catastrophic mistake— Aromashodu fumbling as he neared the goal line—turned into the best possible scenario. If he had scored on the play, Georgia would have gotten the ball back with nearly a minute to go and only needing a field goal to win. Instead, Auburn got the ball on the one yard line, ran the clock down, kicked the field goal for the win, and walked off. The Dawgs offense never got back on the field.

9. Georgia Tech, Atlanta, 1987 season.

John: This will be forever remembered as the Aundray Bruce game. This is the game that convinced the Falcons to make him the first overall pick in the NFL Draft—much to their later dismay.

Van: Auburn had battled Tech in some memorable games over the years, and this was to be the final game of the series overall (Tech didn't want to play us anymore), so it had special significance. Auburn had won quite a few in a row in the series and Tech's coach, Bill Curry, had never beaten Auburn or Pat Dye (and never would). The Yellowjackets desperately wanted to win, and for most of the game, it looked as if they would. Tech led Auburn 10-7 with only 24 seconds remaining in the game when Jeff Burger found Lawyer Tillman in the back of the end zone. Jim Fyffe said it best: "TILLMAN TILLMAN TILLMAN! TOUCHDOWN AUBURN! A BULLET BY BURGER!" And then, as Tech tried desperately to come back down the field in the closing seconds, OLB Aundray Bruce picked off a pass (his second of the day) and returned it for a touchdown, making the final score 20-10 Auburn after the Tigers had actually trailed only a few seconds earlier.

Astonishingly, this remains Auburn's last win over Georgia Tech.

8. LSU, Baton Rouge, 1997 season.

John: Was this Dameyune Craig's finest hour? Auburn scores the winning touchdown on a Rusty Williams run with thirty seconds left after an eighty-yard drive that started with just over three minutes left in the game. Craig's passing carried Auburn against the strong running of LSU and Cecil Collins.

Van: This was one of those games where it simply didn't look like Auburn was going to win. The trends were against them; LSU had won hard-fought victories in 1995 and 1996, and we all know what a miracle it took to beat them in 1994. Cecil "the Diesel" Collins ran wild on the Auburn defense, gaining 232 yards on 27 carries, yet Auburn somehow managed to limit them to "only" 28 points—and, at the end of the day, Rusty Williams (not exactly astride the top of the Auburn historical rushing charts) had scored just as many touchdowns as Collins, and Craig had thrown for 342 yards. This was a good win against a bitter foe that really needed its win string over us snapped, and the 1997 Tigers got it done.

Two other wins in Tiger Stadium deserve mention: 1993 and 1999. The **1993 LSU game** was Terry Bowden's first big road win and an early component of "the Streak," the twenty straight wins he achieved in his first two seasons. It marked the moment that Stan White stepped up in his senior year and truly became the quarterback we had always hoped he could be. The **1999 LSU game** is the one that Bayou Bengals fans still refer to as the "Cigar Game," in which Tommy Tuberville's first squad absolutely pounded LSU, 41-7, and in all likelihood got Gerry DiNardo fired. The highlight of the game was probably Auburn's first touchdown, a fake field goal in which kicker Damon Duval caught a flip-pass from the holder and ran untouched into the end zone. After the game, Auburn players smoked cigars, somehow offending LSU fans, who have held this up as an egregious insult ever since. Whatever.

7. Florida State, Tallahassee, 1984 season.

John: This game was not on TV, so you had to be there in person or listen on radio. This was the game that started the Tomahawk chop and the most annoying chant in sports history. And that memorable score: 42-41.

Van: This was the game where I and a whole lot of other Auburn people truly fell in love with Jim Fyffe. As John notes, this one wasn't televised, so we had to tune in to "the Auburn *Football* Network" and listen. I tracked the game on a piece of notebook paper and was totally absorbed in every play as Jim laid it out. And what a game to try to keep track of! Back and forth it went; FSU did not yet have Mickey Andrews assembling stout defenses and Auburn's was victimized by a wild and crazy Seminole attack. At the start of the game, Chief Osceola threw the flaming spear at the feet of the Auburn captains, and quarterback Pat Washington later said that gesture ticked him and the other players off. They showed it! The game ended with FSU deep in Auburn territory; had it been played for another hour, the score might have been 100-99.

It's interesting to consider that Florida State has three modern-era wins over Auburn, and each came in a different location: Auburn (1987), New Orleans (1988), and Tallahassee (1989). During that same run of games, Auburn won three over them in Jordan-Hare (1983, 1985, and 1990) along with the above-mentioned victory in Tallahassee.

6. Alabama; Iron Bowl, 1982 season.

John: After nine years of losing, Auburn needed to stand up and win a slugfest-type game with Bama. That's what this was.

Van: This might have been as high as #2 on my list. A win over Alabama for the first time in nine years. (In human terms, put it this way: Alabama started their 9-win streak when I was in first grade. I didn't get to see Auburn win the Iron Bowl until I was in high school and nearly had a driver's license!) A win over the Bear in his final Iron Bowl. Beating him at his own game—running the wishbone attack right at him for sixty minutes. The tables in the state turning, at long last. This was without question the key win in Pat Dye's early career at Auburn. Bo over the top; Pat Dye's tear for the Bear; the goalposts at Legion Field coming down; Jim Fyffe's "monumental victory!" call, not to mention that this is possibly the game where he first began to say "Touchdown Auburn!" every time; Randy Campbell and Lionel James; 23-22 forever.

5. Tennessee, Knoxville, 2004 season.

John: This game marked the first moment in the 2004 season when we all realized how good that team could be. Ronnie Brown running over the defender at the Tennessee goal line is a moment I will never forget.

Van: I'm happy to say this is one of many on this list that I was there to witness in person. It's amazing how quiet the better part of 100,000-plus people can get, very quickly—and how quickly they can evaporate from the stands as things turn against them. The Auburn defense made both of Tennessee's rookie quarterbacks look like middle-schoolers, while Jason Campbell, Ronnie Brown, and Cadillac Williams tore the Vols defense apart time and again. This was simply a beautiful game and a complete team effort. In the locker room pregame, Coach Tuberville told the players, "It'll take a good one, but let's make it a great one." They did.

Speaking of **Tennessee**, let us not overlook the **SEC Championship Game** win over them, later in that **2004** season—Auburn's first-ever win in the conference title game, and wonderful revenge for UT's defeat of the Tigers in the first AU appearance there, in 1997.

And of course one of Pat Dye's major early road wins was at **Tennessee** in **1983**. I still remember Trey Gainous catching a Vols punt and taking it back to the house. Any win in Knoxville should be savored, and this was a great one.

4. Georgia, Athens, 1999 season.

John: The Ronney Daniels game. All that needs to be said. Nothing is better than UGA fans leaving the stadium in droves while booing their own team.

Van: They did indeed leave—if not at halftime, then at the start of the third quarter, when the Tigers came out and stuck yet another touchdown on the board, to go up 38-0. Remember, this was not a great Auburn team by any means; they would finish the year 5-6, missing out on a bowl appearance in Tuberville's first season. They had virtually no running game. Most of the offense was Ben Leard throwing to Ronney Daniels. Yet they absolutely torched a pretty decent Georgia team in Sanford Stadium. It was simply astonishing.

A much more historically significant Auburn win over **Georgia** in Athens came near the end of the **1983** season. Georgia had won the previous three SEC titles in a row, leaning heavily on Herschell Walker on offense and a stout defense. Auburn had narrowly lost at home to the Dawgs the previous year, in the only meeting of Bo and Herschell. With Walker gone to the USFL, Auburn won a game of steel from the Dawgs, 13-7, ending Georgia's dominance of the league and placing the Tigers at the top for most of the rest of the decade.

Also, because it doesn't really fit in anywhere else on this list: **South Carolina, SEC Championship Game, 2010 season**. A beat-down for the ages, setting all kinds of SEC title game records, giving us our second-ever win in this game and our seventh conference title overall, getting us to the National Championship Game, and doing it all against a Steve Spurrier-coached team! What's not to love?

3. Florida, Gainesville, 1994 season.

John: So many things jump out about this game. Steve Spurrier, that great offense, and another high scoring, exciting Auburn win. And it was Spurrier's first-ever SEC loss at home!

Van: Lots of things do come to mind when I recall Florida '94. Auburn was well into what would become a twenty-game winning streak under second-year coach Terry Bowden, who preached to the players before the game that, since the Tigers were not bowl-eligible due to probation, this was their "Super Bowl." Only folks actually inside Jordan-Hare had been able to witness Auburn's shocking upset of the Gators the year before, thanks to those same probation penalties, but in '94 the Tigers were back on the air and looking to impress poll voters.

I had just completed my Master's degree and was still living near the campus, and somehow managed to talk my roommate into scrounging up tickets and riding down to Gainesville with me. Watching it in person, surrounded by shocked and stunned Gators fans, was fun enough; going back and seeing the broadcast with Brent Musberger's shouted "They never quit!" as Frank Sanders catches the final touchdown was possibly even better. I won't describe the festivities after we left Ben Hill Griffin Stadium at Florida Field that evening, but suffice to say I woke up the next morning on the floor of an apartment in Tallahassee—*Tallahassee!*—rolled up in an FSU blanket, with no memory of how I got there.

This was also the game where poor Terry "I wore Auburn pajamas as a kid" Dean's Heisman campaign ended, and Danny Wuerffel's began. Dean had been tearing up opponents all season as the Gators' quarterback, but Auburn shut him down and intercepted his passes repeatedly in the first half. Eventually Spurrier went to his favorite tactic of pulling the starting QB and sending in the backup, and Wuerffel nearly brought Florida back.

Two other big Auburn road wins over **Florida** deserve mention here: **1988** and **2007**.

The 1988 Auburn team, one of the finest units in Auburn history, not only won in the Swamp, where the Tigers hadn't won in a while; they not only exorcised demons from Kerwin Bell's huge comeback win in that stadium in 1986 that knocked us out of the Sugar Bowl; they not only did it during Florida's "Gator Growl" Homecoming celebration; but they did it by shutting out Emmitt Smith's Gators, 16-0.

The 2007 team took down Urban Meyer's and Tim Tebow's defending national champions in the Swamp, with then-freshman Wes Byrum kicking the winning field goal a second time, after Meyer called a quick time-out that nullified the first kick. This win guaranteed that neither Meyer nor Tebow ever defeated Auburn in their Florida careers.

2. Alabama, Tuscaloosa, 2002 season.

John: I think of this as the Tre Smith game. With Ronnie Brown and Cadillac Williams both injured and unable to play, nobody gave Auburn much of a chance. But Tre had a big day at running back. There was a thread on an Alabama message board during the game, in which Tide fans are melting down as the little third string "midget" rips them for lots of yardage. Someone copied it and sent it around the Internet for a while. I have a copy and still enjoy reading it from time to time.

Van: I might not have put this game this high. It was good to win yet again in Tuscaloosa (this game marking the *third* different century in which Auburn had won—and, to that point, not yet lost—in T-Town). It was great to win in a year we weren't supposed to—nobody saw this win coming! It was also great to beat smug Dennis Franchione during the season that he kept referring to Auburn only as "that school down the road," and in a year when he continuously preached to Alabama fans that they should all "hold the rope" –only to see him left holding the bag. And this game did mark the first of six consecutive Iron Bowl wins by Tommy Tuberville's Auburn teams. I'm just not certain it was the second-best ever.

I might have swapped in the **2004 Iron Bowl**, which otherwise doesn't even make our top ten list. That game was important in that it represented another Tigers win in Bryant-Denny, kept that streak alive, finished off an undefeated regular season for Auburn and kept the Tigers in the hunt for the national championship. And like the 2010 edition, the first half was agony until the Tigers got things going just before halftime.

And don't forget the **1986 Iron Bowl**, with Lawyer Tillman's famous "Reverse to Victory" after two earlier Brent Fullwood touchdowns, giving the Tigers the win over a Ray Perkins-led Tide team. But, honestly, a win over Alabama is huge in any season. Which gets us to the biggest of all:

1. Alabama; Tuscaloosa, 2010 season.

John: This was the best road win in Auburn history. The comeback, the stakes—nothing else is close.

Van: I have to agree, this one is definitely the best.

It's funny—I had a number of conversations with Auburn friends in the days after the 2010 season about our pick for the best game of that year. I tended to choose the Arkansas game, which was simply a track meet, back and forth, close all the way—until Auburn exploded on the Hogs and crushed them in the fourth quarter. Most of my friends, on the other hand, unhesitatingly went with this Iron Bowl. My usual response was, "It's hard for me to pick as 'best game of the year' a contest in which I spent most of the first half groaning in agony and wanting to slash my wrists."

Despite how awful the first half looked and felt, however, it did turn into a huge, tremendous, gargantuan win—an almost unfathomable one; a comeback of nearly unthinkable proportions. Starting just before halftime, the Tiger offense outscored Alabama 28-3 in the Tide's own stadium, in front of over a hundred thousand very loud and mostly crimson-clad partisans. (And, let's be honest: Alabama was lucky to get the three!) The Auburn defense, meanwhile, went from making McElroy look like Joe Montana to making him look like Hannah Montana. The Tigers' ticket to Atlanta might already have been punched, following the win over Georgia, but what a hollow trip to the SEC title game it would have been if Auburn had not come back to win this one—and all bets about Glendale would have been off, or at least a whole lot shakier.

13

Twitter Trooper Taylor Spy:
A (Very Short) Novel of Espionage and 'Crootin'

The origins of this chapter and the column from which it came are somewhat convoluted but nevertheless worthwhile, we believe.

In short: John had become annoyed at the talk during the 2011-'12 offseason of all sorts of trickery and chicanery going on in recruiting. The social networking service called Twitter, in particular, was seen as becoming a new arena for meddling with young players during the recruiting process. There was also the whole business with star running back T. J. Yeldon pretending to be committed to Auburn all recruiting season, only to switch to Alabama at the very last second and refuse to take any calls from the Auburn staff. John suggested to Van that they do a Wishbone column addressing this issue—but perhaps in more of a satirical way, getting the point across (hopefully) while presenting it in a more entertaining way than as a simple screed against bad recruiting practices.

Van had recently watched the theatrical remake of "Tinker Tailor Soldier Spy," and the name jumped right out at him. He took John's suggestions and went to work.

Whether the resulting "very short novel of espionage and 'crootin'" makes its larger point, or is even all that entertaining, we leave to you, the reader.

It did, however, get picked up by the popular "Every Day Should Be Saturday" Internet column for that week—something that pleased the authors to no end.

One note of caution: This was written before the 2012 season, when we were all (mostly) still high on Coach Chizik and his staff, and truly believed that Coach VanGorder would have the defense breathing fire that fall.

With all of that in mind, we present our little drama: "Twitter Trooper Taylor Spy!"

*   *   *

"One of our recruits... is a mole...!"

The haggard assistant coach collapsed on the floor, bleeding from multiple gunshot wounds to the abdomen that would have killed a lesser coach but not an SEC assistant because this is the SEC by God.

Gene Chizik leapt to his feet and ran around his trophy-laden desk, which was trophy-laden because this is the SEC by God.

"Trooper! Trooper—speak to me! You say one of our recruits was injured playing Whack-a-Mole??"

Trooper paused in his desperate efforts to stanch the bleeding with a towel, reached up with bloody hands, and—just as Defensive Coordinator Brian VanGorder ran into the room—grasped Chizik by the collar. "No, you fool—a mole! One of our recruits is a mo—URK!"

"Trooper!!"

Chizik and VanGorder exchanged glances heavy with portent that this would be a really dramatic yet somehow ephemeral story.

"He's gone, Gene," VanGorder's mustache, which is nigh-omnipotent, declared.

"But—did you hear what he said?" Chizik demanded. "A mole! We have a mole in our midst!" He rounded his desk and snatched up the red hotline phone. "This is the Chiz," he announced. "We have a situation. Convene the War Council!"

Chizik took the dead silence coming from the other end to mean Aubie would comply with his orders, as always.

"To root out the mole in our Recruiting Circus," Chizik told the assembled crowd of assistant coaches and mascots, "I've decided to bring in a special investigator. Someone who can operate outside the margins and look into everything in a fair and impartial way. Someone who can infiltrate the deepest circles of recruiting and never be noticed."

The special investigator entered the room. He wore a dark blue blazer and striped tie, baseball cap, and white sneakers. As he walked in, he coughed. And coughed. And coughed.

The coaches looked up in shock and awe.

"Coach Dye!" exclaimed Coach Luper.

"RAAAWWK!" screeched Nova.

"..." added Aubie.

Patrick Fain Dye nodded to each of the men and wildlife, and then took a pair of thick, round eyeglasses from his pocket and put them on. Then he handed out bags of Golden Flake potato chips.

"Let us begin," he intoned in his rural Georgia accent. "Coach Chizik has filled me in on the details. Sounds like you fellas have a mole in the Circus."

"A sleeper," Coach Luper interjected.

"Sleeper?" Dye looked over at the running backs coach, eyes wide. "Well, now—Bo used to nap before all the big games, but it didn't really interfere with—"

"He means a sleeper agent," Chizik clarified.

"Oh. Heh. Right." Dye removed his cap and scratched his head. "Okay, well—I'll root this mole out for you." He gazed at each of the coaches in turn. "I know you men can handle the rest."

"You got that right, Coach," VanGorder replied, slipping on a pair of brass knuckles. His mustache was, of course, already wearing a pair.

Carefully Coach Dye set four little plastic football players from one of those old vibrating electric football games out on Chizik's desk.

"Tweeter," he said, and pointed to the first one. Then, "Trooper. Sniper. Troll." He looked up at the coaches. "These represent four of your current recruits. Three of these young men are simply confused—*genuinely* confused—by the chaos that is the college football recruiting process—or else keeping their options open, talking to different schools, trying to make the best decision for themselves and their families. Or waiting to hear if Saban will offer their high school coaches a job." He paused, then, "But one of them is not legit—he's only pretending to be committed to the University of Auburn so he can spy on our activities, use up a scholarship spot, block other recruits—and then switch his commitment at the last minute to one of our rivals."

Chizik absorbed this shocking information, then leaned in close to the lamp on his desk. "What do you think about that, Nick?" he asked.

"That's about ri—ummm, nevermind," the lamp replied.

"Think of the negative publicity," Coach Thigpen uttered in astonishment.

"Exactly," Dye declared. "And that's why we're gonna nip this in the bud. Because," he added, "you read any book on 'crootin, and you'll find it comes down heavy in favor of bud-nippin'."

"How will you find the mole?" Coach Luper asked.

Dye looked around. "Wait a minute. Are we secure here? Nobody's listening in?"

"No," said Chizik.

"No," said the lamp.

"Where's Coach Loeffler?" Dye asked, growing suspicious.

"Oh, it's okay," Chizik replied. "We don't let him into the big-boy meetings yet. He's mowing Jordan-Hare."

Dye nodded. "Good. Good."

"So," Luper said, bringing them back to the topic at hand, "as to your methodology?"

Dye pointed to the little football player figures as he replied.

"All I know how to do is go back to work," he said. "It takes analysis. I'll have to dig deeply. Study patterns of behavior. Did this one linger too long at the ice cream toppings bar with that recruit who's committed to Florida? Did this one Tweet too much about how awesome Georgia's locker room was? Did this one eat grass with Les Miles?" Dye shrugged. "It takes work, men. Hard work."

Chizik nodded and then clasped Dye firmly by the hand. "I know you're the right man for the job, Coach. The Auburn Family thanks you. We're so thankful that you're All In."

Dye snorted. "Oh, I'm All In, all right," he muttered, patting the flask in his jacket pocket. "Now pass the chips."

After two full days of sipping bourbon, munching on Golden Flakes, and watching American Idol reruns, Pat Dye at last rose from his recliner, showered, put on his blue blazer and striped tie, white tennis shoes, and baseball cap, and drove to the nearby Waffle House. He nodded to the other customers as he entered and then slid into the designated booth.

After a few minutes of waiting, another figure slid in across from him. The other patrons at the Waffle House looked over at them briefly but, this being Waffle House at 2 a.m., soon shrugged and got back to their meals.

"The mole," Dye grumbled, his voice low. "You have the name?"

"Oh, I have it, alright," the shadowy figure replied. "But I can give you more than that."

"Is that so?"

The other man nodded. Then he adjusted the paper bag that covered his head. "I can give you the ringleader," he said. I can tell you who Karla is."

"Karla!" Dye exclaimed. "The puppet master! The seemingly-mythical guy who runs all the mole operations for the Evil Empire!" There was a predatory gleam in the coach's eye that hadn't been present since the days of Bill Curry coaching at Alabama. "He really exists? You'll give me his name, too?"

"Absolutely. If the price is right."

"Oh, it's right," Dye said. "So—the names?"

"Wait," the bagman said, holding out a hand. "First things first. You have it with you?"

Dye frowned, then reached under the table and pulled out a sack. Reluctantly he handed it over.

The bagman accepted the sack and stashed it away. "This will come in handy," he said with what might have been a grin, underneath his own bag.

"The names," Dye growled, between coughs. "Give me the names!"

The bagman took a slip of paper from his pocket and handed it to Dye. "That's the mole," he said.

Dye glanced at it, shrugged, and stuffed it in his pocket. "What about Karla?" he asked.

The bagman nodded and handed him another slip. "I think you're gonna like it."

Dye read the name written on the paper. He brightened. His cough fell silent.

"You'll give that to Chizik, then?" the bagman asked.

"This?" Dye chewed his lip for a second. "Oh—I think I'll tend to this," he answered, "personally."

Coach Dye leveled his semi-automatic .45 at Paul Finebaum.

"I knew it, Finebaum," the old coach growled menacingly. "I knew you were Karla. You've been manipulating things—playing the puppet master behind the scenes—all along!"

"I had to do it—don't you understand?" Finebaum clasped his hands together plaintively. "I thought I could control Saban, but he's just too powerful! He made me do things—*terrible* things! And then the SOS turned on me! It was a coup!"

"I don't want to hear it."

"Look in your heart!" Finebaum was sweating profusely now, on his knees, pleading. "You don't have to do this! Look in your heart!"

"The game is up, Karlabaum."

Finebaum looked frantically left and right, seeking any avenue of escape. "Legend!" he cried. "Jim! I-Man!!"

"You think I-Man's coming to your rescue, Finebaum?" Dye asked, scoffing. "I doubt that!"

With a savage scream, Finebaum hurled himself at Dye.

Dye fired once, twice.

Finebaum's bloody body fell to the floor.

Dye stood over him, shaking his head sadly.

The door burst open and Tammy ran in. She looked down at the mess that was Finebaum, then at Dye, then up at the heavens. She raised both fists and screamed in futility.

"PAAAAAAAAWWWWWWLLLLL!!!!!"

Coaches Dye and Chizik sat in a bass boat on Lake Martin. Dye handed a slip of paper to Chizik.

"This is the mole?" Chizik asked, looking at the name on the paper in astonishment.

"You'll be wantin' to memorize that and then destroy it," he rumbled. "And I was never here."

Chizik nodded, read the name over one more time, then put the paper in his mouth and chewed it up.

"So—how did you do it, Coach?" Chizik asked after he'd swallowed. "How did you find the mole?"

Dye eyed him levelly. He coughed a few times, then shrugged. "All I knew how to do was go back to work."

"Right," Chizik said, nodding.

"I searched again. And again. And again." He coughed. "That's what it takes, men."

Chizik frowned and looked around. "It's just you and me here in the boat, Coach."

217

"Work—hard work," Dye continued. "But it was worth it. I've seen you grow up. I've seen ya become men, men."

Chizik pursed his lips, nodded, and picked up the paddle. With deft strokes he turned the boat around and headed back to shore. Along the way they saw Nick Saban approaching in his own dingy, the body of Paul Finebaum laying in the front.

"Burial at sea," Saban offered by way of explanation as the two boats passed one another.

Chizik snapped a quick salute by way of reply and paddled faster. Behind them he heard a splash.

"Looks like you'll end up with a pretty decent 'crootin class," Dye rumbled as they pulled alongside the dock.

Chizik nodded.

"I ain't smart enough to tell ya how much I love ya," Dye concluded.

Chizik nodded again.

As Dye stood and started to climb out of the boat, Chizik looked up at him and his eyes widened.

"Umm.... Coach—what happened to your pants?"

Dye looked down, realized for the first time that he was clad only in a sport coat, tie, cap—and boxer shorts—and blinked in surprise.

"Well. Danged if I know," he muttered. "That seems to happen a lot." He shrugged and reached back toward Chizik. "Now hand me them Golden Flakes."

THE END

The Ten Most Costly Auburn Losses

We won't spend much time on this one. Who wants to dwell on the losses, when this book is (mostly) about the triumphs and the dominance? But the victories wouldn't feel quite so glorious if we Tigers fans hadn't tasted bitter disappointment so often; it has tempered us in the fires of adversity and forged a harder steel in the long run from the crucible of occasional defeat. And it makes the victories that much grander.

Our criteria here are not "games that cost coaches their jobs" but rather "games that hurt the program itself—that knocked us out of national or conference honors, or that simply disappointed us to the point that we still look back in disgust or depression at them to this day.

Here, therefore, are the ten losses in the modern era that cost Auburn the most; the losses that remind us to be all the more grateful and joyous when things go *right*:

Honorable Mentions:

LSU, 2001. This game was delayed until after the Iron Bowl because of 9-11 and ended up becoming a de facto divisional title game. LSU's win meant that they finished with the same record as Auburn, but it gave them the head-to-head tie-breaker for the division title, and knocked Auburn out of an appearance in Atlanta.

Arkansas, 1995. The missed field goal at the end of this one (being played at the same time the Atlanta Braves were clinching their 1995 World Series title) cost Auburn an SEC West Division title and a trip to the Georgia Dome. The Hogs—*again*.

FSU, 1987. Win this game and Auburn has another undefeated season—though, likely, another one that did not result in a national championship, given the tie with Tennessee. (Beat FSU, though, and the Tigers might be playing someone other than Syracuse in the Sugar Bowl—or playing with more than just a bowl trophy on the line...)

Florida OR Georgia, 1986. These two games are interchangeable; both were narrow losses in a two-loss season. Win just one of them and Auburn wins the SEC Championship and goes to the Sugar Bowl, though they wouldn't have played for the national title that season with one loss.

Miss State OR Ole Miss, 1999. All the Tigers would've gained by winning either of these games, in Tommy Tuberville's first season on the Plains, was a winning season (6-5 instead of 5-6) and a bowl trip. But Auburn collapsed at the end of both these very winnable contests and gave them both away.

And now, on to the Top Ten:

10. Florida, 1984.

This one doesn't get as much attention as some of Auburn's more critical losses; even the Iron Bowl that year is more often thought of as a costly loss, being the infamous 17-15 "Wrong Way Bo" game. But a win would've given Auburn the undisputed SEC Championship, even over ineligible Florida, since the Tigers' two losses to open the season were to non-SEC opponents Miami and Texas. As it played out, Florida finished with the best record in the conference but LSU went to the Sugar Bowl instead.

9. LSU, 2005.

If just one of John Vaughn's numerous missed field goal kicks makes it through the uprights, the Tigers finish the season undefeated in the SEC, 10-1 overall (with just that almost inexplicable opening-night loss to Georgia Tech blemishing the record), and with a spot in the SEC Championship Game against a Georgia team they'd already beaten in Athens.

It is an absolute crime that of Tommy Tuberville's 2002, 2005, 2006, and 2007 teams, none of them made an appearance in the SEC Championship Game. Each was deserving; arguably, each was at least as deserving as the 2000 squad that did make it. Speaking of which:

8. Georgia, 2002.

The Bulldogs scored in the waning moments of the game, knocking Auburn out of the SEC West title, Florida out of the SEC East title, and both of those teams out of Atlanta, in what (to our knowledge) remains the only time a single play in a single game changed both participants in the conference title game. It also denied the Tigers the chance to avenge their narrow loss to Ron Zook's Gators in Gainesville earlier in the season. This team was loaded, with Ronnie Brown having an epic half-season after Cadillac Williams' injury in Gainesville, and could have won the conference. They did go on to win the Capital One Bowl over Penn State.

7. Georgia, 1982.

The Bulldogs were ranked #1 in the country going into this game, but the unranked Tigers played them down to the wire, very nearly pulling out the huge upset win. Had Auburn scored at the end and prevailed, the Tigers would have actually won a share of the SEC and had the head-to-head tiebreaker over Georgia—though, the way the system worked back then, a 10-1 UGA likely still would have received the invitation to the Sugar Bowl over a 9-2 Auburn. But you never know.

6. Alabama, 1994.

Win this contest in Legion Field and Auburn finishes a run of 22 straight games over two seasons without a single loss. To hear many in the sports media talk, the Tigers had a legitimate shot at a national title by running the table two straight years—though the draw with Georgia the previous week probably would have put an end to that possibility, even with a win over the Tide. At the very least, Auburn could have pointed out that they would've played in the second and third SEC Championship Games in place of Alabama if not for probation those two years.

5. Arkansas, 2006.

The mastermind of this Auburn defeat was none other than Hogs Offensive Coordinator Gus Malzahn—perhaps you've heard of him. With a victory in this game, Auburn wins the SEC West at 7-1 and faces eventual national champion Florida—a team Auburn had already beaten once that season—in the Georgia Dome, with the door open to a BCS title game run.

4. Tennessee, 1989.

A win in the "Blame it on the Rain" game in Knoxville would have given Auburn an undefeated season in the conference, sole possession of the SEC Championship, and a trip to the Sugar Bowl to face eventual national champions Miami. (Beat Miami there, and who knows..?) Because of this loss, the Tigers had to share the conference title with Alabama and Tennessee and ended up in the Hall of Fame Bowl. A conference title is a conference title, even if it's just a one-third share. But just imagine how much better it all could have been.

3. Southern Cal, 2003.

While this loss ended up being mostly inconsequential for the 2003 season, it had to have affected the views of the poll voters the following season, when Auburn was never able to move higher than third in the rankings (and secure a spot in the BCS title game), despite being undefeated.

Depending on how you look at it, this game—a shutout in the Tigers' own stadium by the visiting Trojans—could very well have prejudiced the entire 2004 season against the Tigers in the minds of the voters, trapping them eternally in third place and out of the running for the BCS title. From that perspective, it qualifies as one of the most damaging losses in Auburn history.

2. LSU, 1988.

You know the story. A one-point loss in the final seconds. An earthquake. And Auburn's only regular-season defeat of 1988, denying the Tigers (and their world-class defense) a matchup with undefeated Notre Dame in the Sugar Bowl with the national title on the line. It still hurts, all these years later.

1. Texas, 1983.

A win over Texas and Auburn finishes 1983 as the only undefeated team, having played the toughest schedule in the country by far. Surely a majority of voters would've moved an undefeated Auburn to #1 in the final poll, rather than jumping a 1-loss Miami over them.

Missed tackles and special teams errors ultimately doomed the Tigers on this September afternoon. The offense's failure to put more points on the board didn't help, though, as Texas's stout defense was able to mostly shut down Auburn's then one-dimensional attack.

This game trumps the second-ranked game above, because a win here would have likely *assured* a national championship, while a win over LSU in 1988 would simply have put Auburn in a position to play for it.

15

The Ten Greatest Teams
in Modern Auburn History

As of this writing, thirty-two different groups of players and coaches have taken the field for a season as that year's edition of the Auburn Tigers in what we of the Wishbone consider to be the "Modern Era" of Auburn football, beginning with the arrival of Patrick Fain Dye as the new head coach, prior to the 1981 season. Many of those teams have distinguished themselves with honors and accolades, with All-Americans and championships. Ten have accomplished just a little bit more.

In evaluating these teams, we considered several factors, including overall performance, final record, accomplishments, fulfilled potential at season's end relative to potential at the start, level of performance relative to the team's era and the level of the competition, and the maddening *"But for one or two stupid plays..."* factor. We have ranked them accordingly. You may—and likely will—see at least some of this differently, and that is well and good.

Without further ado, we therefore present our choices for the Ten Greatest Auburn Teams in the Modern Era:

10. 1997: DC's Senior Campaign

Terry Bowden's 1997 squad was the first to win a legitimate SEC Western Division title. They lost only two games in the regular season—to Florida and Mississippi State, both in Jordan-Hare—and came up a single point short to Tennessee in Auburn's first appearance in the SEC Championship Game. They went on to defeat Clemson in the Peach Bowl. Their win over Alabama in the Iron Bowl was certainly heart-stopping, but many felt the game should never have been so close, considering the Tide that year had won only four games. They did secure impressive road wins at LSU and at Georgia, as well as a big win over a good Virginia team in Charlottesville, and double-threat quarterback Dameyune Craig made the team exciting, unpredictable and fun to watch every single week.

9. 2006: Cox and Defense

While the 2006 Tigers won an impressive 11 games and lost only twice, they rank this low simply because their two losses were so unexpected, so relatively lopsided, and so devastating. Big wins over #7 LSU and #3 Florida had them ranked in the top five in the country as late as November 11, and they were in position much of the year to have a shot at playing for the national championship. But a shocking defeat at home at the hands of Arkansas (with an offense conducted by Gus Malzahn) and then a blowout loss to Georgia in Jordan-Hare erased any chances of a BCS berth. The season did end on a pair of high notes, however, as Brandon Cox led the team to big wins over Alabama (in Tuscaloosa) and Nebraska (in the Cotton Bowl).

8. 1986: Air Auburn

Two plays. The 1986 team came within two plays of being undefeated. A last-second two-point conversion by Kerwin Bell,

226

rolling his wheelchair into the end zone at Florida Field, and then a holding call on a Brent Fullwood touchdown run that would have beaten Georgia (in the infamous "wet dawg" game)—those two plays were all that kept the Tigers from an undefeated regular season and a Sugar Bowl berth, possibly for the national championship. And this the very next year after Bo Jackson finished his Auburn career.

All of that aside, the 1986 squad is probably best-remembered by Auburn people for being the first season of "Air Auburn," with Pat Dye moving away from the one-year experiment with the I-Formation (to boost Bo's Heisman chances) to a more pass-friendly offense. Despite the new emphasis on throwing the ball, however, the high points of the year came on the ground, mostly courtesy of the rugged running of Brent Fullwood and his lead blocker, fellow senior Tommie Agee.

For all of that duo's heroics, though, the most famous running play of the year was undoubtedly the "Reverse to Victory" touchdown against Alabama. Auburn had lost perhaps the most heartbreaking Iron Bowl in history the year before, on Van Tiffin's last-second field goal. The Tigers wanted revenge, and they got it, when Lawyer Tillman took a late-fourth-quarter end-around handoff from Jeff Burger (by way of Tim Jessie) and weaved his way into the end zone for the victory.

This team also had the opportunity to play in the Orange Bowl—something Auburn has never done in the Modern Era. But Pat Dye had already promised the folks of the Citrus Bowl in Orlando that the Tigers would come to their bowl instead, and he kept his word. The Tigers proceeded to knock off USC, 16-7, in that game on January 1.

7. 1989: The "First Time Ever" Squad

It's a testament to the quality of the six teams ranked higher here that the 1989 team is only seventh on the list. Their two losses came at Knoxville ("Blame it on the Rain," we sang) and at Tallahassee (against one of the more powerful Florida State squads ever), both by single-digits. Reggie Slack's (and Tracy Rocker's and Quentin Riggins') squad beat everybody else, though, including LSU, Florida, Georgia and Alabama.

Above all else, though, this team will always be remembered for one of the single greatest and most important accomplishments in Auburn history: the 1989 Iron Bowl. Undefeated, second-ranked Alabama came to Jordan-Hare (kicking and screaming) for the "First Time Ever" that year, threatening to do the absolutely unthinkable: beat Auburn in our own house in their first visit. The '89 squad had all of the Auburn Family and all of Auburn history riding on their broad shoulders, and they responded like champions. In Auburn's final game played in the decade of the 1980s, they beat the Tide by double-digits.

Their bowl game—Auburn's first game of the 1990s, on New Year's Day—was almost an afterthought, but they won it, too. We've covered it in depth elsewhere in this book.

6. 1987: They Even Hugged the Ref

The 1987, 1988, and 1989 Auburn teams were three of the strongest, toughest, orneriest teams in Auburn football history, and among the absolute elites in all of college football those three years. (The 1986 team wasn't far behind them.) They had a tough-as-nails defense consistently at or near the top of the national rankings in yardage and points allowed. They had guys like Lawyer Tillman and Freddy Weygand and Duke Donaldson and Walter Reeves and

Alexander Wright catching passes from Jeff Burger. They had the super-reliable Win Lyle kicking field goals.

The one real weakness on those three squads was their lack of an All-SEC caliber, home-run-hitter at running back. Brent Fullwood had moved on to the NFL after '86, and James Bostic and Stephen Davis were still a couple of years down the road. Stacey Danley and James Joseph carried the load admirably, but neither was quite of the caliber of a Bo Jackson or even a Rudi Johnson, able to take over a game when the going got tough. When Emmitt Smith spurned Auburn and chose (at his momma's urging) to stay closer to home and go to Florida, the Tigers lost the player that could have conceivably pushed them over the threshold to one, two, or even (at least in the dreams of the Wishone columnists) three national championships. The best defense in football, that receiving corps, Reggie Slack—and *Emmitt Smith*? Seriously? They would have been up there with the toughest teams of the 1980s from any program in the country. Even without him, they still were.

The '87 bunch had a swagger about them. With a 3-4 defensive front consisting of Tracy Rocker, Benji Roland, and Ron Stallworth, why wouldn't they? They opened up against old enemy Texas in newly expanded Jordan-Hare and beat the Longhorns nearly to death, 31-3 (and star linebacker Kurt Crain even hugged the ref after one play). They gave Florida nightmares in Jordan-Hare on Halloween night, 29-6. Only a late comeback by the Vols in Knoxville (resulting in a 20-20 draw) and an inexplicable lapse against FSU (38-6) spoiled their regular season record.

Everyone remembers how that season ended. Undefeated Syracuse in the Sugar Bowl. Win Lyle and Dick MacPherson. 16-16. "Tie-Dye" and "Sour Grapes." Not the glorious finish this team deserved, but (as Pat Dye himself put it afterward), they deserved better than to go out on a loss, and they certainly didn't. In retrospect, knowing the Orangemen as we've come to know them since, spoiling their season was not a bad way to go out at all.

5. 1993: The Best Team Nobody Saw

What's left to be said about the '93 Undefeateds that hasn't already been said—even by us? Terry Bowden's first season as head coach after Pat Dye stepped down; star players (or reliable and seasoned seniors) at all the key positions including quarterback, center, running back, wide receiver, and even kicker and punter. In retrospect, the shock wasn't that this squad was so good but that the previous three had been so mediocre-to-bad.

They rank fifth and not higher for two simple reasons. One: They were never able to test their mettle in postseason play, either in Atlanta or in a bowl game of any sort, due to probation. So we'll never really know how they would have done in a full season. And two: There's a sense that much of the SEC was "down" that year. They only had to play two truly top-ranked opponents all year— Florida and Alabama—and got them both in Jordan-Hare. They eked out extremely narrow wins against each, and thus deserve every accolade they've ever received, and more.

This is in no way meant as a negative criticism of the 1993 team and its accomplishments. They faced every foe they were allowed to face, and they beat them all. No one could ask for anything more.

4. 1988: Big Blue Defense

It's true that the 1993 squad never lost a game and finished the year with at least a claim to a national championship, while the 1988 team could boast neither of those things. However, the 1988 squad had a legitimate opportunity to play for the big prize—and missed seizing that opportunity by *one single play.* An *earthquake* of a play.

You know the one we're talking about. Tiger Stadium. Fourth Down. 6-0 Auburn. A last-gasp pass for a TD, and LSU wins, 7-6. Gone was the undefeated season. Gone was the inevitable matchup with Lou Holtz's Notre Dame in the Sugar Bowl. Instead they faced a motivated Florida State team that had started slow but was really coming on at the end of the year. Even then, they fell just short at the end, and it took a no-call on a blatant pass interference against Auburn's Freddy Weygand late to seal the deal for the Seminoles.

More than anything they did or did not accomplish, however, the 1988 team ranks this high simply because of what we might call the "eye test." They looked danged impressive every week, particularly on defense. Some facts: They gave up more than one touchdown in a game only *once* all year long. The team that did that—North Carolina, oddly enough—was the only team to score more than ten points on them. They reeled off a stretch of shutouts lasting three weeks, including a 16-0 whitewash of Florida *in Gainesville, on the Gators' homecoming.* They beat Tennessee, Miss State, and Florida by a combined score of 87-6. They played only three away games (!) in the entire regular season, but in those games they allowed their opponents a *combined total* of just 17 points.

The scores would have been even more lopsided but for unforced errors by the offense. The O-line was plagued by motion penalties all season long, meaning the offense was constantly taking two steps forward and then one step back.

The 1988 Tigers weren't perfect. They lost two big games to two very tough teams. But they dominated everyone else, won the SEC for a second year in a row, and made it to the Sugar Bowl—and they looked as impressive as all get-out along the way. Could they have beaten Notre Dame for the National Championship? Your intrepid Wishbone duo have no doubt at all.

3. 1983: Dye's First Dynamo

The 1983 team rightfully deserves this spot. If you aren't so sure, let us make it clear: They won the national championship.

Oh, we are well aware that Auburn doesn't count finishing first in the *New York Times* poll as a "legitimate" title. We're not the sort of people to just randomly count every single #1 ranking, no matter how legit, as a "claimed" national title. Can't imagine how anyone else could, either. (*Cough cough ALABAMA cough.*) But let's be clear: At the start of the day on January 1, 1984, the experts all said one thing: If Nebraska and Texas lose, Auburn is the champion. Guess what? Nebraska and Texas both lost. And yes, we still hate Miami, all these years later.

That '83 squad had a lot going for it, but two things stand out in particular: a very strong defense, and a running game powered by Bo Jackson and Lionel James. Add to that solid line play by future 49er Steve Wallace, steady game management by QB Randy Campbell, a D-line that included Donnie Humphrey and Doug Smith, kicking by Al Del Greco and blocking by fullback Tommie Agee, and you have the makings of a champion. A *national* champion.

If only the Tigers had scheduled Wake Forest or Duke for the second game of the season instead of Texas. If only the special teams units hadn't given the Longhorns such great field position. If only...

Alas, Texas won that early clash and everyone remembered it for the rest of the season. The AP voters jumped Miami from fifth to first, and left Nebraska ahead of Auburn at #2. It's still just as shocking today as it was on January 2, 1984.

This team deserved better. They faced easily the toughest schedule in the nation, including out-of-conference foes Texas, Boomer Esiason's Maryland, a good FSU squad, and the always-solid Georgia Tech and Southern Miss, in addition to Tennessee, Florida, Georgia and Alabama. They beat eighth-ranked Michigan in the Sugar Bowl, in the era when the SEC Champion went to New Orleans to play an at-large team, no matter what.

They didn't get the #1 ranking they had earned when all was said and done, but they had served notice to the football world that Auburn was back, and here to stay. That message, delivered with the savagery of a blue-clad defensive end driving your quarterback six inches into the lush grass of Jordan-Hare, was received loud and clear across the landscape of the SEC and beyond.

2. 2004: Any Time, Anywhere

Perhaps the only thing worse than earning a championship and having it denied by voters is earning the right to *play for* a championship and having even the *opportunity* denied by voters.

The 2004 Tigers beat everyone they faced. There were no "if only" moments. They didn't give up a long kick return to Texas, or a last-second touchdown to LSU. They *won* those kinds of games. *All* of those games. And *still*.

You don't need a history lesson here. As Legolas said in "Fellowship," "For me the pain is still too near." We all know the deal. Jason and Ronnie and Cadillac and Carlos. Ace and Deuce catching the ball. Chizik running the defense. Gorgeous Borges turning around an offensive attack that had been anemic and downright *offensive* the year before and making them into a powerhouse.

And USC and Oklahoma sitting there at #1 and #2 all season long, just taunting us with the knowledge that they weren't going to lose. They simply were not going to get out of the way for a better team to take one of their spots. It was awful and terrible, and of course the other truly sad thing about it is that it made the Auburn Family look at that 2004 team as somehow a team that didn't achieve enough—that came up short somehow—that in some weird way, let us down.

That's just not so. They did what they had to do. It's not fair to them or to the Auburn spirit to remember them in any sort of negative way. They went 13-0. They beat the living snot out of Tennessee in Knoxville, and rang them up again in Atlanta. They beat the Tide in T-Town. They put together a performance for the ages against 1-loss Georgia, holding the Dawgs scoreless until the final seconds.

And yet. And yet, we can't help but thinking... *If only.* If only Cal had held on to beat USC. If only Oklahoma hadn't stolen Bowling Green off our schedule before the season started, leaving Auburn to scramble to find a last-minute replacement and settling for the Citadel; perhaps that would have been enough to lift Auburn's strength of schedule above Oklahoma's.

If only.

Enough of that. Hail the 2004 Auburn Tigers. Honor them and remember them always, for the campaign they waged that year has been topped in the modern era by only one other Tigers squad:

1. 2010: Cam's Champions

We can argue team-vs.-team, players vs. players. We can debate if Cam Newton could have scored against the 2004 defense, or if Nick Fairley's defense could have shut down Jason and Ronnie and

Caddy. We can study the stats and the strength-of-schedule of each team *ad nauseum*, and still one fact stands out that is simply incontrovertible: The 2010 team won 'em all—and then won the big prize. They have a crystal football in a cabinet, while those other spectacular squads—2004 and 1993 and 1988 and 1983, for all their worthiness—do not. The 2010 players and coaches have the rings. They have the hardware. They went to Glendale and faced the fearsome offensive attack of Oregon and they won, and they brought the Coaches' Trophy home aboard that big 747.

There has never been another Auburn team like them. There's never been a college football team quite like them. A quarterback who was simply unstoppable for most of the year, converting third downs with ease and occasionally breaking off a Bo Jackson-style long TD run—and who then cranked up his arm and slung it around and lit up the scoreboard that way, too. A supporting cast of all-timers, including: A young running back who broke Bo's freshman record and won MVP of the BCS Title Game; a defensive tackle who could not be blocked; a lightning-fast back who averaged around ten yards a carry; a corps of no-name receivers who got the job done every week; a senior-laden OL and a senior kicker who could always be counted on when the game was on the line; a tight end who knew how to find the end zone with the ball; a brainy linebacker who managed the defense like a coach on the field; and a complete team that demonstrated on a nearly weekly basis that no deficit was too big, no hole too deep to climb out of, no situation too intimidating and no opponent too talented.

And, on top of all that, a mad scientist and his young apprentice—Gus Malzahn and Rhett Lashlee—who concocted the *don't-blink-your-eyes* offense that took this *"ten"* of a team and boosted it up to *"eleven"*—and so impressed everyone with their schemes that they have now returned to the Plains after a one-year absence as Auburn's new head coach and offensive coordinator.

Plenty has been said about this team. We even wrote a book about them—*Season of Our Dreams*. The point here, however, is to justify why they're ranked #1. We think the answer is simple: They closed the deal, got it done, brought home the big prize, and took us all on the greatest ride of our lives along the way. We will leave it to others to work out elaborate simulations comparing their performance to that of the 2004 or 1983 teams. For us, there's no debate. The 2010 National Champions are the greatest Auburn team in the Modern Era, and their glory will live forever in the hearts of the Auburn Family.

16

The Expectations Game:
Auburn "Season Quotient" Rankings

In this chapter we have taken each season of Auburn Football in the Modern Era and given what our Expectations were going in—what we feel we had realistically been led to believe would be the outcome (in total wins, including all post-season play) for that season, before it started. Then we look at how many wins the team actually achieved. We also award bonus points for bowl wins, conference titles, and national titles, beyond the number of total wins. So, for example, Auburn in 2010 won 14 games including two post-season wins. We award that team 14 total "win" points plus 3 "bonus" points for post-season success (1 bonus point for conference win, 1 for bowl win, and 1 for national title win), for a total of 17.

Of course this is all subjective in terms of "Expectations," but we've tried to be realistic and somewhat conservative. (For example, some fans were talking of "undefeated repeat season" going into 2005—but we were *not*.) You are welcome to use our same formula—or tweak it however you like—and calculate your own Season Quotients.

And yes, we're probably not using "quotient" exactly right here, but we're not mathematicians. You get the idea.

Again, the formula is total wins (*including post-season*) + 1 *bonus* point for a bowl win + 1 *bonus* point for an SEC Championship +1 *bonus* point for a national championship. So, yes, bowl wins and SEC Championship Game wins count as two total points—one point to the base score as a win, another point for it being a post-season win.

So here we go:

1981:
Expectations: 7
Reality: 5
Season Quotient: **-2**

1982:
Expectations: 7 +1 = 8
Reality: 9 +1 = 10
Season Quotient: **+2**

1983:
Expectations: 9 +1 = 10
Reality: 11 +1 +1 +1 = 14
Season Quotient: **+4**

In Pat Dye's opening trio of seasons, his teams increasingly exceeded expectations and raised the bar for Auburn football. But then his next two seasons fell somewhat flat:

1984:
Expectations: 11 +1 +1 = 13

Reality: 9 +1 = 10

Season Quotient: **-3**

1985:

Expectations: 10 +1 +1 = 12

Reality: 8

Season Quotient: **-4**

Following the 1985 season, Dye revamped the offense with a much greater emphasis on passing. The team then embarked on a four-year run of mostly positive results. There is no question the 1986-1989 seasons were spectacularly successful by any objective measurement, but remember—we are comparing pre-season expectations to actual results.

1986:

Expectations: 9 +1 = 10

Reality: 10 +1 = 11

Season Quotient: **+1**

Here we begin to see a period of extremely *good* Auburn teams—and a period of extremely high *expectations*.

1987:

Expectations: 9 + 1 +1 = 11

Reality: 10* + 1 +.5 = 11.5

Season Quotient: **+ 5**

We award 10 base "Reality" points for 1987 for 9 total wins plus two ties. 9 + .5 + .5 = 10. We then award another .5 for the bowl tie itself.

1988:

Expectations: 10 + 1 + 1 = 12

Reality: 10 + 1 = 11
Season Quotient: **-1**

It is fascinating to see the 1988 season result in a negative Season Quotient number. It speaks to just how lofty the expectations were, going into that season, and how disappointing it was to *just barely* miss out on playing Notre Dame for the national championship.

1989:
Expectations: 9 + 1 = 10
Reality: 10 + 1 + 1 = 12
Season Quotient: **+2**

The Tigers went into the 1990 season with some in the national media predicting a national championship. In retrospect, that was far too ambitious a goal for this squad, which had lost many of the star athletes from that terrific 1986-'89 run. We limited our expectations for this exercise to only ten wins plus a conference title and bowl win, but were still disappointed:

1990:
Expectations: 10 + 1 + 1 = 12
Reality: 8.5 +1 = 9.5
Season Quotient: **-2.5**

1991:
Expectations: 9 + 1 = 10
Reality: 5
Season Quotient: **-5**

This team was ranked 17th in the preseason but collapsed after a 3-0 start and won only 2 games the rest of the way.

1992:
Expectations: 8 + 1 = 9

Reality: 5.5
Season Quotient: **- 3.5**

This two-season slide (1991-'92) finished out the Pat Dye Era with a whimper rather than a bang, and probation soon followed. Thus our expectations the following year—Terry Bowden's first—were drastically reduced:

1993:

Expectations: 7
Reality: 11
Season Quotient: **+4***

1994:

Expectations: 10
Reality: 9.5
Season Quotient: **-0.5***

Note that, for 1993 and 1994, post-season play of any kind was disallowed by NCAA sanctions, limiting the possible numbers for Expectations and especially for Reality.

1995:

Expectations: 10 + 1 + 1 = 12
Reality: 8
Season Quotient: **-4**

Bowden loudly proclaimed that 1995 was the Tigers' first "AUthentic" opportunity to play for championships under his tutelage. Given his 20-1-1 start, expectations were fairly high going into that season, and one of the national sports magazines ranked Auburn second in the country in preseason. The eight-win campaign that followed was pretty disappointing.

1996:

Expectations: 9 + 1 = 10

Reality: 8 + 1 = 9
Season Quotient: **-1**

1997:
Expectations: 10 + 1 + 1 = 12
Reality: 10 + 1 = 11
Season Quotient: **-1**

Can a season in which the Tigers played for the SEC Championship be considered disappointing? Yes. Expectations were high in Dameyune Craig's senior year but, even with ten wins and a one-point loss to UT in Atlanta, there was a sense that we should have seen more from this team.

1998:
Expectations: 9 + 1 = 10
Reality: 3
Season Quotient: **-7**

Few truly saw what a precipitous cliff the Tigers were about to slide over, following the graduation of Dameyune Craig. His replacement at quarterback, Ben Leard, endured a horrible season, infamously beginning multiple games by throwing "pick-sixes." Bowden departed midway through the year.

1999:
Expectations: 7
Reality: 5
Season Quotient: **-2**

After a struggle to get his era started in 1999 (including at least two painful last-minute losses, either of which would've gotten the Tigers to a bowl game with a win), Tommy Tuberville found the missing piece of his offense—rugged RB Rudi Johnson—for 2000, and picked things up:

2000:

Expectations: 8 + 1 = 9

Reality: 9

Season Quotient: **0**

To be fair, 2000 probably should have resulted in a positive Quotient. The Tigers made it to the SEC Championship Game and to a good New Year's Day bowl. The problem for their numbers here: They lost both games.

2001:

Expectations: 9 + 1 = 10

Reality: 7

Season Quotient: **-3**

2002:

Expectations: 9 + 1 = 10

Reality: 9 + 1 = 10

Season Quotient: **0**

The 2000 season really was a "break-even" season, as the numbers indicate. Extremely narrow losses to Florida and Georgia were balanced out by nice wins over Alabama and Penn State.

2003:

Expectations: 11 + 1 + 1 +1 = 14

Reality: 8 +1 = 9

Season Quotient: **-5**

We have to be honest with 2003 and state that we expected a national championship run. Instead the offense imploded and the Tigers failed to even win a share of the SEC West.

2004:

Expectations: 10 +1 = 11

Reality: 13 +1 +1 +1 = 16
Season Quotient: **+5**

The 2004 season speaks for itself.

2005:
Expectations: 11 + 1 = 12
Reality: 9
Season Quotient: **-3**

Three losses, all virtually inexplicable, made this season of so much potential into a disappointment. Not starting Kenny Irons against Georgia Tech; missing five field goals in Baton Rouge; not showing up against Wisconsin in the bowl. But the wins over Georgia and Alabama were sweet indeed.

2006:
Expectations: 11 + 1 + 1 = 13
Reality: 11 + 1 = 12
Season Quotient: **-1**

The 2006 season counts as a mild disappointment only because the Tigers flirted with the upper reaches of the BCS rankings all year, only to have Arkansas prevent them from even getting to play in the SEC Championship Game.

2007:
Expectations: 10 + 1 = 11
Reality: 9 + 1 = 10
Season Quotient: **-1**

2008:
Expectations: 9 + 1 = 10
Reality: 5
Season Quotient: **-5**

What we see here in the second half of Tuberville's tenure is an Auburn team doing respectably well each year after the magical 2004 run, but never quite matching the raised level of expectations that came after that season. With 2008, it all fell apart and he was done. And then came Gene Chizik and Gus Malzahn:

2009:
Expectations: 7
Reality: 9 +1 = 10
Season Quotient: **+3**

And then came Cam Newton and a seemingly-transformed Nick Fairley:

2010:
Expectations: 9 +1 = 10
Reality: 14 +1 +1 +1 = 17
Season Quotient: **+7**

And then Cam and Nick left:

2011:
Expectations: 9 +1 = 10
Reality: 8 +1 = 9
Season Quotient: **-1**

And then Gus left:

2012:
Expectations: 9 +1 = 10
Reality: 3
Season Quotient: **-7**

It is interesting to note that 2012 was exactly as disappointing (-7) as 2010 was mind-blowing-ly surprising (+7).

Here now are the Top Ten Disappointing Seasons of the Modern Era (eleven actually, due to ties), based on our Season Quotient formula:

9. **1984 (-3)**
9. **2001 (-3)**
9. **2005 (-3)**
8. **1992 (-3.5)**
6. **1984 (-4)**
6. **1995 (-4)**
3. **1991 (-5)**
3. **2003 (-5)**
3. **2008 (-5)**
1. **1998 (-7)**
1. **2012 (-7)**

It's interesting to note that, as insanely wretchedly horrendous as 2012 was, it wasn't (in these mathematical terms) any more disappointing than the 1998 season.

It's also worth noting that Auburn hired a new head coach following each of the three "worst" years here, and very nearly did so after the fourth one (2003).

And, saving the best for last, here are what we consider to be the Top Ten Most Expectation-Exceeding Seasons of the Modern Era:

10. **2000 (0)**
10. **2002 (0)**
9. **1987 (+.5)**
8. **1986 (+1)**
6. **1982 (+2)**
6. **1989 (+2)**
5. **2009 (+3)**

3. 1983 (+4)
3. 1993 (+4)
2. 2004 (+5)
1. 2010 (+7)

What can we take from the fact that it required the inclusion of two "break even" seasons to round out the Top Ten in this category? Perhaps it says we have our expectations set a tiny bit too high, every season. It also reveals just how remarkable those super-special years truly are, when the team performs far above our expectations going in. We should truly savor them.

17

The History of Jordan-Hare Stadium

FOREWORD

Van originally wrote this history of the Auburn stadium as a "primary sources research paper" for Anthony Carey's History Research Methods course in 1996, while working on a History PhD at Auburn University. Years later, he posted it to his personal Web site for all to see, and over the years it has been linked to by Wikipedia and (reportedly) copied and used by the Auburn University tour guides. Van has occasionally added to it, as new developments occurred. Now we present a newly revised and updated edition of it here.

Van adds:

My first visit to Jordan-Hare came as a kid during the late 1970s, and I've enjoyed a love affair with the grand old edifice from the very start. I hope that love shows through in this chapter. I'm not able to get back to the Loveliest Village nearly as often as I'd like to, these days (my last visit was for the Iron Bowl in 2007), but I was in attendance for some important milestones in recent history, including the opening of the East Deck in 1987 (against Texas), the "First Time Ever" game in 1989 and the dedication of "Pat Dye Field" in 2005. I can't wait to visit again—though it's hardly "visiting" when you consider a place your true home.

Here's the story of that home.

INTRODUCTION

If football is truly a religion in the American South, then Jordan-Hare Stadium is a grand cathedral.

To this special place, the faithful roll in for games like pilgrims headed to Mecca. More than a simple sports arena, the structure holds a special place in the hearts of Auburn people, as the scene of some of the happiest memories of their lives. It indeed borders on a level of spirituality, the attachment of these people to this stadium.

Located in the heart of the campus, this grand edifice has grown along with the University around it, and today ranks among the top facilities of its kind in the nation. With nearly 90,000 in attendance on football Saturdays, the stadium ranked for many years as the fifth largest city in Alabama. (In the 2010 census, the entire city of Tuscaloosa's population was found to have crept just a hair above that of Jordan-Hare's capacity, moving the stadium to sixth-largest.)

Though the feelings elicited by the structure are clear, the reasons for its existence are somewhat more complex. How has a world-class sports arena, capable of holding so vast a population—larger than most NFL stadiums—sprouted up over the past sixty years on the plains of east Alabama? Fragments of the answer can be found in a number of places, including Atlanta, Montgomery, Columbus and Birmingham. Ultimately, however, the answer lies in the vision of a handful of men who, over the years, believed in the potential of

Auburn's football program, and who worked to bring the dream to fruition.

In 2014, Jordan-Hare Stadium will turn seventy-five years old. That fact alone makes it more than worthwhile to take a brief look back at the fascinating history of the construction and growth of this grand edifice.

I. BUILDING A DREAM: "LET'S PUT AUBURN ON THE MAP!"

Before 1939: Drill Field and Drake Field

Before the Tigers came to claim Jordan-Hare as their home, the teams played on two other on-campus fields. Both now lie under concrete, asphalt, and floral arrangements. In the shadows of the chemistry lab building between Samford Hall and Foy Union, which was at last check a park and a parking lot, Auburn hosted football games on what was called the "Drill Field" from 1892 until the 1920s. Abandoning this location, the Tigers moved to Drake Field— an area later to be paved over as part of the Haley Center parking lot, next to the original site of the Eagle's Cage and also near the women's dorms.

Athletic Director Emeritus Jeff Beard, a student at the time, helped assemble the temporary bleachers at Drake Field. "Each year bleachers were erected ten rows high on each side of the field." He recalled, "They held approximately 700 people, the seating capacity for our home games. We had one home game a year."

By the late 1930s, crowds were too large to be adequately accommodated in the temporary bleachers at this location, and Auburn found itself forced to play most of its games on the road, usually in Birmingham's Legion Field, Montgomery's Cramton Bowl, Mobile's Ladd Stadium, and Memorial Stadium in Columbus, Georgia. From this unhappy situation, with the team forced to play its "home games" far from home, came the seeds of the mighty edifice which now graces the Auburn campus.

As the decade of the 1930s drew to a close, Auburn's leaders understood they simply had to build a home stadium for their wandering team—a stadium with the capacity to attract at least some other schools and teams to come to the Plains. "There was a terrible need for a stadium...if we were going to compete with the rest of the schools in the Southern Conference," said Jeff Beard. "Coach Meagher realized something had to be done. He continued to improve the team and the schedule." Winning helped more than anything else: The team's success "began to give Auburn people the feeling that Auburn should have a home stadium to play in and that Auburn's facilities needed to be improved."

As early as 1934, the university's Physical Plant had considered building a "concrete stadium to put Auburn on the map," though with the lingering effects of the Depression, nothing had come of it. The money simply wasn't there. By 1937, the decision had been made to build, should the funds become available. Finally, they were. Moving to a third site, preparations were begun for the construction of a permanent facility: "Auburn Stadium." A young Jeff Beard, helping to survey the area, drove in the first stake to mark off the future stadium. Auburn has played on this site ever since.

By 1938, the economic situation had improved to the point that Auburn President Dr. L.N. Duncan could report the approval by PWA Secretary Ickes of "the most ambitious building program ever undertaken by the Alabama Polytechnic Institute." While much of this new construction would include non-athletic facilities, among items included in the $1,446,900 PWA-funded project was the construction of a $60,000 stadium unit, which included erection of concrete stands, engineering work to prepare the area, and completion of a modern track facility.

Engineering work was indeed needed at the new site. A meandering stream at the bottom of the valley had to be diverted and filled in. In addition, before a stadium and field could be built there, the previous tenants needed evicting. These inhabitants consisted of a herd of goats, belonging to the dean of the school of veterinary medicine, which grazed in the valley. These goats were reported to exhibited a severe nervous condition—one which would be duplicated by supporters of many visiting teams that came to play against Auburn over the years.   (Your intrepid Wishbone columnist has long wondered why Jordan-Hare never came to be nicknamed "Goat Valley," or something to that effect. Then again, we probably don't need yet another nickname to confuse the uninitiated.)

The original concrete grandstand, dubbed "Auburn Stadium," was designed by Arnold G. Wurz, who passed away in 1989, just weeks before the stadium's fiftieth anniversary celebrations. The name choice, "Auburn Stadium," is significant in that it reflects the tendency of all associated to refer to the team and school as "Auburn," even as far back as the 1930s. The school was actually designated Alabama Polytechnic Institute and did not officially become Auburn University until 1960.

1939: Auburn Stadium

By November of 1939, Coach Jack Meagher, who had coached the team on tiny Drake Field, at last had a stadium of his own, modest as it was. Having played Florida in a number of different cities over the previous years, the Gators seemed a good opponent with which to christen the new, 7,290-seat facility. "People wondered what we were going to do with that many people coming to town," Beard said. How would little Auburn, Alabama ever be able to accommodate a couple thousand Gators? Restrooms in particular were a concern, as the town itself had only two gas stations with public facilities at the time.

The field house—later transformed into the Geology building, Petrie Hall—was also under construction and not completed in time for the game. (If you've ever noticed the oddly symmetrical and perfectly perpendicular orientation of Petrie Hall to the north end zone of the stadium—something that puzzled me greatly while I was a student—now you know why.) Florida players were forced to dress in uniform in their hotel in Opelika before riding to the stadium. Incidents such as this over the years further complicated Auburn's efforts to move important games to the campus.

Auburn and Florida tied, 7-7. The staging of the game itself was a success. Those original 7,290 seats remain today as the lower half of the west stands. Only a year later 4,800 wooden bleachers were added to the east side, demonstrating the viability of a home field and dispelling the doubts of the naysayers. Auburn Stadium was open for business, and it seemed there was nowhere to go but up. And around!

II. THE EARLY YEARS

1949: Cliff Hare Stadium

Despite the stadium's success, only twelve home games were played there during the first decade of its existence, between 1939 and 1949, as Auburn continued to struggle to convince other teams to travel to East Alabama to play football.

"We began to play more important games at home," Beard recalled, but notes that most were still played at other sites. The main cause of this was a phenomenon that smaller programs still experience today. "The only advantage we had playing on the road had to do with financing. We could still make more money by playing in the bigger stadiums on the road."

To make matters worse, in the final three years of the decade, the team won only three games. For some programs, that would have marked the kiss of death—the program would have stagnated with poor play and a small facility mutually feeding upon one another and resulting in a second- or third-rate program overall. Fortunately, the Auburn Family was as devoted a bunch of fans then as they are now, and one that demanded the college field a quality team with a quality facility in which that team could play. Even in the lean times of the Forties, the seats had been filled. With such an obvious financial incentive, by the end of 1948, the time had come for expansion.

In a press release issued on New Year's Eve, 1948, the Board of Trustees of A.P.I. "authorized President Ralph Draughon to contract for the construction of 13,000 additional seats at the Auburn Stadium." The wooden bleachers on the east side were to be replaced with concrete seats and the west stands expanded to bring the total capacity to 21,500. The Board also voted to name the newly expanded facility "Cliff Hare Stadium."

Dr. Clifford Leroy Hare served as State Chemist and dean of the School of Chemistry and Pharmacy at A.P.I., as well as faculty chairman of athletics. He also played backup quarterback on Auburn's very first football team, in 1892. The caption in the 1934 Auburn-Georgia game program calls Cliff Hare "one of the most beloved characters connected with athletics in the South." He seemed the perfect choice for whom to name the stadium.

David Housel, writing in the 1973 *Auburn Football Illustrated*, tells of Shug Jordan's long afternoon talks with the aging Cliff Hare. "Fesser Hare told me how he and Dr. Sanford—for whom the stadium in Athens is named—used to come to Auburn every year after the Auburn-Georgia game in Columbus and divide the money. They would sit down in the Hare kitchen, take the money out of an old cigar box, and spread it across a marble table top and say, 'a dollar for you and a dollar for us' until the game proceeds were divided equally between the two schools." (One can only wonder how those two venerable professors would have reacted to today's world of gargantuan stadiums and zillion-dollar television contracts.) From these experiences, Hare saw the advantage of a larger stadium in Auburn at least as clearly as anyone else. He wanted it to happen. The Tigers simply needed to find the right coach to start winning ballgames.

Jordan's First Years: Success Breeds Growth

With the arrival of Coach Ralph "Shug" Jordan in 1951, the stadium's growth was assured. Quickly reversing the Tigers' football fortunes, Jordan took the team to two straight bowl appearances. Success on the field quickly led to financial success.

"In 1955 we had been to a couple of bowl games and we were feeling good," Beard states. "Coach Jordan was building a good program and we had some money jingling in our pockets so we decided to build the west stands up to fifty-four rows high."

The reasoning was actually a bit more complicated than that. The Board of Trustees, in a resolution dated April 29, 1955, gave a number of factors which weighed into the decision. The resolution stated:

"It appears more feasible, economical, and advantageous to plan the scheduling of more football games on a home-and-home basis...

"To accomplish this on a satisfactory basis it appears that approximately 30,000 stadium seats should be available at Cliff Hare Stadium, which would permit us to negotiate for games with almost every member of the Southeastern Conference...

"By having a stadium of proper capacity at Auburn and by scheduling more home-and-home games, we would benefit materially from stadium rental fees which we pay when playing away from Auburn..."

In addition, the resolution called for a new press box "to replace the existing temporary and inadequate press box section." Clearly, this matter was of some importance to the Board and the president. Draughon and Beard had come to realize that by playing at Auburn, they could save the money they were paying Columbus and other cities to rent out their stadiums. Draughon stated that the project would be "started as early as possible...in order to have facilities ready by the opening of the football season."

The resolution was adopted without dissent, although in a bow to the true mission of the college, a resolution adopted several weeks later took pains to note the expansion was actually "for the benefit of the college and the students in attendance thereat."

A memorandum from Beard to Draughon, dated June 3, 1955, shows that Batson-Cook Company of West Point, Georgia, won the contract to build the additions for $275,000.00. Beard remembers that the crews "walked off the job on the last day of August. The stadium was complete."

With the capacity of the stadium having reached 34,500, Auburn could host four home games in 1955: Chattanooga, Florida, Furman, and Mississippi State. (The Tigers won all four games, shutting out Florida and Furman, and would end the year with a regular season record of 8-1-1.) Playing and winning those four games at home, Beard said, "was a great feeling for those of us who were tired of traveling. Four games showed us what a great advantage it was to play at home." The commitment had at last been made to bring Auburn's opponents to the campus.

Even so, still none of the Tigers' major rivals (aside from Florida) would play in Auburn. No Alabama, No Georgia, no Tennessee, no Georgia Tech. Beard and Jordan next would turn their attention to this problem, with their focus falling first on Athens and on Bulldogs Coach Wally Butts.

III. BECOMING A COMPETITIVE ARENA: 1955-1970

Making Room for Georgia

The year 1957 saw Auburn climb to the very pinnacle of football success, going undefeated and winning the AP National Championship. Coach Jordan had demonstrated that the Tigers were a force to be reckoned with, and this gridiron success provided leverage in Auburn's negotiations with other schools.

The first to be persuaded to come was Georgia. "This was pretty hard to do because Coach Wally Butts loved to play in Columbus," Beard remembered. Auburn had played the Bulldogs there nearly every year since 1916, with the only exceptions being a couple of early games in Athens. "But we kept working on it until we got the game changed."

Georgia won the first game played back in Athens in 1959, ironically with a young Georgia guard named Pat Dye recovering a fumble to win the game for the Bulldogs. The next year's game would be played in Auburn, and Jordan and Beard realized they would need still more seats in the stadium.

The time had come to close in one of the end zones, connecting the two stands at one end. A memorandum from L. E. Funchess, Director of the Campus Planning Committee, to Beard, dated March 3, 1960, reports approval of the plan to close in the south end zone, at a cost of nearly a half-million dollars. The bleacher seats which had stood there were moved to the north end, providing still more seats. (The north end would otherwise remain open, allowing access to the field house that would become Petrie Hall.) A large scoreboard replaced the previous one which had been built by an engineering class years earlier. In addition, dressing rooms were built under the new stands.

An overall plan for the stadium's development began to take shape with the 1960 expansion. The sidelines stands had been built into hillsides, so the closing of the end zones would have blocked air circulation within the stadium. To remedy this, risers were left out of the lower seats in the south end zone. This, along with construction of a continuous interior concourse, was modeled on the Rice Stadium in Texas. (It's hard to imagine today that Auburn modeled its premiere athletic facility after something the Rice Owls had built first.) The single-level, continuous concourse allowed direct access for first aid vehicles and transports to any point within the stadium, and also made it easier for attendees to move about the stadium and to and from their seats.

The project was a success. The Georgia game sold out quickly (with Auburn winning this time, 9-6), and both Georgia and Auburn officials were pleased with the results of their new arrangement. The city of Columbus, however, felt betrayed by the move—an attitude that would be repeated by some of the leaders of the city of Birmingham nearly thirty years later.

Horseshoe to Bowl

Winning seasons and bowl invitations continued through the 1960s, and thoughts quickly turned to another expansion. Beard summed up the feelings of Auburn's leaders at the time: "Adding...seats had enabled us to have a representative home schedule and collect the stadium rental that would be so vital to the future of the program." With this in mind, and in view of the continued sellouts in the horseshoe-shaped Cliff Hare Stadium of the 1960s, plans moved forward for the complete enclosure of the stadium by 1970.

The Board of Trustees, on October 25, 1968, unanimously approved a proposal to begin study for again enlarging Cliff Hare Stadium, "due to the continued increase in student enrollments and the demand for football tickets at home games in Auburn." The Board went to great lengths to specify that this was contingent on acquisition of funding, which must not come from the school's general funds.

The Board agreed by June of 1969 that "it appears necessary and advisable to enlarge the capacity of Cliff Hare Stadium, enlarge the present press box facilities, and construct a new running track facility." The resolution also called for modification and enlargement of the dressing facilities.

The south end zone construction in 1960 had produced an unintended consequence: It had obscured from view part of the fine running track which had surrounded the playing field—a development that saddened Auburn's track coach, Wilbur Hutsell. The coach feared visiting track teams might hide fresh runners under the stands, where no one could see them, to sneak in during a race. With the track removed due to stadium expansion, a new, stand-alone track was built in a different location to take its place, and it would be named in Hutsell's honor. (The existence of a running track surrounding the field also explains why Jordan-Hare's stands are so much further back from the sidelines than are stands in many other football stadiums. Compare that layout to, say, Florida Field.)

The June 1969 resolution noted that an act had been passed in the first special session of the 1969 state legislature "to permit such construction and to make provisions for the financing of same." With the money no longer a major concern, plans moved ahead quickly. In the mean time, the Board's Naming of Buildings Committee recommended that the former field house, which would be sealed off from the stadium by the north stands enclosure and which was being renovated for classroom and lab use, be named for the late Dean George Petrie, who had connections with both the sciences and athletics at Auburn.

The Monsanto Company, on March 24, 1969, proposed in a memo to Coach Beard the installation of AstroTurf in Jordan-Hare. Their letter lists the cost of covering Auburn's playing field in artificial turf at $212,500.00. Turf had become popular among colleges in the late 1960s—nearly everyone was doing it, including the University of Alabama. Despite consideration, however, Beard and Jordan rejected the idea. They had misgivings about the safety of the artificial surface. "It turned out that we were right," Beard says. Auburn never went to fake turf, and eventually most schools switched back to natural grass—at least until the most modern and safe artificial surfaces came along in the 1990s and 2000s.

Expansion plans were finalized at a Board meeting on November 22, 1969. The Trustees were clearly enthusiastic about Auburn football: "Dr. Philpott (the university president) reviewed several details concerning Auburn's invitation to play the University of Houston in the Astro-Bluebonnet Bowl on December 31, 1969." When Philpott noted the presence of Coach Jordan and Coach Beard, the Trustees broke out in wild applause. The Board unanimously approved a nineteen year bond issue to finance the north stands construction, and then gathered around Dr. Philpott to look at an artist's conception of the finished stadium.

Auburn added an additional detail to the north end zone enclosure, one that made school officials proud. "It was something that had not been done in any of the stadiums we played in," Beard says. "We made provisions for wheelchairs and handicapped spectators. This really attracted a lot of attention in the state."

The final cost of the addition, including the relocation of Hutsell Track to its new location, was just over one and a quarter million dollars. Tiny Cliff Hare Stadium, formerly only a single set of concrete bleachers, had grown into a full-fledged bowl, and the time had come to honor the coach whose success enabled the growth to occur.

"Today's game will be Auburn's first SEC game in newly-named Jordan-Hare Stadium, which was dedicated in pre-game ceremonies." So wrote Buddy Davidson in the official program for the Ole Miss game of 1973. The honor recognized "Jordan's lasting contributions to Auburn football." Auburn's stadium had become the first in the nation to be named for an active coach. Jordan would coach the remainder of that season and two more before retiring after the 1975 season.

Writing in the program for the dedication game in 1973, David Housel, Sports Information Director and later Athletics Director, reflected back on the competitive advantage Auburn had gained with its fine home stadium. He called the newly-christened Jordan-Hare Stadium "perhaps the hardest place in the country for a visiting football team to win. Bar none." He supported this bold statement with a little history: While the facility was known as Auburn Stadium, from 1939 to 1949, Auburn did not lose a single game of its twelve played there (with two ties.) During the Cliff Hare Stadium period, from 1949 to 1973, Auburn posted a record of 80-13-1, which included a run of thirty straight wins at home (with thirteen shutouts). Housel pointed out that many of those wins came against such powers as Georgia, Florida, and Georgia Tech. Auburn would enjoy a similar run during the 1980s under Coach Pat Dye, and again from the mid-1990s-on under Coaches Terry Bowden, Tommy Tuberville and Gene Chizik.

Housel also wrote of the monetary advantage for visitors playing in Jordan-Hare. Now the shoe was on the other foot—teams wanted to play in Auburn because they could make more money doing so than they could by playing the Tigers at home.

He described Jordan-Hare as "an extremely popular place to play football" in the South, despite Auburn's considerable home field advantage. "The reason," he explains, "is money, the greenstuff without which an athletic program cannot function." With a tremendous season ticket base and consistently large crowds, even the smallest visiting school enjoys a healthy payday, "one of the largest in the United States," according to Housel.

IV. JORDAN-HARE: FIFTH-LARGEST CITY IN ALABAMA

1980: The West Deck

Despite a slight decline in on-field fortunes during the 1970s, two more rivals, Georgia Tech (1970) and Tennessee (1974), finally made the trip to the Plains. Auburn had played its home game with each of them in Birmingham's Legion Field for a number of years, a situation used by Alabama to argue that Legion Field was a "neutral site" for the Auburn-Alabama game, since Auburn already played occasional games there.

Jordan-Hare was an unqualified success, selling out despite a dearth of championships and Sugar Bowl trips during the 1960s and 1970s. With six home games a year by 1970 and revenues increasing, thoughts once again turned to expansion. An upper deck would be added to the west stands by 1980, credited by the Auburn Media Guide as due to the exploits of players such as James Brooks and Joe Cribbs. For whatever reason, the stadium's success despite the Tigers' mediocrity and probation during the late 1970s proves that Auburn had finally come into its own.

The Trustees of 1977 were slightly less enthusiastic over the prospect of expansion than their counterparts of earlier years had been. When Coach Lee Hayley, Chairman of the Stadium Expansion Committee, presented the recommendation of the committee for an upper deck and electric lighting for night games to be installed, "a lengthy discussion ensued." Finally, Coach Jordan, who by now served as a Board member, motioned for a vote, and the Board authorized preliminary working plans by a majority of only six to three. The days of instant unanimous votes for stadium growth had ended.

The Board discussed the possibility of authorizing the president to develop a bond plan for funding the additions on June 5, 1978. Once again Coach Jordan motioned for a vote, and the Board approved the measure, eight to one. The matter came to a head on November 29, 1978. Once again, Coach Jordan asked for a vote of the Trustees, and by a margin of only four to three, the Board authorized the expansion. The resolution stated that expansion and lighting of the stadium were "felt to be in the best interest for a quality athletic program at Auburn University." The resolution went on to defend its position on the grounds that the move was "recommended by a special committee," and had obtained the approval of the Auburn Alumni Executive Committee. Approval at last obtained, construction began before the year was out.

The *Auburn Bulletin* reported specifics on the new addition in late 1979. The completed stadium would hold over 72,000 people, with the additions coming in at a cost of approximately $7 million. The new West Deck towered 150 feet above the field and projected twenty feet out over Donahue Drive. The article describes the West Deck's combination of press and television area, president's and athletic director's boxes, concession and reception areas, and a deck of over 10,000 new seats. Light stands were incorporated into the West Deck while three light towers stood 140 feet over the east stands. These three towers would stand only seven years before making way for the East Deck.

The lights would not be used until Auburn's first night game, September 19, 1981, against Wake Forest. The stadium itself, however, opened in renovated form to begin the 1980 season and was an immediate success.

1987: The East Deck

Soon after the West Deck was completed, Auburn hired a new head football coach and athletic director: Patrick Fain Dye. A tough competitor who had coached at Alabama under "Bear" Bryant and played at Georgia under Wally Butts, Dye understood the importance of making Auburn's home game with Alabama a true home game.

Jordan-Hare Stadium, though at this point holding over 72,000 fans, still trailed Birmingham's Legion Field in capacity. Dye knew that a stadium larger than Alabama's would be a lever with which he could move the heretofore intransigent Tide. Almost immediately after taking the reins at Auburn, he set out to make that goal a reality.

In late 1984, with a feasibility study completed, Dye's proposal came before the Board. Though the West Deck had only been completed four years earlier, the Trustees voted (with no totals listed) to establish a budget of not more than $15 million for the project, with none of the funds to come from "the general fund, student fees, nor the full faith and credit of Auburn University." The resolution specifically mentions Dye's recommendation, as well as the demand for additional seats in the stadium.

On July 2, 1985, the Board met in a special called meeting in Foy Union, on the Auburn campus, with much of the administration and the media present, in order to clarify the financial aspects of the expansion. The new resolution pledged funds from revenue-generating sports, executive suite revenue, other concessions, and a portion of student fees to underwrite the stadium bond issue. On September 20, by a vote of eight to one, the Board approved issuance of $30,115,000 in bonds.

Clearly the Alabama game figured prominently in the actions of the Trustees as well as in those of Dye. On December 21, 1985, (significantly only days after Alabama had defeated Auburn on a last-second field goal, in Birmingham, and on an Auburn "home" year,) the Board voted unanimously to "endorse the recommendation of the Athletic Director [Dye] and the President of Auburn University and instructs that a contract be negotiated with the University of Alabama to have the Alabama game played in Auburn's Jordan-Hare Stadium when Auburn University is the home team." The resolution specifically pointed out the planned increase in seating capacity of Jordan-Hare, and declared that "it is in the best interest of Auburn University to play this game in Jordan-Hare Stadium." The Trustees had taken the step of resolving the game site a vital matter to the University itself, in effect firing a warning shot over Alabama's bow that Auburn was determined to resolve the matter, once and for all.

With the posturing and paperwork complete, construction of an east upper deck began. This expansion also saw installation of a mammoth new scoreboard, complete with animated display screen and massive public address system, over the south stands. Jordan-Hare, one of the few stadiums in the country with absolutely no interior advertising at that time and for years afterward, would not allow a scoreboard which contained advertising. The Coca-Cola Company proposed in 1985 to erect the new scoreboard, free of any advertising, for $1 million. Coca-Cola made the offer contingent on the right to sole distribution of Coke products in the stadium for the next ten years. The Board agreed.

The eighth expansion, this construction would bring the stadium's capacity to 85,214. In addition to the deck of seats, more than a thousand scholarship donor seats and seventy-one luxury executive suites were built.

Those skyboxes, expected to be leased by corporations entertaining clients, would figure significantly in the funding of the expansion. Sixty-five of them held twelve persons and rented (in 1987) for $24,000 a season. Four held eighteen guests and rented for $36,000 per year. One held thirty people and rented for $48,000 a year. The University used the seventy-first. The suites were carpeted, with theater seats, a kitchenette, bathrooms, heat and air conditioning, and a closed-circuit television. Food and alcoholic beverages were available in the suites as well (though alcohol was prohibited anywhere else in the stadium).

In addition to the suites and a new section for high school recruits, former Associate Athletic Director Oval Jaynes saw other benefits to the 1987 expansion: "[It] will allow Auburn to move ahead with its scholarship donor program. Last season 160 scholarship donors had to sit in the stands rather than in the special section on both sides of the press box." Jaynes noted that the scholarship program was nearly deemphasized in the early 1980s because many new donors, who were giving $3,000 a year, could not be guaranteed sideline seats. Room had existed for them within the stadium, but older season ticket holders would have had to be relocated to the end zones. This would not have been a popular move.

Pat Dye called the East Deck "the most positive step we have taken for our total athletic program since we've been at Auburn." He went on to predict that the new income would benefit all aspects of athletics at Auburn, as well as providing much-needed seats for scholarship donors. "It will also give us room to grow in the future. This is the result of four years of coming together by the entire Auburn family, students, faculty, alumni and friends."

The East and West Decks were indeed designed with future growth in mind; they could have been connected at either end (or both) to create a second "bowl" of seats, similar to the layout of fully expanded Neyland Stadium in Knoxville. Given the width of Auburn's stadium, however, a double-ringed design would have given Jordan-Hare a larger capacity even than mighty Neyland.

The Auburn Tigers kicked off the 1987 season in newly-expanded Jordan-Hare Stadium against the University of Texas, who had been added to the schedule prior to the season in order to provide a "name" opponent for the opener. Over 80,000 fans filled the stadium (including this intrepid columnist), the largest crowd ever to witness a football game in the state of Alabama at that time. (Auburn utterly dominated the Longhorns and won, 31-3). By the end of the season, the stadium had been nearly filled twice, in games against Florida and Florida State.

The next season, against Georgia, Jordan-Hare sold out. Even so, one matter remained to be settled. The Alabama Crimson Tide had to play in Auburn.

On December 2, 1984, Auburn's Sports Information Department had issued a press release first announcing the expansion of the stadium. Dye's unannounced goal, even before then, was to bring Alabama to Auburn to play. Five years to the day after that announcement, he would have his wish.

V. THE LAST BRICK IN OUR HOUSE

1989: First Time Ever

The Florida game at Auburn late in the 1989 season featured the commemoration of Jordan-Hare's fiftieth anniversary. Florida was chosen because it had been the very first opponent, way back in 1939, to play in Auburn Stadium. (At halftime, the two players who scored Auburn's first touchdown in that game re-enacted their feat with a touchdown pass.) The Tigers went on to win that game in dramatic (and remarkably similar)fashion with a last-second touchdown pass from Reggie Slack to Shane Wasden. In any other year, this might have been the premiere event of the season. But another game that year attracted much more attention from all concerned. On December 2, Alabama would be coming to Auburn.

By the late 1980s, with all of Auburn's other opponents now playing in Auburn, Alabama's longstanding argument that Legion Field represented a "neutral site" had lost much of its grounding. No longer a second home for the Tigers, as it still was for the Tide, Legion Field only served as a home field for Auburn once every two years. Even then, the tickets were split down the middle, with half to Auburn and half to Alabama. The only real sign that it was a home game for Auburn was the fact that on odd years the Tigers wore blue jerseys.

Jordan-Hare Stadium was now the largest football facility in the state, and the Tide could no longer deny the truth: They must play the Tigers in Auburn. A change of coaches and athletic directors in Tuscaloosa in 1987 smoothed the way, but the move had at this point become inevitable. Former Tide Coach Ray Perkins had said, "It won't happen," shortly before leaving the Capstone for Tampa Bay in 1986. A scant year later, on paper at least, it happened.

The move would be incremental, with 1987 seeing the last of the fifty-fifty split of tickets at Legion Field as Auburn was the home team. The next year would be a true Alabama home game in the stadium that had always been home to them anyway, and they kept most of the tickets for themselves. At last, in December of 1989, Auburn's nemesis, the Crimson Tide, finally visited Jordan-Hare Stadium, in a game that quickly became known simply as "First Time Ever." The fact that Auburn won the game—knocking off a second-ranked and undefeated Crimson Tide in the process—almost takes a backseat to the fact that it was played there at all.

It was an event unlike any before on the Plains. Pat Dye, referring to the completion of the second upper deck two years earlier and the subsequent capitulation of Alabama to agree to come to Auburn, called that day, "the last brick in our house." The task was completed. Auburn finally hosted *all* of its home football games. As one observer put it, this was "the story of how a people and a football program wandered across the Southeast in search of a home, and how they came to find that home."

The Tide had one final degradation in store for their rivals before they would agree to come to the Plains in 1989. They insisted that although the 1989 game could be played in Auburn, the following Tigers home game (in 1991) would have to be played back in Birmingham. Exhausted with the bickering, Auburn agreed, simply to put the matter to rest. Thus in 1991, Auburn came to decorate Alabama's beloved Legion Field in orange and blue, or as close to it as the Tide-oriented electronics on the scoreboard could come. A giant AU was painted on the cheap AstroTurf at midfield, a pale mockery of the one gracing the lush grass of Jordan-Hare. Alabama won the game, but Auburn fans almost didn't care. It was over. Legion Field was history; from then on it would be just another place to visit—and *that* not for very much longer.

VI: FURTHER EXPANSION

Jordan-Hare's story has been one of constant growth and expansion from the beginning. And yet, in all the years following the 1987 expansion with the East Deck and related facilities, only slight and mostly cosmetic upgrades have been undertaken.

Until the 1990s, the stadium averaged an expansion every eight years, eventually ranking among the top ten on-campus facilities of its kind. In 1990, for the second year in a row, Auburn sold all 75,000 season ticket books and turned away still more applicants. At that time, ticket manager Bill Beckwith envisioned the addition of more enclosed and air-conditioned club level seats, which would sell for more than $2,000 apiece, in the south end zone. "The revenue from those additional club level seats could be used to fund future construction of an upper deck in the *south* end zone to handle the overflow of students and demand for regular tickets." With student ticket purchases up by 4,000 between 1985 and 1989, demand for seats was seen as continuously rising.

Importantly, the 1990 sellout was achieved without the added "hook" of a home Alabama game, as there had been for the first time in 1989. Beckwith found this aspect "particularly gratifying." For many years, officials and supporters of the University of Alabama had claimed Auburn was incapable of supporting a major football program without the draw of playing Alabama every year. Many felt Jordan-Hare would fall far short of selling out its many seats on years without a visit by the Crimson Tide. Consistent sellouts in the years after 1989 served as evidence that Auburn football had become a tremendous draw in its own right. "We have reached the point where we no longer need something like the Alabama game to help us sell out," Beckwith said at the time. "We've gone up to a higher level. Auburn football is selling itself."

1996: The World's Largest Classroom: Dr. Kicklighter Fulfills a Dream (or a least an idle fancy)

On June 3, 1996, squirrels knocked out Auburn's campus electricity (they were forever getting into the transformers and blowing them up), just as Dr. Joseph Kicklighter prepared to administer final exams for his freshman history class. As he later put it, he was "fulfilling my lifelong fantasy to teach in the stadium" when he led his 325 students out of their darkened classroom and across the street. There, in the bright sunshine, he turned Jordan-Hare Stadium into the world's largest classroom.

1998: Murals, Upgrades and Ads

As part of an overall stadium upgrade prior to the start of the 1998 season, and in conjunction with upgrades to Plainsman Park (the baseball facility), the long ban on interior advertising gave way to a "corporate sponsorship package" that included a variety of ads for companies such as Alabama Power and HealthSouth. During this time, the concourses were somewhat upgraded, including the addition of small televisions overhead along the walkway, and the interior of the stadium experienced a new paint job. (Fortunately, this paint job was carried off more successfully than the one back in the early 1990s, done on a very windy day, and resulting in many cars all across campus—including mine!—being covered in a thin film of gray paint!)

The 1998 overhaul also included the addition of a big-screen television to the scoreboard (all the big programs were adding them that year), within an attractive display filling nearly the entire width above the South Stands. The display included pictures of past Auburn greats such as Bo Jackson, Tracy Rocker, Pat Sullivan, and Pat Dye, above featured advertisers' logos. The stadium's sound system enjoyed an upgrade that year, too—a custom-built, computer-driven system that filled a small room and was capable of directing roughly the same level of sound to any point within the stadium (though admittedly, at times, it fluctuated due to wind conditions and computer readjustments).

Ten giant (eleven by twenty-nine foot) black-and-white murals covering Auburn's football history to that point, by artist Michael Taylor, were also added to the exterior of the East Stands that year.

2001: Reconfiguring the Locker Rooms and Restoring the End Zones

The capacity of Jordan-Hare Stadium actually increased by a relatively small amount, to 86,063, prior to the 2001 season, as Coach Tommy Tuberville ordered the locker rooms to be reconfigured. This operation moved the visitors' locker room from underneath the South Stands to a new location in the northeast corner, giving the visitors a new tunnel from which to emerge onto the field. The home locker room was dramatically upgraded and expanded, and a new tunnel was added, allowing Auburn's team to come onto the field from the center of the South Stands. A giant "AU" logo in the center of the home locker room floor was declared off-limits to foot traffic by that year's seniors, and was roped off.

2002-Present: A North Upper Deck, or What?

The plan assembled during the Dye years had called for the eventual enclosure of each end of the stadium by connecting the Upper East and Upper West decks across the end zones. Had this been done, Jordan-Hare would surely have surpassed even Neyland Stadium in Knoxville in capacity, given the wider distance between the decks in Auburn. The University came very close during the 1990s to enclosing the south end in this manner, which would have taken the capacity to 91,714, making it the fourth-largest stadium in the country at that time, but for various reasons this never came to fruition.

A study after the 2002 season, however, revealed that scholarship seating and additional skyboxes were the real items in demand, not more general seating. In response, Auburn prepared new plans to build a free-standing smaller deck and skybox enclosure above the North Stands within the next couple of years, in a configuration similar to what Florida added to Ben Hill Griffin Stadium during the 1990s. This addition would have taken Jordan-Hare's capacity closer to 90,000, though probably not much over that total. (The section numbers 62-99 had been saved for any newly-constructed seating in that manner.)

At the end of the 2004 season, work began on a compromise solution to the need for more skyboxes. The existing East Deck was expanded slightly, lengthening it at each end. This provided more space underneath for additional skyboxes, while also adding a relatively modest number of general (open air) seats above. The stadium's capacity following this modest project reached 87,451.

Between the 2006 and 2007 seasons, a major renovation of the walkways and related facilities underneath the stadium was set to overhaul the appearance and capacity of the pedestrian areas. A major portion of this project included the addition of many new, and much-needed, women's restrooms.

Before the 2007 season, a massive, $2.9 million, thirty-by-seventy-four foot high definition video display replaced the existing large scoreboard above the south stands. Jordan-Hare thus became the first SEC stadium to feature an HD video display and the second in all of the NCAA after Texas.

At the Alabama game at the end of the 2007 season, the field itself was named in honor of former Head Football Coach Pat Dye— the man most responsible for bringing the Alabama game to Auburn on a permanent basis.

Following the 2010 National Championship season, Coach Gene Chizik and Athletics Director Jay Jacobs had the stadium's external decorations renovated to reflect Auburn's various football achievements, including conference and national titles and Heisman and other individual trophy winners.

The issue of possible further major expansions to the stadium remained an open question.

CONCLUSION

The evidence shows the main motivation for expanding the stadium over the years has been to persuade larger or more prestigious schools to come to Auburn to play Auburn's home games. This in turn increased Auburn's prestige and share of the profits. Unfortunately, accomplishing this was never easy. Visitors such as Georgia and Tennessee and especially Alabama much preferred to play at nearby neutral sites, especially if as many or more seats were available there.

To bring the teams to Auburn, the stadium was expanded. To secure the Alabama game, Pat Dye virtually forced through a second deck only seven years after the first was added. Eventually all of the teams, even the Crimson Tide, could no longer refuse to come. All of their excuses had evaporated.

Yet even as Auburn's stadium grew to a size competitive with the others, Auburn still needed fans buying tickets and sitting in the seats. Anyone can build a large stadium only to have it stand half-empty on game day. Auburn built a large stadium to attract big home games, but for the program to be successful, the seats had to be filled. To fill the stadium, the team's success on the field became a priority.

The Tigers have indeed been successful on the field, winning conference and national titles and many individual honors. The one factor has fed the other. The teams have been competitive, the fans have come, and the stadium has grown.

SOURCES

This history of Jordan-Hare Stadium was originally written as part of my coursework in Auburn's History PhD program, back in 1996. Most of the research involved sifting through boxes of original items (primary sources) held by the Auburn University Archives at Ralph B. Draughon Library.*   Additional information has been added over the years.   Sources consulted for this project are listed in the Appendix to this book.

* At the same time I was in the Archives room, digging through old press clippings and game programs, the great Auburn Journalism prof, Jack Simms, was seated at the next table over, preparing his wonderful *Auburn: A Pictorial History of the Loveliest Village*. Talk about inspiration!

18

The Gus Bus and Beyond:
The Future of Auburn Football

The future of Auburn football rests on the firm foundation provided by the past—by the glorious accomplishments of the Modern Era and the equally resonant achievements of players and coaches stretching back across the breadth of the Twentieth Century and even into the Nineteenth. For most of this book, we have explored that rich modern history; now we look ahead to the *future* of Auburn Football, in a conversation between the authors.

What are the biggest challenges Auburn Football faces in next five to ten years?

John: Rebuilding the toughness and physicality on defense that was a trademark of Auburn in the 1980s and in the early 2000s. Auburn's defense must become stronger, mentally and physically tougher, more disciplined and more talented. Some of this change will come from new players entering the program. Some of it will come from new coaches pushing the new and returning players.

And some will come from the returning players changing their bodies and improving how they play the game.

Over the last two years the Auburn defense has become a shell of the proud units that once wore that same uniform. Auburn gave up more yards, first downs and points in 2011 and 2012 than in any other two seasons in the school's history. The number one way to improve that is by getting tougher and more physical – but it is a major challenge and won't be easy.

How bad is it? The Auburn defense has been on a downward trend for nine years since the magical 2004 season. The defense has allowed more yards and yards per play each year – leading to the last two seasons when Auburn allowed 5.73 yards per play (2011) and 5.99 yards per play (2012). So in 2012 the opponent was able to average *six yards per play* every time they snapped the ball.

Yes, defensive statistics across college football have gotten worse as offenses have gotten better. But we know that Auburn cannot be an SEC contender with that kind of defensive futility.

Van: It's hard to argue with that. Even in an era of super-duper offenses, defenses still win championships. Even in 2010, when *offense* led the way to our national championship, we still needed Nick Fairley and company on the other side of the ball, to keep the score within reach of that super-offense every single week.

Another challenge Auburn faces is the problem of public perceptions. Most Auburn people know all too well that the national media are not terribly fond of our program to begin with; they've always been quick to believe any bad thing that comes along, no matter how far-fetched or ridiculous it might be. That phenomenon reached a crescendo with the BCS National Championship season in 2010: At the heights of our glory and national prominence, the Cam Newton "pay for play" rumors exploded and virtually the entire rest of the country instantly declared Auburn "guilty." Many confidently predicted that Auburn's hard-won title would always carry an "asterisk" and that it was only a matter of weeks, perhaps even days, until the championship would be stripped. If only the NCAA's unprecedented announcement, many months later, that neither Cam nor Auburn had done anything wrong had received a thousandth of the publicity the original, false allegations were given.

In retrospect it seems obvious that Gene Chizik believed nothing but positives—overwhelming positives—would result for Auburn from that 2010 season. He clearly thought he could use it to sell the program to the nation's elite players who wouldn't have considered Auburn before, and that he could use that leverage to completely change the personality of the offense and be given the time to make it work (if it ever would have). He also believed he could challenge Alabama at their own game—at playing a pro-style offense and recruiting the top players in the state—and go toe-to-toe with them and win, or at least break even. It didn't work. One (generally acknowledged) national championship in fifty-three years is not enough, as it turns out, to put our program on a par in the nation's perceptions with a team across the state that has won (at current count) the other three titles in the last four years. Which brings us to the big red elephants in the room...

John: Yes. Auburn finds itself in the situation of needing to improve its program and return to greatness at the same time Alabama is in a position of dominance. Historically it is has been easier for Auburn to rise to the highest levels when Alabama was down or having problems. But now Auburn must compete for in-state recruits with the team that is winning national titles and churning out first round draft picks. No other school in the nation faces the kind of in-state challenge that Auburn faces.

Van: The good news, at least from Auburn's current viewpoint, is that dominance in the Iron Bowl series never remains with just one side for terribly long. Auburn has risen to the challenge of a dominant coach in Tuscaloosa winning multiple national titles before, and will do so again. Is Gus Malzahn the coach to get that done? You and I think so; time will tell if we are correct.

Where do you see the football program in five or ten years?

John: Associated Press report from January 12, 2020: Coach Gus Malzahn and the Auburn Tigers have completed an amazing journey that began when Malzahn took over the program following the worst season in Auburn history. And tonight the Tigers came all the way back from that historical low to win the program's latest national championship. "I always knew that we could get it done here," claimed an excited Malzhan after the game. "We've had some good seasons since I have been at Auburn — winning the conference in 2016 was huge. But this year it all came together with a very special team." Auburn's 2020 squad broke the all-time scoring record in college football for points in a season and shredded SEC defenses on the way to the eight-team college football playoff. With the retirement of Nick Saban in 2017 after losing to Auburn in his final three seasons, Auburn has fully eclipsed Alabama as the dominant team in the SEC and as a perennial national title contender. "When I look back over my time at Auburn leading up to this victory," Malzahn said, "it all began with that 2013 team. They weren't the greatest team in Auburn history but they played their guts out and fought hard to the end in every game and I know that the fans and I will always remember them as the team that laid the foundation for all our future success…"

Van: (Sniffling) Excuse me, but I have to wipe away a little tear of happiness from that. Well done.

During what would turn out to be Gene Chizik's final season, 2012, I was experiencing deep doubts about the future of our program. After all, here was a coach who had led us to a national championship in his second season on the Plains, who had turned in acceptable 8-win campaigns on either side of it, and who was bringing in a number of allegedly big-time recruits every season. And despite all that, it was obvious to everyone that the program was in disarray, disintegrating before our eyes, and that the team itself was going nowhere fast. Nowhere, that is, but down—downhill with no brakes, no steering wheel, and no real prospects for turning things around. (Chizik's final record as Auburn's head coach was 33-19, for a .635 winning percentage. Remarkably, however, without the 2010 season, his record was 19-19, and in his final two seasons, it was a dismal 11-14.)

Bringing in Gus Malzahn has provided a tremendous boost to the morale of the Auburn Family. He's likeable, he won a conference title during his one season at Arkansas State before returning to Auburn, and (rightly or wrongly) he's widely viewed as being much more responsible for the successes of 2010 than Gene Chizik. The fact that Auburn fired Chizik and immediately hired Malzahn speaks volumes about that last point. The powers-that-be couldn't have made it clearer if they'd publicly stated, "We blame Chizik for the bad stuff and credit Gus for the good stuff over the last four years."

Whether Malzahn ultimately will be successful in bringing championships to Auburn—or even wins over our major rivals in the conference—we cannot yet say. There's no question, though, that his arrival has provided a spark and a ray of hope. By cleaning house entirely in terms of assistant coaches and support staff—by doing what you and I said should be done by the next coach, which was washing the Football Complex out and fumigating the place— he's given everyone reason to believe the future will be different from the immediate past. There's also something to be said for being "the new guy." If Auburn's coach in 2013 was Chizik for another year, his leash would be very short and the pressure on him would be intense to improve the team's performance and to improve it dramatically. With Gus, as a brand new head coach with a new staff in place, he has a great deal more room to maneuver. The pressure won't be nearly as intense; he merely needs to show the program is going in the right direction, and it could hardly go in a more *wrong* direction than it was last year. He will be seen as the potential solution to the problem, rather than its cause, and will be given multiple seasons to get things going.

Unless something remarkably unexpected happens—either the team actually performs worse in 2013 than it did in 2012 (which seems impossible), or Gus immediately wins three national championships in his first three seasons—I expect him to still be the head coach in five years. In that time, I expect that Auburn will have returned to Atlanta at least once, and perhaps two or three times (though that may be too much to expect from any team not coached by Nick Saban in this day and age of seven-team divisions and Western Division play). I fully expect that the Tigers will have appeared in a bowl game every season of his tenure, though he may need some luck in 2013, given the state of the program as he found it, and the strength of the schedule.

Whether Gus will still be at Auburn in ten years is a tough call to make, this early, regardless of his success or failure. Roughly every other Auburn coach in recent years has made it that long. Shug Jordan? Yes. Doug Barfield? No. Pat Dye? Yes. Terry Bowden? No. Tommy Tuberville? Yes—exactly ten. Gene Chizik? No.

Let's put it this way: If Gus Malzahn is still Auburn's head coach for the 2022 season, it will mean he has been at least as successful as Tommy Tuberville—and I think just about any Auburn person would be happy with that result.

What do you see happening with Jordan-Hare Stadium in the next five to ten years?

John: The lesson of what is happening at the University of Tennessee is an important one for Auburn to learn from. Auburn has done an excellent job of building new athletic facilities in many other sports over the last ten years. But expanding a stadium the size of Jordan-Hare would be incredibly expensive—and it would only be worth it if you were absolutely certain that you were going to sell those seats. Tennessee expanded Neyland stadium and borrowed a lot of money to do so. Then the football team had an extended period of crappiness and the fans stopped buying all the season tickets and donating as much money. So now the athletic department at Tennessee is $200 million in debt. And the pressure on the new coach there is intense because of it. So I would be concerned about Auburn expanding unless we were in a period of stability and were not worried about selling the tickets.

Van: Tennessee is a great cautionary tale, indeed. They have become a 90,000-fan program with a 102,000-seat stadium.

I would dearly love to see Jordan-Hare gain at least an upper deck across the North End. That alone would push capacity close to 100,000, because the stadium was constructed in such a manner that the East and West Stands are farther apart than in many other SEC stadiums, thus allowing room for many, many more seats and for a North Upper Deck almost as wide, or even wider, than the East and West Uppers.

That, of course, will remain only a fantasy for the foreseeable future. Studies conducted during the Tuberville years revealed a demand for additional deluxe scholarship seating—some of which he added—not for more regular seats. It's instructive (and remarkable) to go back and look at the attendance numbers even during the Pat Dye era, when Auburn was winning big. Fewer home games were sellouts than you might suspect during the 1980s, when the Tigers were at the height of their powers. That's not an indictment of Auburn in particular; with attendance in much of the country on a downward trend, given both economic factors and more and more comprehensive television coverage of college football, there's simply no impetus to expand the stadium.

Coaches Tuberville and Chizik did, however, do a lot of great work at beautifying the exterior of the stadium and renovating portions of the interior, and it will be interesting to see what additions and alterations Coach Malzahn makes during his tenure.

What are your thoughts on SEC expansion a year later?

John: I don't like change. I wear the same clothes, drive the exact same way to work and eat the same food all the time. So I don't like new teams in my football conference. And I am still talking about Arkansas and South Carolina!! As far as Texas A&M and Missouri go, it went about like we expected. The Aggies have the resources and the excellent young coach to compete (although they won't always win ten games per year in the SEC West and it may be harder for them to live with that after tasting so much success their first year.) But as long as Kevin Sumlin hangs around, they will be competitive.

The same cannot be said for Missouri. While I think they will certainly have better seasons in the future and 2012 was the worst year of quarterback play at Missouri in twelve years, this team is going to have problems in the SEC and will be lucky to finish over .500 in the East in the next few years. I expect Missouri fans may regret the move to the new conference soon if they do not already.

Auburn's annihilation at the hands of Johnny Manziel and Texas A&M left a bad taste in the mouths of Auburn players and fans. I expect that Auburn will want to prove to the new kid on the SEC

West block that the Tigers aren't the creampuff that they seemed to be in 2012. While Texas A&M still seems like the SEC school that Auburn has the most in common with, the way the Aggies strolled into Jordan-Hare and put more than 60 points on the scoreboard will not be forgotten. In the minds of Texas A&M fans, their program has already moved past Auburn and they think they will now be the team to annually contend with Alabama and LSU for the Western Division title. Auburn needs to step up over the next two years and show the "new kids" that this belief is not correct.

Van: While never thrilled with the idea of a fourteen-team league—too many teams vying for only two spots in Atlanta and for one conference trophy—I was at least happy to have a program like Texas A&M in the SEC, because they obviously fit. My reasons for welcoming Missouri, on the other hand, were entirely selfish: I live near St Louis, and was thrilled with the idea of having Auburn come visiting the area every now and then.

Little did I realize at first just how seldom "now and then" would turn out to be. With fourteen teams, with Mizzou in the opposite division, and with the SEC retaining an eight-game conference schedule, it suddenly dawned on me that the good Tigers would be up here visiting the new Tigers only once every twelve years! Consider this: We have played Clemson of the ACC more often in the last six years than Auburn will play Missouri in Columbia *in the next thirty-five years!*

Those things aside, I do like the idea of having new blood in the conference, and I don't mind another "white meat" team to beat up on—assuming we ever do play Missouri, and assuming they remain beatable and Auburn becomes formidable again.

And consider this: Texas A&M in their first season in the SEC, came within a hair's breadth of playing for the national championship. A win over Florida or LSU and they go to Atlanta instead of Alabama. It's remarkable.

The SEC remains the toughest conference in the land, and Auburn remains in the tougher half of that conference, forced to deal on an annual basis with Alabama, Arkansas, LSU, Texas A&M, and a revitalized Ole Miss, along with better-than-normal Mississippi State. The level of competition in the conference, and particularly in the West, is simply astonishing and the Tigers have no choice but to return to a nationally competitive level of performance if they simply want to survive conference play over the next few years. I think it can be done and I'm confident at this moment that Gus Malzahn is the man for the job. Time will tell how true that turns out to be.

But all it takes is a quick flip back through the pages of this book to see that Auburn's football history is a grand one, filled with glorious victories, trophies and titles, and some of the greatest players ever to put on pads and helmets. The Tigers have achieved great things in the past, and there is no reason whatsoever that we the proud members of the Auburn Family cannot look to the future and expect to experience *even more* decades of dominance.

Appendix 1:
All Games, 1981-2012

1981:

5-6 overall; 2-4 SEC

9/5	TCU	W	24-16
9/19	Wake Forest	L	21-24
9/26	at Tennessee	L	7-10
10/3	at Nebraska	L	3-17
10/10	LSU	W	19-7
10/17	at Georgia Tech	W	31-7
10/24	Miss State	L	17-21
10/31	Florida	W	14-12
11/7	N Texas	W	20-0
11/14	at Georgia	L	13-24
11/28	Alabama (Bham)	L	17-28

1982:

9-3 overall; 4-2 SEC

9/11	Wake Forest	W	28-10
9/18	Southern Miss	W	21-19
9/25	Tennessee	W	24-14
10/2	Nebraska	L	7-41
10/9	Kentucky	W	18-3
10/16	Georgia Tech	W	24-0
10/23	at Miss State	W	35-17
10/30	at Florida	L	17-19
11/6	Rutgers	W	30-7
11/13	Georgia	L	14-19
11/27	at Alabama (Bham)	W	23-22
12/18	Boston College*	W	33-26

Tangerine Bowl, Orlando, FL

1983:

11-1 overall; 6-0 SEC
National Champions*; SEC Champions

9/7	Southern Miss	W	24-3
9/17	Texas	L	7-20
9/24	at Tennessee	W	37-14
10/1	Florida State	W	27-24
10/8	at Kentucky	W	49–21
10/15	at Georgia Tech	W	31-13
10/22	Miss State	W	28-13
10/29	Florida	W	28-21
11/5	Maryland	W	35-23
11/12	at Georgia	W	13-7
12/3	Alabama (Bham)	W	23-20
1/2	Michigan**	W	9-7

New York Times Poll

** *Sugar Bowl, New Orleans, LA*

1984:

9-4 overall; 4-2 SEC

8/28	Miami*	L	18-20
9/15	at Texas	L	27-35
9/22	Southern Miss	W	35-12
9/29	Tennessee	W	29-10
10/6	at Ole Miss	W	17-13
10/13	at Florida State	W	42-41
10/20	Georgia Tech	W	48-34
10/27	at Miss State	W	24-21
11/3	at Florida	L	3-24
11/10	Cincinnati	W	60-0
11/17	Georgia	W	21-12
12/1	at Alabama (Bham)	L	15-17
12/27	Arkansas**	W	21-15

*Kickoff Classic, E Rutherford, NJ
**Liberty Bowl, Memphis, TN

1985:

8-4 overall; 3-3 SEC

9/7	SW Louisiana	W	49-7
9/14	Southern Miss	W	29-18
9/28	at Tennessee	L	20-38
10/5	Ole Miss	W	41-0
10/12	Florida State	W	59-27
10/19	at Georgia Tech	W	17-14
10/26	Miss State	W	21-9
11/2	Florida	L	10-14
11/9	East Carolina	W	35-10
11/16	at Georgia	W	24-10
11/30	Alabama (Bham)	L	23-25
1/1	Texas A&M*	L	16-36

*Cotton Bowl, Dallas, TX

1986:

10-2 overall; 4-2 SEC

9/6	UT Chattanooga	W	42-14
9/17	East Carolina	W	45-0
9/27	Tennessee	W	34-8
10/4	W Carolina	W	55-6
10/11	at Vanderbilt	W	31-9
10/18	Georgia Tech	W	31-10
10/25	at Miss State	W	35-6
11/1	at Florida	L	17-18
11/8	Cincinnati	W	52-7
11/15	Georgia	L	16-20
11/29	at Alabama (Bham)	W	21-17
1/1	USC*	W	16-7

Citrus Bowl, Orlando, FL

1987:

9-1-2 overall; 5-0-1 SEC
SEC Champions

9/5	Texas	W	31-3
9/12	Kansas	W	49-0
9/26	at Tennessee	T	20-20
10/3	at North Carolina	W	20-10
10/10	Vanderbilt	W	48-15
10/17	at Georgia Tech	W	20-10
10/24	Miss State	W	38-7
10/31	Florida	W	29-6
11/7	Florida State	L	6-34
11/14	at Georgia	W	27-11
11/27	Alabama (Bham)	W	10-0
1/1	Syracuse*	T	16-16

Sugar Bowl; New Orleans, LA

1988:

10-2 overall; 5-1 SEC
SEC Champions

9/10	Kentucky	W	20-10
9/17	Kansas	W	56-7
9/24	Tennessee	W	38-6
10/1	North Carolina	W	47-21
10/8	at LSU	L	6-7
10/15	Akron	W	42-0
10/22	Miss State	W	33-0
10/29	at Florida	W	16-0
11/5	Southern Miss	W	38-8
11/12	Georgia	W	20-10
11/25	at Alabama (Bham)	W	15-10
1/2	Florida State*	L	7-13

Sugar Bowl, New Orleans, LA

1989:

10-2 overall; 5-1 SEC
SEC Champions

9/9	Pacific	W	55-0
9/16	Southern Miss	W	24-3
9/30	at Tennessee	L	14-21
10/7	at Kentucky	W	24-12
10/14	LSU	W	10-6
10/21	at Florida State	L	14-22
10/28	Miss State	W	14-0
11/4	Florida	W	10-7
11/11	Louisiana Tech	W	38-23
11/18	at Georgia	W	20-3
12/2	Alabama*	W	30-20
1/1	Ohio State**	W	31-14

"First Time Ever" in Auburn, AL

**Hall of Fame Bowl, Tampa, FL*

1990:

8-3-1 overall; 4-2-1 SEC

9/8	Cal St Fullerton	W	38-17
9/15	at Ole Miss	W	24-10
9/29	Tennessee	T	26-26
10/6	Louisiana Tech	W	16-14
10/13	Vanderbilt	W	56-6
10/20	Florida State	W	20-17
10/27	at Miss State	W	17-16
11/3	at Florida	L	7-48
11/10	Southern Miss	L	12-13
11/17	Georgia	W	33-10
12/1	at Alabama (Bham)	L	7-16
12/29	Indiana *	W	27-23

Peach Bowl, Atlanta, GA

1991:

5-6 overall; 2-5 SEC

8/31	Georgia Southern	W	32-17
9/14	Ole Miss	W	23-13
9/21	at Texas	W	14-10
9/28	at Tennessee	L	21-30
10/5	Southern Miss	L	9-10
10/12	at Vanderbilt	W	24-22
10/26	Miss State	L	17-24
11/2	Florida	L	10-31
11/9	SW Louisiana	W	50-7
11/16	at Georgia	L	27-37
11/30	Alabama (Bham)*	L	6-13

Final Auburn "home" game in Legion Field

1992:

5-5-1 overall; 2-5-1 SEC

9/5	at Ole Miss	L	21-45
9/12	Samford	W	55-0
9/19	LSU	W	30-28
9/26	Southern Miss	W	16-8
10/3	Vanderbilt	W	31-7
10/10	at Miss State	L	7-14
10/17	at Florida	L	9-24
10/24	SW Louisiana	W	25-24
10/31	Arkansas	T	24-24
11/14	Georgia	L	10-14
11/26	at Alabama (Bham)	L	0-17

1993:

11-0; 8-0 SEC
National Champions*
Undefeated Season**

9/2	Ole Miss	W	16-12
9/11	Samford	W	35-7
9/18	at LSU	W	34-10
9/25	Southern Miss	W	35-24
10/2	at Vanderbilt	W	14-10
10/9	Miss State	W	31-17
10/16	Florida	W	38-35
10/30	at Arkansas	W	31-21
11/6	New Mexico St	W	55-14
11/13	at Georgia	W	42-28
11/20	Alabama	W	22-14

Named National Champions by five polls and organizations
**Not eligible for post-season play due to NCAA sanctions*

1994:

9-1-1; 4-1-1 SEC*

9/3	at Ole Miss	W	22-17
9/10	NE Louisiana	W	44-12
9/17	LSU	W	30-26
9/24	East Tenn State	W	38-0
9/29	Kentucky	W	41-14
10/8	at Miss State	W	42-18
10/15	at Florida	W	36-33
10/29	Arkansas	W	31-14
11/5	East Carolina	W	38-21
11/12	Georgia	T	23-23
11/19	at Alabama (Bham)	L	14-21

**Not eligible for post-season play due to NCAA sanctions*

1995:

8-4 overall; 5-3 SEC

9/2	Ole Miss	W	46-13
9/9	Chattanooga	W	76-10
9/16	at LSU	L	6-12
9/30	at Kentucky	W	42-21
10/7	Miss State	W	48-20
10/14	Florida	L	38-49
10/21	Western Michigan	W	34-13
10/28	at Arkansas	L	21-26
11/4	NE Louisiana	W	38-14
11/11	at Georgia	W	37-31
11/18	Alabama	W	31-27
1/1	Penn State*	L	14-43

Outback Bowl, Tampa, FL

1996:

8-4 overall; 4-4 SEC

8/31	UAB	W	29-0
9/7	Fresno State	W	62-0
9/14	at Ole Miss	W	45-28
9/21	LSU	L	15-19
10/5	South Carolina	W	28-24
10/12	at Miss State	W	49-15
10/19	at Florida	L	10-51
11/2	Arkansas	W	28-7
11/9	NE Louisiana	W	28-24
11/16	Georgia	L	49-56 (4OT)
11/23	at Alabama (Bham)	L	23-24
12/31	Army*	W	32-29

Independence Bowl, Shreveport, LA

1997:

10-3 overall; 6-3 SEC

SEC Western Division Champions

9/4	at Virginia	W	28-17
9/13	Ole Miss	W	19-9
9/20	at LSU	W	31-28
9/27	Central Florida	W	41-14
10/4	at South Carolina	W	23-6
10/11	Louisiana Tech	W	49-13
10/18	Florida	L	10-24
10/25	at Arkansas	W	26-21
11/1	Miss State	L	0-20
11/15	at Georgia	W	45-34
11/22	Alabama	W	18-17
12/6	Tennessee*	L	29-30
1/2	Clemson**	W	27-17

SEC Championship Game, Atlanta, GA

**Peach Bowl, Atlanta, GA

1998:
3-8 overall; 1-7 SEC
9/3	Virginia	L	0-19
9/12	at Ole Miss	W	17-0
9/19	LSU	L	19-31
10/3	Tennessee	L	9-17
10/10	at Miss State	L	21-38
10/17	at Florida	L	3-24
10/24	Louisiana Tech	W	32-17
10/31	Arkansas	L	21-24
11/7	Central Florida	W	10-6
11/14	Georgia	L	17-28
11/21	at Alabama (Bham)	L	17-31

1999:
5-6 overall; 2-6 SEC
9/4	Appalachian State	W	22–15
9/11	Idaho	W	30-23
9/18	at LSU	W	41-7
9/25	Ole Miss	L	17-24 (OT)
10/2	at Tennessee	L	0-24
10/9	Miss State	L	16-18
10/16	Florida	L	14-32
10/30	at Arkansas	L	10-34
11/6	Central Florida	W	28-10
11/13	at Georgia	W	38-21
11/20	Alabama	L	17-28

2000:

9-4 overall; 6-2 SEC
SEC Western Division Champions

8/31	Wyoming	W	35-21
9/9	at Ole Miss	W	35-27
9/16	LSU	W	34-17
9/23	Northern Illinois	W	31-14
9/30	Vanderbilt	W	33-0
10/7	at Miss State	L	10-17
10/14	at Florida	L	7-38
10/21	Louisiana Tech	W	38-28
10/28	Arkansas	W	21-19
11/11	Georgia	W	29-26 (OT)
11/23	at Alabama	W	9-0
12/2	Florida*	L	6-28
1/1	Michigan**	L	28-31

*SEC Championship Game, Atlanta, GA
**Citrus Bowl, Orlando, FL

2001:

7-5 overall; 5-3 SEC
SEC Western Division Co-Champions

9/1	Ball State	W	30-0
9/8	Ole Miss	W	27-21
9/22	at Syracuse	L	14-31
9/29	at Vanderbilt	W	24-21
10/6	Miss State	W	16-14
10/13	Florida	W	23-20
10/20	Louisiana Tech	W	48–41 (OT)
10/27	at Arkansas	L	17–42
11/10	at Georgia	W	24–17
11/17	Alabama	L	7–31
12/1	at LSU*	L	14-27

12/31	North Carolina**	L	10-16

Rescheduled from 9/15 due to Sept. 11 attacks
**Peach Bowl, Atlanta, GA*

2002:

9-4 overall; 5-3 SEC
SEC Western Division Co-Champions

9/2	at USC	L	17-24
9/7	Western Carolina	W	56-0
9/14	Vanderbilt	W	31-6
9/19	at Miss State	W	42-14
9/28	Syracuse	W	37-34 (OT)
10/12	Arkansas	L	17-38
10/19	at Florida	L	23-30 (OT)
10/26	LSU	W	31-7
11/2	at Ole Miss	W	31-24
11/9	Louisiana–Monroe	W	52–14
11/16	Georgia	L	21-24
11/23	at Alabama	W	17-7
1/1	Penn State*	W	13-9

Citrus Bowl, Orlando, FL

2003:

8-5 overall; 5-3 SEC

8/30	USC	L	0-23
9/6	at Georgia Tech	L	3-17
9/13	at Vanderbilt	W	45-7
9/27	Western Kentucky	W	48-3
10/4	Tennessee	W	28-21
10/11	at Arkansas	W	10-3
10/18	Miss State	W	45-13
10/25	at LSU	L	7-31
11/1	Louisiana-Monroe	W	73-7

11/8	Ole Miss	L	20-24
11/15	at Georgia	L	7-26
11/22	Alabama	W	28-23
12/31	Wisconsin*	W	28-14

*Music City Bowl, Nashville, TN

2004:

13-0 overall; 9-0 SEC
National Champions*
SEC Champions
SEC Western Division Champions
Undefeated Season

9/4	Louisiana–Monroe	W	31–0
9/11	Miss State	W	43–14
9/18	LSU	W	10-9
9/25	The Citadel	W	33-3
10/2	at Tennessee	W	34-10
10/9	Louisiana Tech	W	52–7
10/16	Arkansas	W	38-20
10/23	Kentucky	W	42-10
10/30	at Ole Miss	W	35-14
11/13	Georgia	W	24-6
11/20	at Alabama	W	21-13
12/4	Tennessee**	W	38-28
1/3	Virginia Tech***	W	16-13

*Named National Champions by numerous polls and organizations.
**SEC Championship Game, Atlanta, GA
***Sugar Bowl, New Orleans, LA

2005:

9-3 overall; 7-1 SEC

SEC Western Division Co-Champions

9/3	Georgia Tech	L	14-23
9/10	Miss State	W	28-0
9/17	Ball State	W	63-3
9/24	Western Kentucky	W	37-14
10/1	South Carolina	W	48-7
10/15	at Arkansas	W	34-17
10/22	at LSU	L	17-20 (OT)
10/29	Ole Miss	W	27-3
11/5	Kentucky	W	49-27
11/12	at Georgia	W	31-30
11/19	Alabama	W	28-18
1/1	Wisconsin*	L	10-24

Capital One Bowl, Orlando, FL

2006:

11-2 overall; 6-2 SEC

9/2	Washington State	W	40-14
9/9	at Miss State	W	34-0
9/16	LSU	W	7-3
9/23	Buffalo	W	38-7
9/28	at South Carolina	W	24-17
10/7	Arkansas	L	10-27
10/14	Florida	W	27-17
10/21	Tulane	W	38-13
10/28	at Ole Miss	W	23-17
11/4	Arkansas State	W	27-0
11/11	Georgia	L	15-37
11/18	at Alabama	W	22-15
1/1	Nebraska*	W	17-14

Cotton Bowl, Dallas, TX

2007:

9-4 overall; 5-3 SEC

9/1	Kansas State	W	23-13
9/8	South Florida	L	23-26 (OT)
9/15	Miss State	L	14-19
9/22	New Mexico State	W	55-20
9/29	at Florida	W	20-17
10/6	Vanderbilt	W	35-7
10/13	at Arkansas	W	9-7
10/20	at LSU	L	24-30
10/27	Ole Miss	W	17-3
11/3	Tennessee Tech	W	35-3
11/10	at Georgia	L	20-45
11/24	Alabama	W	17-10
12/31	Clemson*	W	23-20 (OT)

*Chick-Fil-A Bowl, Atlanta, GA

2008:

5-7 overall; 2-6 SEC

8/30	Louisiana–Monroe	W	34–0
9/6	Southern Miss	W	27–13
9/13	at Miss State	W	3–2
9/20	LSU	L	21–26
9/27	Tennessee	W	14–12
10/4	Vanderbilt	L	13–14
10/11	Arkansas	L	22–25
10/23	at West Virginia	L	17-34
11/1	at Ole Miss	L	7–17
11/8	Tennessee–Martin	W	37–20
11/15	Georgia	L	13–17
11/29	at Alabama	L	0–36

2009:

8-5 overall; 3-5 SEC

9/5	Louisiana Tech	W	37–13
9/12	Miss State	W	49–24
9/19	West Virginia	W	41-30
9/26	Ball State	W	54-30
10/3	at Tennessee	W	26-22
10/10	at Arkansas	L	23-44
10/17	Kentucky	L	14-21
10/24	at LSU	L	10-31
10/31	Ole Miss	W	33-20
11/7	Furman	W	63-31
11/14	at Georgia	L	24–31
11/27	Alabama	L	21–26
1/1	Northwestern*	W	38–35 (OT)

*Outback Bowl, Tampa, FL

2010:

14-0 overall; 8-0 SEC
BCS National Champions
SEC Champions
SEC Western Division Champions
Undefeated Season

9/4	Arkansas State	W	52–26
9/9	at Mississippi State	W	17–14
9/18	Clemson	W	27–24 (OT)
9/25	South Carolina	W	35–27
10/2	Louisiana–Monroe	W	52-3
10/9	at Kentucky	W	37–34
10/16	Arkansas	W	65–43
10/23	LSU	W	24–17
10/30	at Ole Miss	W	51-31
11/6	Chattanooga	W	62–24
11/13	Georgia	W	49–31
11/26	at Alabama	W	28–27
12/4	South Carolina*	W	56–17
1/10	Oregon**	W	22-19

SEC Championship Game, Atlanta, GA
**BCS National Championship Game, Glendale, AZ*

2011:

8-5 overall; 4-4 SEC

9/3	Utah State	W	42–38
9/10	Miss State	W	41–34
9/17	at Clemson	L	24–38
9/24	Florida Atlantic	W	30–14
10/1	at South Carolina	W	16–13
10/8	at Arkansas	L	14–38
10/15	Florida	W	17–6
10/22	at LSU	L	10–45
10/29	Ole Miss	W	41–23
11/12	at Georgia	L	7–45
11/19	Samford	W	35–16
11/26	Alabama	L	14–42
12/31	Virginia*	W	43–24

Chick-Fil-A Bowl, Atlanta, GA

2012:

3-9 overall; 0-8 SEC

9/1	Clemson*	L	19–26
9/8	at Miss State	L	10–28
9/15	Louisiana–Monroe	W	31–28 (OT)
9/22	LSU	L	10–12
10/6	Arkansas	L	7–24
10/13	at Ole Miss	L	20–41
10/20	at Vanderbilt	L	13–17
10/27	Texas A&M	L	21–63
11/3	New Mexico State	W	42–7
11/10	Georgia	L	0–38
11/17	Alabama A&M	W	51–7
11/24	at Alabama	L	0–49

* Chick-Fil-A College Kickoff, Atlanta, GA

Appendix 2:
Auburn vs. the SEC, 1981-2012

TEAM	AU WINS	AU LOSSES	DRAWS
SEC WEST			
ALABAMA	17	15	
ARKANSAS	11*	10	1
LSU	12	12	
OLE MISS	20	5	
MISS STATE	23	9	
TEXAS A&M	0	2*	
SEC EAST			
FLORIDA	11	15	
GEORGIA	16	15	1
KENTUCKY	9	1	
MISSOURI	0	0	
SOUTH CAROLINA	7	0	
TENNESSEE	10	7	2
VANDERBILT	11	2	

Includes games prior to team joining SEC.

Appendix 3:
Auburn vs. the Conferences,
Overall Record, 1981-2012

TEAM	AU WINS	AU LOSSES	DRAWS
ACC	15	7	
Big East	2	3	
Big Ten	6	3	
Big West	3	0	
Big XII	4	2	
Conf USA	2	0	
MAC	6	0	
MWC	1	0	
PAC 12	3	2	
SEC	146	92	4
Sun Belt	9	0	
SWC	4	3	
WAC	7	0	

Appendix 4:
Auburn vs. the Conferences, Average Score, 1981-2012

TEAM	AU SCORE	OPP SCORE
ACC	23.9	19.2
Big East	26.4	31
Big Ten	22	22.2
Big West	46.7	12.3
Big XII	25.8	15.3
Conf USA	32.5	13
MAC	41.7	11.2
MWC	35	21
PAC 12	19	17.4
SEC	23.3	19.9
Sun Belt	42.4	10.2
SWC	20	19.3
WAC	48.3	18

Appendix 5:
Sources Consulted for the
History of Jordan-Hare Stadium

"Jordan-Hare Stadium Compared to Alabama Cities," *1995 Auburn Football Media Guide* (1995): 239.

Jeff Beard, "Jordan-Hare Stadium Down Through the Years," *Auburn University Football Illustrated* (1989): 10, Buildings, Jordan-Hare Stadium Miscellaneous Folder, Series I, Auburn University Archives.

Deborah J. Miller-Wood, "Remembering...Auburn's Stadium Through the Years," Display script, University Archives exhibit at Foy Union Building, (Summer, 1987): 1, Buildings, Jordan Hare Stadium Miscellaneous Folder, Series II, Auburn University Archives.

Dru McGowen, "Anniversary," *Inside the Auburn Tigers* (March 1989): 12, Buildings, Jordan-Hare Stadium Miscellaneous Folder, Series II, Auburn University Archives.

"Vast Program of Building on at A.P.I.," Miscellaneous newspaper clipping, (Dec. 18, 1938): 1, Buildings, Jordan Hare Stadium Miscellaneous Folder, Series I, Auburn University Archives.

Mark Murphy, "Jordan-Hare," *Inside the Auburn* Tigers (Jan. 1985): 21, Buildings, Jordan Hare Stadium Miscellaneous Folder, Series II, Auburn University Archives.

"Mr. Arnold G. Wurz, 82, Retired Engineer and General Contractor" (obit), *Atlanta Journal-Constitution*, (Aug. 19, 1989): C-6, Buildings, Jordan-Hare Stadium Miscellaneous Folder, Series I, Auburn University Archives.

Dan Hollis, *Auburn Football, the Complete History*, 1892-1987, (Auburn: Auburn Sports Publications, 1987), 233.

"Auburn Stadium is Named Cliff Hare," News Bureau, Alabama Polytechnic Institute, Release to Weeklies (Dec. 31, 1948): 1, Buildings, Jordan-Hare Stadium Miscellaneous Folder, Series I, Auburn University Archives.

"Alabama Poly Faculty Chairman Athletics," Auburn-Georgia Official Program (1934): 5, Buildings, Jordan-Hare Stadium Miscellaneous Folder, Series I, Auburn University Archives.

David Housel, "Jordan-Hare: Afternoon Talks," Auburn Football (Oct. 6, 1973): 40, Buildings, Jordan-Hare Stadium Miscellaneous Folder, Series I, Auburn University Archives.

Minutes of the Board of Trustees, April 29, 1955, Alabama Polytechnic Institute (Oct. 30, 1955-March 14, 1957): Vol. 14, Auburn University Archives.

Minutes of the Board of Trustees, Alabama Polytechnic Institute, (July 26, 1955): Vol. 14 (Oct. 30, 1953-March 14, 1957), Auburn University Archives.

Jeff Beard, Memorandum to President Ralph B. Draughon, (June 3, 1955), Buildings, Jordan-Hare Stadium Miscellaneous Folder, Series II, Auburn University Archives.

L. E. Funchess, Memorandum to G.W. Beard, (March 3, 1960), Buildings, Jordan-Hare Stadium Miscellaneous Folder, Series I, Auburn University Archives.

Minutes of the Board of Trustees, Auburn University, (Oct. 25, 1968), Vol. 17 1965-1969, Auburn University Archives.

John S. Moore, letter to G.W. Beard, (March 24, 1969): 1, Buildings, Jordan-Hare Stadium, Miscellaneous Folder, Series I, Auburn University Archives.

Minutes of Recessed Meeting of the Board of Trustees of Auburn University, (Nov. 22, 1969), Vol. 17, 1965-1969, Auburn University Archives.

John R. Burgess, Memorandum to Col. L. E. Funchess, (March 31, 1971): 2, Buildings, Jordan-Hare Stadium Miscellaneous Folder, Series II, Auburn University Archives.

Buddy Davidson, "The Game Today," *Auburn Football Illustrated*, (Oct. 6, 1973): 25, Buildings, Jordan-Hare Stadium Miscellaneous Folder, Series I, Auburn University Archives.

Misc. Papers (untitled, no author given), (1980), Buildings, Jordan-Hare Stadium, Miscellaneous Folder, Series I, Auburn University Archives.

David Housel, "Jordan-Hare: A Tiger Trap," *Auburn Football Illustrated* (Oct. 6, 1973): 46, Buildings, Jordan-Hare Stadium Miscellaneous Folder, Series I, Auburn University Archives.

"Jordan-Hare Stadium," *Auburn Football Media Guide* (1989): 228, Buildings, Jordan-Hare Stadium Miscellaneous Folder, Series I, Auburn University Archives.

Minutes of the Board of Trustees, Auburn University, Dec. 3, 1977, Vault F-2, Box 1, 1977-1983, Auburn University Archives.

"Facts and Figures on Stadium," *Auburn Bulletin*, (Sept. 23, 1979): A-6, Buildings, Jordan-Hare Stadium Miscellaneous Folder, Series II, Auburn University Archives.

Minutes of the Board of Trustees, Auburn University, Dec. 3, 1984, Vault F-2, Box 2, 1984-1987, Auburn University Archives.

Murphy, Mark, sidebar to "Jordan-Hare," *Inside the Auburn Tigers*, (Jan., 1985): 20-21, Buildings, Jordan-Hare Stadium Miscellaneous Folder, Series II, Auburn University Archives.

"Jordan-Hare Stadium to be Expanded," press release, Auburn Sports Information (Dec. 2, 1984): 1, Buildings, Jordan-Hare Stadium, Miscellaneous Folder, Series II, Auburn University Archives.

Keith Jackson, CBS Sports television interview (Dec. 2, 1989), video recording, author's collection.

Perry Ballard, "Jordan-Hare: More Seats Needed?" *Opelika-Auburn News* (Sept. 30, 1990), Buildings, Jordan-Hare Stadium Miscellaneous Folder, Series II, Auburn University Archives.

Jason Sasser, "Jordan-Hare Addition Ahead of Schedule," press release, Auburn Sports Information, (April 15, 1987): 1, Buildings, Jordan-Hare Stadium, Miscellaneous Folder, Series II, Auburn University Archives.

ABOUT THE AUTHORS

Van Allen Plexico is an award-winning author and editor who managed to attend Auburn (and score student football tickets) for some portion of every year between 1986 and 1996. He realizes that's probably not something one should brag about, but hey. He teaches college near St Louis (because ten years as a student was somehow just not enough time to spend at school) and writes and edits for a variety of publishers. Find links to his various projects at *www.plexico.net*.

John Ringer graduated from Auburn in 1991 (which may be the greatest time ever to be an Auburn student – SEC titles in 1987, 88 and 89 and the 1989 Iron Bowl). His family has had season tickets every year since well before he was born and he grew up wandering around Jordan-Hare on game days. He currently lives in Richmond, Virginia where he spends way too much time reading about college football on the internet and teaching his children to love Auburn football.

Van and John's previous book about Auburn football, ***Season of Our Dreams: The 2010 Auburn Tigers***, reached fifteenth on the Amazon.com Sports Best Sellers List in the summer of 2011, and for that (and so much more), they sincerely thank the Auburn Family. You can read their semi-regular columns as well as accessing their "Wishbone Podcast" audio show at *www.thewareaglereader.com*.

Made in the USA
Lexington, KY
23 October 2015